PRAISE FOR *High Society*

"A fascinating account of Kelly's difficult transition from Hollywood royalty to the real deal."
   —*USA Today*

"Addictively readable, perceptive, eloquent."
   —*Philadelphia Inquirer*

"An intimate and detailed account of Grace Kelly's life and career."
   —*Elle*

"The author smartly manages to correct errors and confirm (or negate) rumors that plagued Kelly throughout her life. . . . Spoto's ace in the hole is that some of the narrative is peppered with Kelly's own words."
   —*Chicago Sun-Times*

"It's hard to imagine that any subsequent biography could do such consummate justice to Grace's life and career."
   —*The Times* (London)

"As definitive a biography as we are likely to get. Spoto tells her story movingly and well. Highest recommendation."
   —*The Sunday Express* (London)

"Brilliantly structured and elegantly written. This biographer knows his craft and loves it."
   —*Weekend Avisen* (Copenhagen)

"A meticulously researched, carefully phrased insight into the life of a complex woman."
   —*Canberra Times* (Australia)

Spellbound by Beauty: Alfred Hitchcock and His Leading Ladies

Otherwise Engaged: The Life of Alan Bates

Joan: The Mysterious Life of a Heretic Who Became a Saint

Enchantment: The Life of Audrey Hepburn

In Silence: Why We Pray

Reluctant Saint: The Life of Francis of Assisi

Jacqueline Bouvier Kennedy Onassis: A Life

The Hidden Jesus: A New Life

Diana—The Last Year

Notorious: The Life of Ingrid Bergman

Rebel: The Life and Legend of James Dean

The Decline and Fall of the House of Windsor

A Passion for Life: The Biography of Elizabeth Taylor

Marilyn Monroe: The Biography

Blue Angel: The Life of Marlene Dietrich

Laurence Olivier: A Biography

Madcap: The Life of Preston Sturges

Lenya: A Life

Falling in Love Again—Marlene Dietrich (A Photo-Essay)

The Kindness of Strangers: The Life of Tennessee Williams

The Dark Side of Genius: The Life of Alfred Hitchcock

Stanley Kramer, Film Maker

Camerado: Hollywood and the American Man

The Art of Alfred Hitchcock

The LIFE of GRACE KELLY

 THREE RIVERS PRESS • NEW YORK

High Society

DONALD SPOTO

CONTENTS

ACKNOWLEDGMENTS

My major debt of gratitude is to Grace Kelly Grimaldi, Princess of Monaco, who granted interviews without which this book would not be possible.

Many of those who knew or collaborated with her are no longer with us, but I was able to discuss Grace with the following before or during research for several other books. I acknowledge, therefore, the late Jay Presson Allen, Peggy Ashcroft, Anne Baxter, Ingrid Bergman, Herbert Coleman, Joseph Cotten, Hume Cronyn, Cary Grant, Tom Helmore, Alfred Hitchcock, Evan Hunter, Stanley Kramer, Ernest Lehman, Simon Oakland, Gregory Peck, Peggy Robertson, James Stewart, Jessica Tandy, Samuel Taylor, Teresa Wright and Fred Zinnemann.

All of Grace's directors, along with almost everyone who acted with her, are deceased. I am especially grateful, therefore, for the reminiscences of those actors and friends of Grace still available to supplement my interviews—among them, John Ericson, Rita Gam, Edward Meeks and Jacqueline Monsigny.

Thanks to Gary Browning, assistant visitor services manager at the Museum of Television and Radio, Beverly Hills, I was able to see many of Grace's television appearances. Mark Gens and the staff of the Archive and Research Study Center at the University of California, Los Angeles, made additional kinescopes of her performances available to me.

As so often, I was welcomed and helped by the dedicated staff at the Margaret Herrick Library of the Academy of Motion Picture Arts and Sciences, Beverly Hills—in particular by Stacey Behlmer and Barbara Hall.

Tom Smith provided research assistance in England, and Jonathan Boone in the United States; I acknowledge their thoroughness and alacrity.

In 2007 the Forum Grimaldi, Monte-Carlo, mounted a tribute in dozens of rooms of its vast conference hall—a celebration of Grace's life and career twenty-five years after her death. For the first time, Prince Albert and Princesses Caroline and Stéphanie made public some very important documents, letters and photos.

Claus Kjær and Stine Nielsen at the Danish Film Institute, Copenhagen, provided important assistance during my research.

My friend the actress Diane Baker first introduced me to the prolific French writer Jacqueline Monsigny and her husband, the actor Edward Meeks. At Grace's request, Jacqueline wrote and Edward costarred in Grace's last film—*Rearranged,* which has remained unavailable to the public since its production not long before the death of the princess. Thanks to Jacqueline and Edward, I was able to see this remarkable movie several times and to treat it at length in this book. They were close friends of Grace for over twenty years, and my interviews with them have provided unique and valuable material.

Not for the first time, and surely not for the last, my brother-in-law John Møller devoted his time and considerable talents to several important tasks in preparing this book for publication. Once again, I salute his artistic and technical gifts.

For various acts of kindness, I am grateful to John Darretta, Lewis Falb, Sue Jett, Irene Mahoney and Gerald Pinciss.

MY NEW YORK AGENT, ELAINE MARKSON, has been a devoted friend and trusted confidante for over thirty years. I am equally fortunate in the constant help and affectionate encouragement of her associates, Gary Johnson, Geri Thoma and Julia Kenny.

Elaine introduced me to the good people at the Harmony Books division of Random House, where my publisher is the highly respected and perceptive Shaye Areheart. Shaye and my superbly attentive and ever-vigilant editor, Julia Pastore, have offered warm support of me and my work. They have my great gratitude.

THIS BOOK IS DEDICATED to my sisters-in-law, Lissi Andersen and Hanne Møller, who have been as devoted to me as they have been enthusiastic followers of my career. They and their husbands, Søren Andersen and John Møller, welcomed me with open arms from my first day in Denmark, where I am blessed to share my life with Lissi and Hanne's brother, Ole Flemming Larsen. He watched Grace's movies with me, he listened patiently to portions of the manuscript, and he provided pointed suggestions for its improvement. Ole's artistic eye for detail and his amazing language proficiency are but a few of his many talents, and his commitment to me and to our life together means more than I can say. Grace, who always placed family first in her life, would have admired and loved Lissi, Hanne and Ole, as does . . .

D.S.
Sjælland, Denmark
Christmas 2008

High Society

INTRODUCTION

DURING OUR LAST MEETING, I ASKED GRACE KELLY GRIMALDI if she planned to write an autobiography or to authorize a writer to compose her life story. "I'd like to think I'm still too young for that!" she said with a laugh. Without any hint of a dark premonition, she then added, "Donald, you really ought to wait until twenty-five years after I'm gone, and then *you* tell the whole story." I have honored her request for a delay: Grace left us in September 1982, and I started work on this book early in 2007.

I spent many hours with this remarkable woman over several years, beginning with our first meeting during the afternoon of September 22, 1975; in a short time she offered me a friendship that deepened over the years. At our introduction, at her home in Paris, she was preparing to relocate from her apartment on the Avenue Foch to another residence nearby. There were packing boxes, and movers working with quiet efficiency, and my tape recording of that afternoon indicates that there were only three brief interruptions in our long conversation.

First, an elderly attendant, the only servant I saw that day, inquired what he might offer for refreshment, and Grace asked if I would like tea and biscuits. Then, a few moments after we began the interview, Grace apologized as she went over to a sliding glass door to the terrace, to admit her cat, eager to check out a visitor. Later, Grace's youngest child, ten-year-old Princess

Stéphanie, emerged from her room. "Mommy, I can't find my yellow sweater." Grace told her to try the obvious place—the drawers of her dresser. Stéphanie returned a few moments later, unable to find the beloved sweater. Grace excused herself, went to Stéphanie's aid and returned moments later, the wardrobe problem having been quickly resolved.

The matter had not been attended to by a servant, nor had one been looking after the child during my visit. "I hope you don't mind these little interruptions," Grace said that afternoon. "We just don't like the idea of turning the children over to nannies and minders. We like to help them ourselves—and then of course we know what to tell them when they ought to do something on their own. They don't always have everything done for them, I can tell you that!"

My visit that day was an important part of the research for my first book, *The Art of Alfred Hitchcock,* the first full-length treatment of all the director's movies. Knowing that she gave interviews but rarely, I had not much hope when I wrote from my home in New York to Grace's secretary at the palace in Monaco. Up to 1975, my writing résumé listed only a few magazine articles and one essay in a book—hence I had little hope for an interview with the princess, who was constantly besieged with such requests.

Two weeks after I wrote, however, I received a reply from her secretary, Paul Choisit, asking if I would like to meet with Her Serene Highness in Paris that September. You bet I would. I went to visit Grace shortly after spending two weeks with Alfred Hitchcock, while he was directing (as it turned out) his last film, *Family Plot,* that summer of 1975. I told him that I had an appointment to interview Grace. "That should be interesting," he said with a wry smile.

❧

MY FIRST CONVERSATION with Grace that September afternoon was mostly about her three films for Alfred Hitchcock, made between July 1953 and August 1954. Her memories were sharp, picturesque, amusing and full of telling anecdotes. That day and later, she also spoke about other directors, especially Fred Zinnemann and John Ford, mostly to compare their methods and manners with Hitchcock's. There was no doubt about her deep respect, affection and acute understanding of Alfred Hitchcock the director and the man. Later she also spoke quite frankly to me about her life and about incidents for which she asked my confidence "as long as I'm around," as she said. I gave her my word.

At that first meeting, Grace impressed me with her total lack of affectation and of anything like a regal manner. She wore a simple navy blue suit and, as I recall, very little jewelry. She put on no airs, she was funny and ironic, she had an extraordinary memory for detail, she told some delightfully risqué tales of Hollywood, she was realistic and completely unstuffy—and she was as interested in my life as I was in hers. I was completely at ease with her. We sat on a comfortable sofa, and we sipped tea and munched delicious little cookies, on and off, all through the afternoon until dusk.

But there was one enormous surprise for me as I prepared to depart.

As we came to the end of the afternoon, Grace asked if anyone was going to write a foreword or introduction to my work. I replied that, as *The Art of Alfred Hitchcock* would be my first book, I had given no thought to the matter of a foreword by anyone—I had been lucky just to find a small independent publisher. "I am constantly asked to endorse products," she continued, "and to comment on books, or to say something about a movie. I cannot do that, for many reasons. However, in your case, I would make an exception. If you will send me your manuscript when it's finished, would you like me to write a foreword to your book?"

In December, I sent her the final draft of *The Art of Alfred Hitchcock,* and on January 16, 1976, a diplomatic courier arrived at my New York apartment, bearing her introduction to the book and a charming cover letter: "I am enclosing the foreword," she wrote, "as well as the galley sheets that I very much enjoyed reading. It will certainly be a great book about Alfred Hitchcock." The book was published in August of that year, with Grace's remarks right up front. Thirty-three years later it is still in print. Doubleday purchased it from the original publisher; foreign translations appeared; and Grace's introduction still honors my debut as a writer. Her generosity was a significant addition and brought the book attention from some who, I am certain, would otherwise have ignored it. And yes, she said, of course I could exploit both her words and her name in promoting the book.

IN THE SUMMER of 1976, Grace invited me to the palace in Monaco, where I presented her with the second copy of the published book—the first, of course, went to Hitchcock. It was a torrid, humid day, and she returned from her country house especially for our reunion. As I was shown into the family quarters, Grace was standing in an orange chiffon outfit, trying, with difficulty, to fasten a bracelet. "Oh, Donald," she said, smiling and extending her wrist when she saw me, "would you please help me with this?"

"What shall we have to drink?" she said afterwards, as we settled onto a settee facing open French doors to a terrace and trying to catch a breeze. We decided on sparkling water. That day I also met Princess Caroline, who came in, fresh and alarmingly beautiful, and briefly joined us. Her mother was proud to show off her intelligent, poised daughter, then a university student in Paris. I was booked into Grace's schedule for an hour in the late morning, but she insisted that I remain for lunch.

From 1975 until Hitchcock's death in 1980, I was a kind of go-between, delivering messages back and forth from Monaco to Hollywood during my various visits with Hitch and Grace. With the probable exception of his wife, he did not easily confide in anyone—but I was an acolyte, and he dropped the mask of diffidence with me, especially at the elaborate lunches prepared just for the two of us in the dining room of his offices at Universal Studios. At such times he was more frank than if we were doing a formal interview. He rarely laughed, but I saw tears run down his face when he spoke, for example, of his recently deceased sister.

Grace, on the other hand, was consistently more forthright and unguarded once she felt confident of my trust. I think this was one of the reasons she offered to write the foreword to my book, and to entrust me with details of her association with Hitch and of her life and career.

WHEN GRACE DIED, I was asked by National Public Radio in the United States to compose and broadcast a tribute to her. It was one of the most difficult assignments of my life, before or since. I spoke briefly of our friendship and of our many conversations about the great and small things of life.

The book you are holding is the story of a working life, from Grace's days as a model and television actress to her final film, made not long before her death. Although that last movie has never been released, it leaves no doubt that Grace was one of the foremost talents of her time, our time, any time. I am fortunate to be able to treat this last, unavailable movie in considerable detail here, as well as a wide selection of her television appearances, which have been, up to now, completely ignored by biographers.

With very few exceptions, Grace's story has not, I think, been generally well served by writers. Apart from an astonishing array of factual errors and omissions, there has been an accumulation of imagined events and fantasies about all kinds of things—love affairs particularly, most of which turn out to be utterly without basis in fact. She was, as I have written here, certainly a healthy, beautiful young woman with normal desires—and most of all, a deep capacity to love and to be loved. As she told me, she "fell in love all the time" before she married Prince Rainier of Monaco. But falling in love did not always mean falling into bed. I have tried to correct the record on this and other more important issues, without fudging the truth—she would have hated that.

Grace's achievements were singular in several ways—not least in the sheer volume of her movie work within a very short period. She worked for two days on a film during the summer of 1950, and then—from September 1951 to March 1956—she appeared in ten films in just four years and six months. But there was a one-year hiatus during this period, so it is more accurate to state that she made ten films in forty-two months. By any standard of assessment, that is a formidable record. In addition, she also appeared in no fewer than thirty-six live television dramas and two Broadway plays between 1948 and 1954.

High Society: The Life of Grace Kelly has been a privilege to write, for it is both a testament to our friendship as well as a biography. To exploit a cliché: Grace was far more than just a pretty face.

"The idea of my life as a fairy tale
is itself a fairy tale."

—Grace Kelly Grimaldi, Princess of Monaco,
to Donald Spoto

Fade-In

1929—1951

ONE

Off the Main Line

I never really felt pretty, bright or socially adept.
— GRACE

IN THE LATE 1920S, THE HAHNEMANN MEDICAL COLLEGE, at the corner of Broad and Vine Streets in Philadelphia, was one of the largest private hospitals in the United States. Unusual luxuries characterized the private rooms: a telephone and radio were installed at every bedside; nurses could be summoned and addressed by call-buttons and two-way speakers; and high-speed elevators whisked visitors to the wards. Although Hahnemann accepted emergency cases from every socioeconomic class, it catered, unofficially but famously, to the demands of the rich from the counties of eastern Pennsylvania.

Early in the morning of Tuesday, November 12, 1929, John B. Kelly escorted his wife, Margaret Majer Kelly, to Hahnemann, where, after an unexceptional labor, she bore her third child and second daughter. On December 1, the Kellys took the baby to St. Bridget's Roman Catholic Church, a three-minute, half-mile drive from their home in the upscale neighborhood of Philadelphia known as East Falls. The infant was baptized

Grace Patricia, in memory of an aunt who had died young, and (so Grace Kelly believed) "because I was Tuesday's child"—who, according to Mother Goose, was "full of grace."

On the banks of the Schuylkill River, East Falls has always been a quiet residential neighborhood, known for its easy commute to downtown Philadelphia. The most respected, established families—Protestants with "old money" like the Drexels, Biddles, Clarks, Cadwaladers and Wideners—lived across the river, in western suburbs along the so-called Main Line, in eighteen communities (among them, Overbrook, Merion, Wynnewood, Ardmore, Haverford, Bryn Mawr, Rosemont and Radnor). The river was very like a social dividing line.

But membership in Philadelphia's élite depended more on history than geography: one was "in society" only if a family could be traced back to colonial times, before the War of Independence. The class distinctions were so immutable that the Kellys knew they would never be accepted into high society, no matter the extent of their wealth. The Kellys were Irish, Roman Catholic and Democrats; Philadelphia society was English, Episcopalian and Republican. "We could have been members of the social register—the so-called Four Hundred—if we'd wanted to," Grace Kelly's mother said. "But we had other things to do." If she really believed this, she was astonishingly naïve. Her husband knew otherwise; instead, he set out to "do well" in business, athletics and politics.

WHEN GRACE WAS born, the entire country was in the throes of a terrible financial crisis. At the end of October the stock market was in almost total collapse, signaling an economic disaster that led to the Great Depression. Scores of banks failed overnight; innumerable companies shut their doors forever; and millions of Americans were suddenly homeless and jobless, pitchforked into abject poverty and facing a future without prospects. The United States was steeped in despair, and newspapers chronicled a tragic epidemic of suicides.

Some families, however, were untouched by the gruesome facts of national life, and Grace's was among them. Her father, John B. Kelly, had never speculated in the stock market, and his wealth—achieved in the construction trade during the boom time after the Great War—was held in cash and government bonds. His seventeen-room brick mansion at 3901 Henry Avenue was set amid lush, undulating lawns, and the property featured a tennis court and elaborate recreational equipment for active children. The house was mortgage-free, like Kelly's seaside vacation home in Ocean City, New Jersey. The family sailed through the Depression enjoying a genteel, privileged life: the Kelly children attended private academies; there were household servants and workers to tend the grounds and gardens; and the children wore only the finest new seasonal wardrobes.

Grace had two older siblings: Margaret ("Peggy"), born in September 1925; and John junior ("Kell"), born in May 1927. The family was complete with the birth of Elizabeth Anne ("Lizanne") in June 1933. "I wasn't a strong child like my sisters and brother," Grace said years later, "and my family told me they thought I was practically born with a cold—I was always sniffling and sneezing, clearing my throat and fighting some kind of respiratory ailment." Her mother routinely reserved the juices of the family roasts for fragile young Grace, in a constant effort to improve the child's strength and stamina.

"My other children were the strong ones, the extroverts, but Gracie was shy and retiring," her mother recalled. "She was also frail and sickly a good deal of the time." The girl filled the hours of her frequent confinements by making up stories and plays for her collection of dolls. "Grace could change her voice for each doll, giving it a different character. She loved attention for all this, but she didn't cry if she didn't get it."

Thin and withdrawn, Grace preferred to read myths, fairy tales and books about dancers and dancing; indeed, her favorite dolls were fashioned like tiny ballerinas, complete with pointe shoes and delicate tutus. She also loved to read poetry and tried her hand at verses:

> *I hate to see the sun go down*
> *And squeeze itself into the ground,*
> *Since some warm night it might get stuck*
> *And in the morning not get up!*

Grace was largely indifferent to physical activity: "I liked to swim, but did my best to avoid other sports and games." This attitude made her something of an outsider. Her father had been an Olympic athlete, her mother a champion swimmer and physical education teacher, and their children were strongly encouraged—indeed, they were expected—to excel at competitive sports. Grace's preference for books and imaginative games did not go down well with her father, a man who had little interest in cultural or intellectual matters.

BORN IN 1889, John B. "Jack" Kelly was the youngest of ten children born to Irish immigrants. Quitting school in early adolescence, he worked in the family firm as a bricklayer while perfecting his skill at sculling (rowing on the river), and during army service in the World War, he became a champion boxer. Returning to civilian life, Jack rejoined his father's company, Kelly for Brickwork, and the postwar building boom of the

1920s quickly made him a millionaire. He did not, however, achieve this on his own, as he often implied, nor was he a self-made American success story. "They've latched on to the brick-layer theme and won't let go of this Horatio Alger idea," said his brother George, who directly confronted Jack's self-glorification. "What's all this talk about you getting callused hands laying bricks? The only times I remember you having calluses were from long hours of scull practice on the Schuylkill River!"

Wealth freed Jack to spend those long hours rowing. After winning six national championships, he headed for the Henley Regatta in England, the most celebrated event in the sport of sculling. But in 1920 his application for inclusion was rejected at the last minute when the judges determined that his years of manual labor and muscular development as a bricklayer gave him an unfair advantage over "gentleman" athletes. The true reason for his dismissal, however, was that the English authorities did not want to risk giving a prize to an Irish-American Catholic. The consequential outcry was so loud that by 1937 the rules at Henley no longer excluded manual laborers, mechanics or artisans as unfit for the competition.

More determined than ever after this rejection, Kelly proceeded to the 1920 summer Olympics at Antwerp, Belgium, where he won a gold medal in the single scull and, half an hour later, a second gold medal in the double scull, in which he rowed with a cousin. His family later swore to the truth of the anecdote that he mailed his racing cap to King George V with the message, "Greetings from a bricklayer." Four years later, during the summer of 1924, Kelly and his cousin repeated their success at the Paris Olympics—an achievement that made "the Irish bricklayer" the first rower to win three Olympic gold medals. With that, he became one of the most famous athletes of his generation, and his name was included in the United

States Olympic Hall of Fame. Later he was appointed National Physical Fitness Director by President Franklin D. Roosevelt, who regarded him as a good friend.

Before his Paris triumph, Kelly renounced bachelorhood (but not his avocation as a womanizer) when he married Margaret Majer on January 30, 1924, at St. Bridget's Church. She was nine years his junior and as strikingly beautiful as he was darkly handsome. They had first met at a swim club, where she successfully competed; she was also one of Philadelphia's most successful cover-girl models. With her degree in physical education, she became the first woman to teach that field at the University of Pennsylvania and at Women's Medical College. She converted from Lutheranism to her fiancé's religion just before their wedding.

"I had a good stiff German background," Margaret said years later. "My parents believed in discipline and so do I—no tyranny or anything like that, but a certain firmness." Proper appearances, unfailing decorum, the importance of manners: these were almost religious observances for Margaret Majer Kelly. She trained her children to control themselves, to hide pain and disappointment, to suppress their emotions in public, to disguise effort and to strive for perfection without seeming to do so. Her tutoring was more successful with Grace than with the others.

Margaret's discipline was apparently unremitting. Kell nicknamed her "the Prussian general" for her heavy hand, and Grace recalled her mother's insistence that her daughters learn not only the fine points of competitive sports but also those of sewing, cooking, dressmaking and gardening. "My mother was the disciplinarian in our family," she said. "My father was very gentle, never the one to spank or scold. My mother did that. But when my father spoke—boy, you moved." Life among the Kellys was to be enjoyed by the constant development of new skills and by the quiet assumption of responsibilities, and Margaret's chief occupation became the training of her children. Jack, meanwhile, was involved in local politics, business, sports and a social (and amorous) life that excluded his family.

When Jack was at home, famous athletes from all over the world frequently visited. For the parents and for Peggy, Kell and Lizanne, these people were stimulating company; for Grace, they were tiresome and left her feeling more alienated than ever. "I never really felt pretty, bright or socially adept, and all that talk of sports, politics and business left me cold." People often mistook Grace's shyness for an attitude of superiority and, later, of snobbery. The truth was that, in addition to her quite different interests and hobbies, she was exceedingly nearsighted: without her hated glasses, very little was clear and she could not recognize people. "She was so myopic she couldn't see ten feet in front of her" without glasses, recalled Howell Conant, who later became her favorite photographer.

Grace's estimation of herself was also formed by her father's favoritism, and this, as with any child, caused her some insecurity. "My older sister was my father's favorite," Grace reflected years later, "and then there was the boy, the only son. Then I came. After that, I had a baby sister, and I was terribly jealous of the attention she got. I was always on my mother's knee, the clinging type. But I was pushed away [by my mother], and so I resented my sister for years."

"Of the four children, Peggy was Jack's favorite," recalled Dorothea Sitley, a longtime family friend. "Grace was the introvert, the quiet, serene one, and she felt left out. It was always Peggy and her father together." Jack admitted his preference for his firstborn child: "I thought it would be Peggy whose name would be up in lights one day. Anything that Grace could do, Peggy could always do better"—or so he thought.

"According to him, Peggy was destined to be the star of the

family," recalled Grace's close friend and publicist, Rupert Allan (later also the Monégasque consul general in Los Angeles). "Jack never paid much attention to Grace—he accepted her, but he never understood her. But she adored him and always sought his approval." Jack Kelly was "a very nice man," recalled Grace's friend Judith Balaban Kanter Quine, "but he was a man without much sensitivity."

As much as she must have been aware of her father's preference for Peggy, Grace longed for her older sister's approval as much as for his. "I used to help my sister sell flowers to passersby to raise money for my mother's pet charity, Women's Medical College and Hospital of Pennsylvania. Naturally, most of our customers were the neighbors. Little did they know that some of the flowers came from their own gardens. I used to be sent by my big sister Peggy to raid the nearby gardens at night, and quite unashamedly we sold these same flowers back to their owners next morning."

Just as she tried to befriend her sister, "Grace admired her father," according to her close friend, the actress Rita Gam. "But she thought he really never appreciated her. He always preferred Peggy and never approved of Grace's career—and her mother was a very tough lady, rather critical and not terribly warm. Both her parents said they were surprised and puzzled by Grace's later success. When she talked about this, there was a certain wistfulness in her voice, but she was an extremely loyal person and very protective of her family." What might be called Grace's marginal status in a family of hardy, rah-rah competitors evoked a touching desire for demonstrative affection. "As a child," recalled her sister Lizanne, "she loved to be held and cuddled and kissed." This longing for physical tokens of affection increased with the years.

Grace and her father remained virtual strangers to each other until his death in 1960. She never addressed the topic directly, but she said that her father liked to be with rough, self-confident children who could tumble on a playing field and bounce right back up. The implication was clear: that was not a description of Grace at any age, and she felt outside the orbit of his approval. Judy Quine agreed: "Jack Kelly didn't cozy up to Grace. He understood business, politics and sports. He knew what these things were about, but he never 'got it' about Grace. Toward the end of his life, he accepted her. He saw her impact on the world and he showed her some respect. That's what they shared at the end of his life—deep respect."

It was perhaps inevitable, then, that a senior family servant named Godfrey Ford became something of a father figure. Addressed as "Fordie," he was the Kelly chauffeur and factotum, evoking enormous affection from all the youngsters—and especially from Grace. "He kept their cars polished," recalled the Kellys' childhood friend Elaine Cruice Beyer. "He could serve, put on a big party, supervise bartenders and buffets and keep the gardens in beautiful condition." Grace's respect and fondness for the African-American Fordie instilled in her a lifelong hatred of racism.

On Thursdays, when the children's nanny was off duty, Fordie was entrusted with the task of putting the children to bed. "Gracie asked my opinions about this and that," he recalled years later. "I'd tell her what I thought, and she'd usually follow my advice." Later he gave her driving lessons in front of the house and in the long driveway, "but she was never good at parking."

SHORTLY BEFORE Grace marked her sixth birthday, in November 1935, she began her education, joining Peggy at the Ravenhill Academy, a convent school for girls less than a half-mile away, on School House Lane. Built in the nineteenth century as a family home by the millionaire William Weightman, Raven-hill is a grand High Victorian Gothic mansion with dark panel-ing, ornate fireplaces, dramatic staircases and formal parlors. Weightman's daughter later donated the vast residence to the Roman Catholic archdiocese of Philadelphia, and when Dennis Dougherty was appointed archbishop in 1918, one of his first acts was to invite the Religious of the Assumption—an order of teaching nuns with whom he had worked as a bishop in the Philippines—to come from Manila and establish a school for girls at Ravenhill, which they did in 1919. Admission was strictly controlled, and at its peak there were but fifty students in the entire first through twelfth grades.

"They were remarkable women," Grace said, "and I was enormously fond of them. They were strict about our studies, but also very, very kind. Their long black habits were simply the formal garb of an exceptional group of teachers, and however rigorous their religious life, the nuns understood young girls and devoted themselves completely to our educational and spiritual welfare." The nuns insisted, among other elements of proper decorum, that the girls wear white gloves to and from school—a convention already familiar to Grace from her mother's home training.

At Ravenhill, Grace's teachers encouraged her wide read-ing, her drawing, her hobby of learning to arrange flowers for classroom and chapel, and her custom of filling a notebook with simple lyrics:

> *Little flower, you're the lucky one—*
> *you soak in all the lovely sun,*
> *you stand and watch it all go by*
> *and never once do bat an eye*
> *while others have to fight and strain*

against the world and its every pain
of living.

But you too must have wars to fight
the cold bleak darkness of every night,
of a bigger vine that seeks to grow
and is able to stand the rain and snow
and yet you never let it show
on your pretty face.

In 1943, Grace began four years of high school at the nearby, nonsectarian Stevens School. At that time it was unusual for a Catholic family to send a child to a non-Catholic school, especially after the years at Ravenhill. But the Kellys were not particularly devout. "Aside from going to Mass on Sundays and saying our prayers before going to bed, we didn't do anything else," Lizanne recalled. "We didn't eat meat on Friday, but even then Mother wasn't too demanding. She said, 'If you happen to be visiting someone and it's Friday and they serve meat, eat it. I don't want them feeling uncomfortable because of you.'" To Margaret's credit, this was good religious common sense—and such a "liberal" viewpoint was not the common attitude of the day among American Catholics.

"My dad was not a very great religious person," Kell said years later. "He attended church more for the children, my sisters and myself, rather than for great sincerity in his beliefs. My mother, of course, was not a Catholic until she married my father. She went through the routine and did the basic minimum, but she is not an active Catholic today [1976]. People who don't know her are inclined to think she is [devout]. But she is not upset over my separation from the Catholic religious point of view—except that it makes her look like something less than a perfect mother." As for Grace, thanks to both her family and the wise nuns at Ravenhill, she never had the neurotic, haunted sense of guilt that often afflicts the scrupulous. On the other hand, she always took her faith seriously—even more so as demands and disappointments accumulated.

At fourteen she had nearly reached her full adult height of five feet, six inches; blue-eyed, lithe and poised, with blond hair turning light brown, she had mostly outgrown her childhood respiratory ailments, but they had left her with a flat, nasal tone it would take years to counter.

As local hospitals were crowded with World War II casualties, volunteers appeared from every station in life, and many schoolgirls devoted several hours each week to helping overworked nurses and aides. Shy and sensitive, Grace was nevertheless coolly efficient when dispatching indelicate chores in the wards. In addition, she quickly understood how much her presence meant to the young men, for she was, after all, a disarmingly attractive young woman.

The Stevens School, located on Walnut Lane in the adjacent neighborhood of Germantown, had been established "for young matrons who are interested in establishing ideal, satisfying homes and in administering them efficiently and scientifically." This rather grandly stated agenda, written at the turn of the twentieth century, was effectively the program for little more than a finishing school for the daughters of wealthy Philadelphians, although by Grace's time things had taken a somewhat more academic turn. She did well in her four-year course of studies, except in science and mathematics, which bored her.

"She is one of the beauties of our class," states the school yearbook for 1947. "Full of fun and always ready for a good laugh, she has no trouble making friends. A born mimic, she is well known for her acting ability, which reached its peak this year in her portrayal of Peter Pan in our Spring Play." Grace was also a member of the glee club and the hockey and swim teams, she excelled at modern dancing, and she was named "Chairman of the Dress and Good Behavior Committee," which must have pleased her mother. Her favorite actress and actor, she said that year, were Ingrid Bergman and Joseph Cotten, who had appeared together in *Gaslight,* a picture she saw many times. "Ingrid Bergman made an enormous impression on me," Grace said. "I couldn't imagine where that kind of acting talent came from." Her favorite summer resort was Ocean City, the family's summer residence; her preferred drink was a chocolate milkshake; among classical music selections, she loved Debussy's "Clair de Lune"; her favorite orchestra was Benny Goodman's; and she especially liked the singer Jo Stafford.

But it was acting with the school drama society, and the parts she played with local amateur groups, that most appealed to Grace. Her parents were almost mute with astonishment as their shy, retiring daughter flourished not by competing, but by participating in the joint effort that a cast makes onstage to create a memorable impact on an audience. As it happened, she drew her primary inspiration from one of her father's brothers.

Her theatrical mentor was not, as is commonly believed, her uncle Walter Kelly, who was sixteen years older than Grace's father. The family had seen him act onstage and in a few films, but he was something of an embarrassment. A nationally known vaudevillian, he had made his fame in a series of monologues that could not be performed in later decades, for they were openly and frankly racist. Dough-faced and corpulent, Walter Kelly played "The Virginia Judge" in a constantly changing series of sketches in which he mimicked not only the judge but also a legion of black men characterized as ignorant and slothful.

Both the magistrate and the malefactors, all played by Kelly, appeared in a mock court where the "colored folks" tried unsuccessfully to defend themselves against various specious accusations.

Walter's sketches about "darkies" and "pickaninnies" (his words) were a staple of clubs, theatres and music halls for over twenty-five years. He also made a number of wildly successful recordings, and he appeared in seven Broadway shows and a half-dozen movies. Grace saw some of his acts and a few of his pictures, but she found only one production both amusing and oddly congruent: the 1935 film *McFadden's Flats,* about a successful bricklayer who earns his fortune as a builder of apartments. Walter Kelly died in January 1939, succumbing to injuries after being hit by a speeding truck on a Los Angeles street. He was sixty-five, had never married, and, owing to his sumptuous living, had depleted a fortune.

The mentorship offered to Grace came from another of her father's brothers, whose fame has more deservedly survived— George Kelly, who became Grace's theatrical guru and lifelong champion. First as an actor and then as one of America's most successful playwrights, George was a completely different man from Walter; indeed, they had so little in common that they never made any efforts to keep in touch.

"George Kelly was a very gracious, highly educated person," recalled Rupert Allan, "well read and very witty, but also exceptionally elegant and cultivated. Grace just adored him." Rita Gam agreed: "George was a perceptive and enormously kind man, and he took a great interest in Grace's youthful dramatic escapades."

George Kelly was born in 1887 and toured nationally as an actor from 1911 on. After military service in France during World War I, he wrote, directed and starred in his own one-act plays, several of which (*The Flattering Word, Poor Aubrey, Mrs.*

Ritter Appears and *The Weak Spot*) have stood time's test and are occasionally presented in repertory and by school and amateur groups. His first full-length Broadway play, *The Torch-Bearers* (1922), which he also directed, is a mordantly funny indictment of amateur theatricals and self-absorbed nonprofessionals. The play reflects George's profound respect for the stage and his lightly veiled contempt for untalented amateurs; ironically, ever since its premiere it has been most often performed by precisely the nonprofessional "little theatre" groups it skewers. "I loved that play as much as I loved Uncle George," Grace said, passing over any mention of Walter when she discussed family history.

Two years after *The Torch-Bearers,* Kelly directed his play *The Show-Off,* which had a Broadway run of almost six hundred performances and was staged with equal success in London; like *The Torch-Bearers,* it has been revived very often. This was soon followed by his production of *Craig's Wife,* which won the 1926 Pulitzer Prize for drama and was the basis for the 1950 movie *Harriet Craig,* which gave Joan Crawford one of her most intense roles as the archetypal middle-class, middle-aged, domineering wife who places domestic perfection above all relationships.

More plays followed, but the last decades of George Kelly's life, while comfortable and personally fulfilling, were professionally static. His plays were neither epigrammatic nor vulgar, and audiences had to sit patiently, listening to long acts in which both characters and social commentaries were revealed through dialogue. He was, in other words, a man of a specific kind of theatre, ferociously moralistic and poorly suited to the later different styles of (for example) Arthur Miller, Tennessee Williams and William Inge. "I won't put my plays out for production because the theater has changed so much," he said in 1970. "I just don't want to become involved [in an era] that is frightful, shallow and sensationalistic." The truth was that the styles of popular comedy and drama had moved beyond him, and he had no desire to keep up with changing theatrical fashion.

One might presume that Margaret and Jack Kelly took pride in their connection to George. But in fact they were less than enthusiastic about him, for he was exclusively homosexual, living for decades with his partner, William Weagley. At that time, having a gay relative was too terrible to contemplate for all but a few enlightened American families, and a man who was "sensitive" (the tip-off code word) could be endured only if the most insistent silence about the awful truth was maintained. When George died in 1974, Weagley was not invited to the funeral; he crept into the church and took a back seat, weeping quietly and completely ignored. He died a year later.

During her childhood and adolescence, Grace heard the whispers and cruel giggles about Uncle George. These she deeply resented, cherishing his visits to Henry Avenue, when he advised her on plays to read, cued her lines when she was in rehearsal, made lists of roles she might undertake in the future and was the only one in the family to take her acting aspirations seriously. "I am so proud of my niece Grace," he said toward the end of his life. "She is not only a very fine actress but is a human being with considerable qualities. Had she stayed on the stage and continued her career, I think we would have seen some very fine performances from her."

Even on his deathbed, George could give quite a performance on his own. When another niece came to visit him, he addressed her with words worthy of Oscar Wilde: "My dear, before you kiss me good-bye, fix your hair—it's a mess."

"To me, he was the most wonderful person," Grace said. "I could sit and listen to him for hours, and I often did. He introduced me to all kinds of things I would never have considered or been exposed to—classic literature, poetry and great plays. He loved beautiful things and refined language, and these he shared with me in ways I never forgot. He was also one of the few people who stood up to my father, disagreed with him, contradicted him. I thought Uncle George was fearless."

George spoke to Jack about allowing Grace to act in local amateur productions: her grades at school were fine, so why should she not indulge her love of the theatre? And so, soon after she entered Stevens, Grace was seen in a one-act comedy, now forgotten, called *Don't Feed the Animals,* written by Bob Wellington and staged by the Old Academy Players on Indian Queen Lane, East Falls. It was no coincidence that the Players—a group that had performed every season since 1923 (and still maintains an impressive schedule)—were passionate partisans of George Kelly, with repeated productions of his works already in their history.

Uncle George remained Grace's favorite member of the family. She persuaded the entire Kelly clan to travel to New York on February 12, 1947, for the opening night of a Broadway revival of *Craig's Wife,* which George directed. (The title role was played by Judith Evelyn, who later assumed the role of "Miss Lonelyhearts" in Alfred Hitchcock's *Rear Window.*)

Grace's teenage scrapbooks, which she preserved and which her children placed on exhibit in 2007, give some idea of her love of theatre during her school years. On December 9, 1943, for example, she saw F. Hugh Herbert's comedy *Kiss and Tell,* at the Locust Theatre in Philadelphia, and she went to as many productions of Uncle George's plays as she could.

IN 1943, Grace's social life flourished. At that time, the word "dating" did not imply a casual sexual affair, but innocent activities like moviegoing, dancing and parties. According to her mother, "Grace's first date was with a young man named Harper Davis, who went to the William Penn Charter School and often took her out to a basketball game or a dance." Three years older than Grace, Harper was one of the most popular and handsome young men in her social orbit, and her scrapbook includes many souvenirs of her dates with this good-looking teenager. He gave her a bottle of perfume at Christmas and signed the gift card, "To Grace with love, Harper." She pasted into her scrapbook the school dance programs for which Harper was her date, a stick of the chewing gum package he gave her on New Year's Eve, and the business card from the store at which he bought her a silver charm on Valentine's Day. She also pressed into her memory book remnants of the flowers he brought her on this or that occasion. Grace's passion for floral arrangements and preservation dates from these early years and was later the subject of her volume *My Book of Flowers,* published in 1980.

At that time, dating among polite young people was conducted according to a complex etiquette that was in fact a subject taught at schools like Stevens and William Penn. Girls and boys learned to dance and were told which subjects were appropriate for civilized conversation. Young ladies were instructed on proper posture, how to walk and sit, how they should hold their white-gloved hands, and what to say to a young man at the door, at the end of an evening. Boys were trained in the right way to ask a girl to dance, and classes in decorum were routinely held in schools.

In the spring of 1944, at the height of World War II, Harper graduated from school, joined the navy and was sent abroad. Not long after returning, he contracted multiple sclerosis, from which he suffered until his death in 1953. Grace visited him often during his confinement and attended his funeral. "He was the first boy I ever loved, and I'll never forget him," she said.

The relationship with Harper, like other dates during her high school years, was entirely chaste, for Grace had not yet tested the waters of sexual experience. Such reticence was typical of the time, especially in polite circles: young people's sexual urges did not tend to lurch into full throttle, nor did they race, as it was said, to go "all the way." Reliable methods of contraception were not readily or widely available, and the fear of pregnancy, venereal disease and an indecent reputation kept the reins on youthful impulses. In addition, penicillin, later the drug of choice against sexually transmitted infections, had only recently been developed, and it was reserved for men injured in combat. Civilian physicians had access to it for the general public only after 1946.

This is not to say that the standards of Queen Victoria and Mrs. Grundy were everywhere observed; it is simply to state the obvious—that sexual intercourse for American teenagers in the 1940s was not as commonplace as it later became. When Grace graduated from high school, she was still a virgin, although she had easily and often fallen in love. "My sister Lizanne loved only one, the boy she married—but Peggy and I were in and out of love every other day."

On June 5, 1947, Grace graduated from Stevens; her classmates predicted, in the senior yearbook, that she was certain "to become a stage and screen star." The following month, she made her first trip to Europe, along with her entire family. The journey was occasioned by Kell's entry into the Henley Regatta after he had received the James E. Sullivan Award earlier that year, which named him the foremost amateur athlete in America. Before and after his navy service during World War II, Kell was relentlessly, even ruthlessly, trained and driven by his father. He won the United States single sculls title in 1946, and Jack Kelly got his revenge for the episode of 1920 during that summer of 1947, when Kell won the Diamond Challenge

Sculls—a victory he repeated two years later. "There was never any doubt what Jack wanted," Margaret said later. "He always insisted he would have a son to make the Diamond Sculls."

Despite impressive post-Henley achievements, Kell never won an Olympic gold medal. "It was a failure my father's contemporaries won't let me forget," he said in 1971. "My father was a tough act to follow—a big, strong guy, fine-looking, eminently successful. There was always pressure to excel, to keep up. I've been competing with him all my life. Living in his shadow made losing harder when I lost, which wasn't very often, but I was humiliated for both of us." That summer, Jack saw that his son's presence in England was documented by the press. "I could never understand my father, letting photographers take pictures of Kell shaving in the bathroom," Grace said. Jack's influence, added Margaret, "was not always good for Kell. I often told Jack that he leaned too hard on the boy, trained him too hard for the Olympics—and it hurt Kell." Arthur Lewis, who knew the whole family, was blunter: Jack "messed up his only son's life by forging him into an instrument of personal revenge."

As also required by his father, Kell later joined the family business while continuing an involvement in sports. He was president of the Amateur Athletic Union, and he won a bronze medal in the 1956 summer Olympics. He became a Philadelphia city councilman, and, briefly, he was president of the United States Olympic Committee.

Kell's personal life was complicated and disordered. He married a champion swimmer and had six children, but then one day, without warning or explanation, he walked out on his family and never returned. He became a notorious playboy, had a serious problem with alcohol, and on May 2, 1985, at the age of fifty-seven, John B. Kelly Jr. dropped down dead while jogging to the Athletic Club after his customary morning row on the Schuylkill River. He was posthumously inducted into the U.S. Olympic Hall of Fame, and Philadelphia's Kelly Drive was named in his honor. He and his father are the only parent-child athletes in the Olympic Hall of Fame.

"Kell never had to grow up," Grace said. "He was naïve, he confused attention with loyalty, he tried too hard to make people like him—and he didn't have Father's toughness, sense of humor or resilience."

Peggy's story, too, was unhappy. After two failed marriages, she sank into alcoholism and died of a stroke at the age of sixty-six, in 1991. Lizanne was then the only surviving offspring of the Kelly-Majer marriage.

AFTER HENLEY that summer of 1947, Margaret took her daughters to Switzerland while the men returned to Philadelphia. The holiday was intended as a kind of consolation prize for Grace, whose low grades in mathematics prevented her matriculation to Bennington College in Vermont, to which she had applied because of its highly regarded drama department.

But Grace really needed no solace. As soon as she received the exceedingly polite rejection letter from Bennington, she began making inquiries about enrollment at the American Academy of Dramatic Arts in New York City. When she finally brought up the subject with her parents, they were not at all pleased—perhaps because of the unorthodox, unconventional life of Jack's brother George. "Daddy was uncomfortable around theatre people for one simple reason: he didn't understand them," said Lizanne. Judith Quine was more explicit: "Jack Kelly saw acting as a slim cut above streetwalker."

"She wouldn't let her Uncle George help her prepare" for

the American Academy, recalled Jack. "She was determined to go places without leaning on anybody or using influence." Added Judith, "She left a prominent Philadelphia family to become a struggling actress in New York. It was an independent move. She had a certain amount of maverick in her, and she was entirely self-sufficient. She knew how to depend on herself." Grace was single-minded in her ambition to succeed as a professional actress. "I rebelled against my family and went to New York to find out who I was—and who I wasn't."

Margaret intervened to temper her husband's disapproval, which could have become an outright veto. "Oh, Jack—it's not as if she's going to *Hollywood,* after all," her daughters remembered their mother saying. "Let Grace go—this won't amount to anything, and she'll be home in a week."

The idea of a career in the theatre was disturbing enough to her father, but pursuing it in New York, and not just with an amateur group in the Pennsylvania provinces—well, that combined Sodom with Gomorrah. Manhattan was no more than ninety minutes by train from Philadelphia, but it was no place for a proper young lady on her own. Why wouldn't she settle down in Philadelphia and marry a nice, rich Catholic boy? "I hear some of your school chums are coming out," Jack said to Grace, raising the prospect of the formal entrance into polite society that was common at the time. "Do you want to come out, too?"

Her reply was firm: "I *am* out! Do you think that to get a date I have to use those women who sell mailing lists of boys' names?" No, she had other plans and was not to be stopped.

"I was saved from professional perdition," Grace said, "because there happened to be a place in New York that my parents thought would preserve, protect and defend me, as if I were the Constitution. It was a residential hotel for women only, and to have my father's consent to audition for the American Academy of Dramatic Arts, I had to agree to live at that hotel—not in an apartment on my own." Perhaps because of his own philandering, Jack was not inclined to trust his children. A hotel for women, which denied access to men above the street-level foyer, would keep careful watch and ward over young Miss Kelly.

TWO

The Student Model

*I don't want to have your mind and will, Father—I want
to be myself.*

    —GRACE (AS BERTHA) IN STRINDBERG'S *THE FATHER*

THE TWENTY-THREE-STORY BARBIZON HOTEL FOR
Women, at Lexington Avenue and 63rd Street, was
designed using an imaginative blend of Italian Ren-
aissance, Gothic and Islamic architectural styles. Admitting its
first residents in 1927, it represented an alternative for young
women arriving in New York in the Roaring Twenties, leaving
home·in search of new professional opportunities but wanting
a safe, respectable place to live. The owners and managers created and reinforced the values of the mostly wealthy families
from which these women had come; in 1947, few others could
afford the rate of twelve dollars a week.

Three letters of reference were required from applicants, and
there was always a long waiting list. Dress codes and house rules
were strictly enforced; liquor was forbidden on the premises; and
men could visit only on the ground floor. Despite—or perhaps

because of—these apparent constraints, the Barbizon was considered a very desirable place to live. "If a girl put on her résumé that she lived at the Barbizon," recalled Margaret Campbell, the longtime executive housekeeper, "that was almost enough, morally and socially," to guarantee employment; at the least, residents had access to some of New York's higher social life. Several of the Beale and Bouvier daughters lived there in the 1920s and 1930s, and over the years its tenant list included the writer Sylvia Plath and many aspiring or working actresses, among them Lauren Bacall, Barbara Bel Geddes, Gene Tierney, Candice Bergen and Liza Minnelli.

The accommodations were certainly not luxurious, and a new girl's first impression might have been that her austere quarters resembled a convent cell or a house of correction. The nine-by-twelve-foot rooms were little more than cubicles, with space only for a narrow bed, an armless chair, a clothes rack, a floor lamp and a small writing desk. Fewer than eighty of the 686 rooms had private baths—the rest shared common facilities on each floor. But everyone had the use of the hotel's gymnasium and swimming pool, library, music studio, kitchen and dining room. Complimentary afternoon tea with tiny sandwiches was served in a large parlor—close to dinnertime, for the benefit of those on tight budgets. The place was lively with news, gossip and music played on a phonograph that had seen better days.

Grace settled into the Barbizon in late August 1947. "She kept a great deal to herself," recalled Hugh Connor, the manager during the years of her residency; he added that she seemed very shy, sitting alone, wearing glasses as she read or knitted. Grace kept a wire recorder in her room and listened to herself reading so that she might improve her diction. But she was not antisocial and established several friendships that endured for the rest of her life: close companions knew her, skill at droll imitations and responded to her infectious laughter. Carolyn Scott, an aspiring model who also lived at the Barbizon, remembered Grace as being sedate in public, given to tweed suits, sensible shoes and a hat with a veil—an image recalled by many that year. "Grace's usual outfit," according to another friend, Alice Godfrey, "was a sweater or cardigan, a bandanna or scarf, a simple skirt and always her glasses—nothing glamorous."

BEFORE HER eighteenth birthday that autumn, and after several auditions and interviews, the American Academy of Dramatic Arts accepted Grace's application for enrollment and handed over a copy of their rating of her abilities:

> *Voice: Improperly placed*
> *Temperament: Sensitive*
> *Spontaneity: Youthful*
> *Dramatic instinct: Expressive*
> *Intelligence: Good*
> *General remarks: Good, full of potential and freshness*

Founded in 1884 and still successfully operating 125 years later, the Academy was the first school to offer a professional education in theatre arts and was considered a prestigious institute for students and working actors in the United States. When Grace arrived, its alumni list included scores of successful actors, among them Spencer Tracy, Katharine Hepburn, Edward G. Robinson, Ruth Gordon, Rosalind Russell and Kirk Douglas. Students enrolled in a two-year program, attending classes several hours for two or three days a week in the cavernous upper floors of Carnegie Hall, at the corner of Seventh Avenue and 57th Street.*

"As I remember, our lessons, exercises and rehearsals were rather loosely structured," Grace recalled. "We read and analyzed scenes from the classics and from modern plays, we improvised and from time to time we presented fully staged plays for alumni and teachers. There were classes in voice, fencing, makeup, mime—nothing was omitted. And discount tickets were available to Broadway theatres." During her first year at the Academy, Grace remembered seeing the New York productions of *Finian's Rainbow, All My Sons, Brigadoon, The Heiress, A Streetcar Named Desire* and *Mister Roberts.*

Tuition at the American Academy cost $1,000 a year, an enormous sum in 1947. Almost every student held down a job, and Grace was no exception, for she never wavered in her refusal to accept family support. That year, several residents at the Barbizon were working as models, and they insisted that she, too, could earn good money in print ads and commercials. She needed only some good photos to show to modeling agencies.

In 1946 and 1947, peacetime prosperity brought an increase in leisure time and more disposable income for household appliances and entertainment. At once, there was an enormous upsurge in the production of television sets, as wartime manufacturing freezes were lifted. At the same time, the New York–based television networks pushed westward to cover the entire country, and the price of TV sets continued to fall with the boom in mass production. Whereas only 0.5 percent of U.S.

---

* When I began a year of Saturday acting classes for teenagers at the Academy in the fall of 1956, it occupied space above the Alvin (later rechristened the Neil Simon) Theatre, at 250 West 52nd Street. I remember a wall of alumni photos, among which Grace's portrait was prominently displayed. By that time she had won an Oscar and was Princess of Monaco.

households had a television set in 1946, 35 percent had one by 1947. This astonishing growth was accompanied by a proliferation of advertising agencies like BBDO and Young & Rubicam, and modeling agencies like those founded by Eileen Ford, which needed many more attractive young women to promote and publicize products. Ford, for example, had two clients in 1946 and thirty-four the following year.*

Grace's friends at Barbizon were on the mark. With her restraint and poise, her bright, blue-green eyes, her alabaster complexion, and a glorious smile that made everyone want to smile with her, she was precisely the image Middle America adored and wanted to replicate. Without any difficulty, Grace found work as a model from 1947 through 1949, signing with the John Robert Powers modeling agency. Founded in Philadelphia in 1923, the agency had briefly represented her mother, who frequently had Powers agents photograph her children. By 1947 the agency had a New York office, and along with Grace, the actress Rita Gam joined its client list. "I thought she was the most gorgeous creature I ever met," recalled Rita. "She was also entirely unaffected, completely without vanity."

Grace began working at $7.50 an hour, and her pay rose quickly to $25.00 an hour—and then to more than $400 a week (approximately $4,000 a week in 2009 valuation). She thus became one of the highest-paid models in New York, and the income covered her tuition bills at the American Academy of Dramatic Arts while enabling her to save healthy sums each month. "She absolutely did not want to be supported by the

---

* In 1946, a good automobile cost $1,400; gasoline was twenty-one cents a gallon; a fine new home could be purchased for $12,500; bread cost ten cents a loaf; a first-class postage stamp was three cents; the minimum wage was forty cents an hour; a respectable annual salary was $3,150; and the stock market was booming at 177.

family," said Lizanne. "I remember her saying, 'If I can't have a career on my own, by my own means, I don't want to have one at all.' " Grace appeared in five-minute-long fashion movies filmed in Paris and Bermuda; she was on the covers of *Cosmopolitan* and *Redbook;* she was photographed for advertisements for Max Factor lipstick, Lustre Creme shampoo, Cashmere Bouquet and Lux soaps, Rheingold beer, Ipana toothpaste, Talbot beauty creams and Old Gold cigarettes—and she often acted in TV commercials.

"My still photographs were okay," she said years later, "but in the TV commercials I was—honestly and truly—just terrible. I think anyone watching me promote Ipana toothpaste must have run out to buy Colgate, or if they saw my Old Gold commercial, they would have bought Lucky Strikes or Chesterfields. It would be nice to think I was not believable in them because I didn't believe in the products, but the truth is that I was simply awkward in reciting the words and stiff in my gestures. My first TV commercial was for an insecticide, and I had to run around a room smiling like an idiot and spraying like a demon. It wasn't exactly what the Academy was preparing me for." When I told Grace that it was very difficult to find any surviving TV commercials in which she had appeared, she said, "Thank God for that!"

GRACE'S ROMANTIC life has been the stuff of considerable tabloid speculation since her death, and the number of her lovers has been greatly exaggerated. But an intimate relationship did begin in late 1948, when she fell in love with Don Richardson, one of her teachers at the Academy. Eleven years her senior, he was a sophisticated New Yorker who completely charmed her, and their affair continued intensely over almost two years. "It came as no surprise when she asked permission to bring him home for the weekend," Lizanne recalled. "The visit was in April 1949, and it was a disaster. At the dinner table, the sound of knives and forks was deafening. The silence was virtually absolute. Every now and then, somebody tried to start up a conversation, but it didn't last. Mr. Richardson, for his part, was racking his brain for any topic of conversation that was not theatre. Again, silence. He just didn't fit in and never did."

There may have been several reasons for the collective cold-shouldering of Don Richardson. Separated but not yet divorced from his wife, he was an actor, a director and a Jewish New Yorker. In addition, Margaret implied that Grace was using Richardson to advance her career. "Honey," she told her daughter, "you can make it on your own. You don't need anyone." Grace was horrified at her mother's suspicions, but her mother's words planted the seeds of doubt about her intentions with Richardson. "The whole situation couldn't have been more gruesome," Grace wrote to Prudy Wise, a friend at the Barbizon who later became her secretary. "The fact that I could fall in love with a Jew was just beyond them." Grace ended the affair when Richardson persisted in pursuing other romances at the same time, and because he was not free to marry; most of all, she became enormously confused about their respective motives.

Graduation from the Academy in the spring of 1949, when she was nineteen, gave her the opportunity to break off all contact with Richardson. "We were typical young drama students," Grace told me. "When we graduated, we were all saying that soon we would be signing autographs for millions of fans, and we tried out all kinds of ways to write our signatures. Oh, it was just a question of time before we'd have fame and fortune! There would be nothing between us and stardom except a few city blocks—from the Academy to Broadway theatres, an easy five-minute walk." At the commencement party was a young man named John Cassavetes, who was a year behind Grace at the Academy and who soon launched a significant career as an actor and director. He was surprised when another student said to him, "That Grace Kelly is such a pretty little thing. Isn't it a shame she's too shy ever to amount to anything?"

In fact, she was amounting to something that same week, and it had nothing to do with modeling or her connection to Richardson.

Every spring, the producer Theron Bamberger came to the Academy to select a young man and woman for roles at the Bucks County Playhouse in New Hope, Pennsylvania—a venerable institution for repertory theatre and a good place to be noticed as a fledgling actor. After visiting a few classes and interviewing students, Bamberger wrote to Grace on June 22, 1949, offering her summer employment in two plays, with rehearsals beginning July 19. Somehow this reached the press, for the *New York Times* noted briefly that "Grace Kelly, niece of George Kelly, the playwright, will make her professional stage debut beginning July 25, at the Bucks County Playhouse, in Mr. Kelly's comedy, 'The Torch-Bearers.' "

The printed program for the week of performances identified Grace by detailing the achievements of her family. "She is the daughter of John B. Kelly, of Philadelphia. Her brother recently figured in the news by winning the Diamond Sculls at the Henley Regatta in England. Her father was a champion oarsman and is well known as the former chairman of the Democratic Party in Philadelphia."

In her uncle's satire on amateur theatricals, Grace played the role of Florence McCrickett, described by the playwright in the 1922 edition as "a very gorgeous-looking thing, in a sleeveless gown of canary-colored metallic silk, made quite daringly severe, to exploit the long, lithe lines of her greyhound figure. She has a perfect shock of hair—rather striking—a kind of suspicious auburn, and she has it bobbed."

Florence has the eponymous role in *The Doctor's Wife*, the play-within-the-play, a group vehicle chosen for a one-time performance by an amateur company and hilariously (and badly) rehearsed as both dark tragedy and high comedy. Grace was instructed to speak with a kind of wan, affectless detachment, and this she evidently did to deliberate comic perfection. "For a young lady whose previous experience was slim," wrote a local critic, "Miss Kelly came through this footlight baptism of fire splendidly. Although father and mother beamed at Grace from the front rows and other friends were scattered through the house, it was largely a theatrical crowd this girl faced. From where we sat, it appeared as if Grace Kelly should become the theatrical torch-bearer for her family." This was the only review taking note of Grace, and it was written by a woman who knew her family.

She had another small but attractive role in New Hope that season—as Marian Almond, Catherine Sloper's cousin, in the taut drama *The Heiress* (based on Henry James's novel *Washington Square*), which was not reviewed. For these summer productions, she was paid the standard playhouse fee—a total of $100 for two plays, including rehearsals. Again, her family was in the audience. Their reaction to her performances has not been recorded, but for Grace, the support she most sought—her father's—was never forthcoming. He continued to tell interviewers, time and again over the years, that Grace's success astonished him. "I've always thought that Peggy was the daughter with the most on the ball," he said. "I thought all the success would come to Peggy."

~

DURING A BRIEF late-summer holiday with her family at the New Jersey seaside, Grace read a news item: Raymond Massey was about to direct and act in a Broadway revival of August Strindberg's *The Father* (1887), the Swedish playwright's most widely read and performed work, and his darkest, angriest tragedy. In taut, suspenseful dialogue, it tells of Captain Adolph and his wife Laura, who disagree on the education of their daughter Bertha: the father believes his daughter would benefit most from leaving home to study, but the mother wants her to remain. This apparently undramatic premise is but the pretext for the couple's increasingly bitter struggle for power. Laura insists that the final decision must be hers alone because Adolph may not actually be Bertha's father. Hearing this, the captain becomes angrier, more perplexed, and then more violent before dying of a stroke.

Grace hurried to New York to read for the role of Bertha. With no Broadway experience and only her recent summer roles to her credit, she knew that it would be difficult to land a significant part in an important classic, with no less a director and costar than the respected Massey. But Grace had read and reread the play, and she went to the audition with a calm intensity and intelligence that won over Massey and the producers, who chose her over twenty-three other candidates. Rehearsals began in mid-October for a November 16 opening at the Cort Theatre on West 48th Street.

Brooks Atkinson, the senior drama critic of the *New York Times,* felt that the production was fine as far as it went, but that it had too much gentility, that Massey's acting and direction lacked the implacable ferocity necessary for a successful presentation of Strindberg's "thunderbolt of wrath and hatred." On the other hand, Atkinson singled out the twenty-year-old making her Broadway debut: "Grace Kelly gives a charming, pliable performance of the bewildered and broken-hearted daughter." Another critic wrote that Grace had "a naturalness that owes nothing to artifice—no airs, simply a charming freshness." But *The Father* is a difficult and demanding play, and the production failed to attract audiences for longer than two months; it closed on January 14, 1950, after sixty-nine performances.

Later, Grace was typically modest about her debut: "For two years before this, I had been told so often that I was too tall for this part or that part—even at the Academy. Fortunately, Raymond Massey and Mady Christians [who played her parents] were tall actors. If they had been just a few inches shorter, I'm sure I wouldn't have been in the cast." Massey completely discounted her assessment: "She got the part because she showed the most promise. All through the rehearsal period, we were impressed with her earnestness, her professionalism and her good manners. She was organized and dedicated. Between rehearsals, she would ask Mady if she could sit in her dressing room and talk about the theatre. She was a delight to have in the company—a rare kind of young person who had a hunger to learn and to improve herself."

It's interesting to ask why Grace so desperately wanted to play Bertha in this gloomy, haunted play. The obvious answer is that it was a serious classic with two experienced major players in the cast. But she may also have been attracted to the play's theme, which she knew from her own life: a daughter's struggle for independence from a severe and possessive family.

THE FATHER. I believe that it is for your future good that you should leave home, go to town and learn something useful. Will you?

THE DAUGHTER. Oh yes—I should love to go to town, away from here, anywhere. If I can only see you sometimes . . .

THE FATHER. But if Mother doesn't want you to go?

THE DAUGHTER. But she must let me.

THE FATHER. But if she won't?

THE DAUGHTER. Well, then, I don't know what will happen. But she must—she must! You must ask her very nicely—she wouldn't pay any attention to my asking.

The play insists that true parenthood does not consist in shaping a child according to one's will, but in providing the freedom to learn and grow according to her own lights. "I want to be myself!" cries Bertha—a line to which Grace could relate, and which she apparently spoke with great poignancy. In the case of the Kellys, the parents' opinions were the reverse of the characters in the play: Jack had not wanted his daughter "to go to town," and Grace had been able to do so only because Margaret predicted that, after a trial run, their daughter would soon be home. Like Bertha, Grace needed from her parents the freedom to be herself and to determine her own path in life—an autonomy that Grace later struggled to give her own children. In other words, Strindberg's central motif struck close to her heart, and she was far too sensitive and perceptive not to have noticed that the play's family was a virtual mirror image of her own. As Judith Quine recalled, "Grace's father wanted her to be re-created in his image."

This parallel may explain her reticence to discuss the play, her role in it, and the auspicious New York theatrical debut that effectively jump-started her career. With a dismissive smile, she referred only to the matter of her height: if the leading players had not been so tall, "I wouldn't have been in the cast."

HER GOOD reviews earned Grace the attention of New York's increasing number of television producers. Like advertising and modeling agencies, they were being asked to provide more "product" for live TV and its startling increase in the number of comedy and quiz shows, news commentaries, children's programs and live dramas.

In early 1950, many highly successful (and eventually long-running) shows in various genres were already in place. *The Howdy Doody Show* and *Kukla, Fran and Ollie* were both ostensibly for children, but much of the humor was spontaneous, unrehearsed and appreciated only by their parents. Milton Berle's variety show reflected his vaudeville background. Arthur Godfrey was a ukulele-strumming humorist who successfully cultivated an image of bumptious friendliness—until he began to fire his cast on live TV. Baseball games dominated the sports season.

Perhaps most memorable, however, were the many live TV dramas, all of them sponsored by companies that majestically exploited their names—among them *Westinghouse Studio One, The Kraft Television Theatre, The Lux Video Theatre, The Armstrong Circle Theatre, The Goodyear Television Playhouse* and *The Philco Television Playhouse*. Every night, viewers had a choice of several half-hour and hour-long live programs for grown-ups, many of them written and directed by people with theatrical and radio experience, and many who later went on to successful careers in Hollywood. As for the actors, there were old hands (Robert Montgomery, Ronald Reagan) and new (James Dean, Eva Marie Saint, Paul Newman, Walter Matthau, Rod Steiger, Steve McQueen). Theatrical producers and talent agents regularly attended Broadway plays, hoping to sign up good new talent before a movie offer came in, as the major studios—already engaged in a bitter struggle with TV for audience dominance—would not allow contract players to appear on the home screen.

A theatrical agent named Edith Van Cleve, who had been Marlon Brando's agent, was on the lookout for new talent to represent. (After his long run in *A Streetcar Named Desire*, Brando went to Hollywood in late 1949 and never again worked in the theatre.) Grace, who did not have an agent, was performing in *The Father* when Edith saw her onstage and offered to represent her.* Grace was receiving offers for future employment almost daily in early 1950, and she realized she needed a good representative; Edith, a well-born former actress, suited her needs and personality.

"I had just done a screen test," Grace recalled, "and then I had a call to go to a barnlike studio somewhere on the far West Side of Manhattan, where I did another test, with Robert Alda, for a picture called *Taxi*. I was eager to do it because it was going to be filmed in New York, not Hollywood, and it was a one-picture deal. At that point in my career, I tried to avoid signing a long-term contract with a studio. Also, it was an interesting part—that of an Irish girl who has come to New York with her baby and goes around in a cab trying to find her husband. I wanted to try an Irish accent, and I found the character very sympathetic. I didn't get the job, but the test survived for a few years and helped me later on."

Taxi's director, Gregory Ratoff, heartily endorsed Grace for the role of Mary Turner, but after seeing the test, the executives at Twentieth Century-Fox in Hollywood decided she was too elegant and sophisticated for the role of a simple country lass; the job went to Constance Smith, an experienced Irish actress who had already appeared in a dozen pictures. "I was in the 'too' category for a very long time," Grace recalled. "I was too tall, too leggy, too chinny. I remember that Mr. Ratoff kept yelling, 'She's perfect! What I love about this girl is that she's *not pretty*!' "

Edith was soon on the phone, however, and she arranged for Grace to audition for a supporting role in director Joshua

---

* Grace, who had a keen eye and good business sense, apparently negotiated the terms of her own quite straightforward, two-page contract for *The Father,* which had none of the complications of a typical Hollywood agreement.

Logan's production of *The Wisteria Trees,* starring Helen Hayes. Rehearsals were scheduled for February and the opening night for late March. But Grace lost the role because Hayes, who had cast approval, judged that she could not project her voice and was therefore unsuited to stage acting. There had been no vocal problems at the 1,102-seat Cort Theatre during the run of *The Father,* but when she was asked to reach the 1,437 seats of the Martin Beck Theatre from its empty stage at the audition for *The Wisteria Trees,* she may indeed have sounded strained—or merely inaudible. "She quickly brushed aside such setbacks," according to her longtime friend Gant Gaither, "and refused to waste any time wallowing in self-pity." Instead, Grace considered what her next opportunity might be.

She did not have to wait long—indeed, from 1950 to 1954, she acted in three dozen live TV dramas, which made her one of the busiest actresses working in the medium who was not cast in a weekly series.*

She began the busy year of TV work during the run of *The Father,* when she rehearsed for a week during the mornings and then appeared live on the evening of Sunday, January 8, on the *Philco Television Playhouse,* in the title role of "Bethel Merriday," based on the 1940 novel by Sinclair Lewis. The teleplay by William Kendall Clarke moved the story quickly from fifteen-year-old Bethel as a student in 1931, through her college

---

* Grace's TV debut, of which no copy has survived, was on November 3, 1948, in a *Kraft Television Playhouse* production of Albert G. Miller's "Old Lady Robbins," costarring Ethel Owen. It seems to have been unremarkable, for she scarcely recalled it thirty years later. She made no TV appearances in 1949, eleven in 1950, five in 1951, fifteen in 1952, three in 1953 and one in 1954. For years, most sources have erroneously stated that Grace appeared in more than sixty TV programs; the actual number appears to have been thirty-six, most of which have not survived in the kinescope recordings made at the time of live broadcast, which were the precursor to videotape and filming for TV.

years, in which she discovers her love for the stage. She then embarks on a tour as a professional actress, and we follow her transformation from a star-struck girl into a seasoned trouper. The role seemed made for Grace.

"Despite the quickness of the preparation and the broadcast, she really studied and applied herself to understanding the character," recalled the episode's director, Delbert Mann. "In fact, she did brilliantly, and immediately joined the kind of unofficial TV stock company we had in those days, made up of the actors we cast over and over again because they were reliable professionals."

Fred Coe, who produced many of Grace's TV projects, added that Grace "had talent and attractiveness, but so do a lot of other young people in the theatre who never become stars. The thing that made her stand out was something we call 'style.' She wasn't just another beautiful girl, she was the essence of freshness—the kind of girl every man dreams of marrying. All of us who worked with her just loved her. You couldn't work with Grace Kelly without falling a little in love with her." That sentiment was often repeated. "Everyone in the production company of *Rear Window* and *To Catch a Thief* fell for her," recalled Alfred Hitchcock's associate producer, Herbert Coleman, a few years later. "Not only Hitch, most of all. Just about everyone wanted to bring her a cup of tea or run an errand for her or do *something*. She never asked, much less did she demand anything, but everyone wanted to show how much they loved and admired her. I think sometimes it made her uncomfortable."

"Off-camera, she reminded me of a small-town high school teacher," recalled Rita Gam. "Her hair was pulled back into a ponytail, her face was scrubbed clean except for a little dash of lipstick, and she wore glasses. She seemed very likable to me— and very shy. But as we became friends, I saw that along with her determination to succeed as an actress, she had a certain inner calm. She accepted the world as it really was, not what she wanted it to be. I remember thinking that this was something unique in someone so young."

During the last week of *The Father,* Grace rehearsed with director Franklin Schaffner on the production of "The Rockingham Tea Set," based on a story by Virginia Douglas Dawson; it was broadcast live (as were all her performances) on Monday evening, January 23, and it is the earliest extant example we have of a performance by Grace Kelly.

In this hour-long drama ("introducing Grace Kelly as Miss Mappin"), Grace plays the nurse-companion to an elderly lady. Miss Mappin is suspected of killing her previous patient—a bitter woman who faked paralysis in order to keep her husband housebound (in which of course she failed). Grace has a long introductory speech leading to the story as a flashback, and to see it almost sixty years later is to be deeply impressed by her unmannered delivery and unaffected diction. She subsequently appeared in ten more TV dramas during 1950.*

---

* On February 2, she was the eponymous "Ann Rutledge," allegedly Abraham Lincoln's great love until her death at twenty-two—a performance of enormous tenderness balanced by youthful high spirits. On March 3, the ABC network presented her in "The Apple Tree" (no connection to the 1966 Broadway musical); and on April 25, she appeared in a half-hour episode of a series called *Cads, Scoundrels and Charming Ladies.* On May 26, she was seen in "The Token," and the July 17 episode of the suspense series *Lights Out* presented her in an installment called "The Devil to Pay." On September 6, she appeared in an abbreviated version of Ferenc Molnár's play *The Swan.* On October 5, Grace appeared in "The Pay-Off," an episode of the series *Big Town.* Viewers who tuned in on November 1 could have seen her on the "Mirror of Delusion" episode of the series *The Web;* and two weeks later she appeared on *The Somerset Maugham Television Theatre* in "Episode," in which she portrayed the daughter of social-climbing parents who falls in love with a working-class boy. Her New Year's Eve was spent acting in "Leaf Out of a Book."

Things were happening quickly. On May 22, she was one of a dozen actors named by *Theatre World* magazine as a "most promising personality of the Broadway stage for 1950." Others honored that evening during ceremonies at the Algonquin Hotel included Charlton Heston and his wife, Lydia Clarke.

That spring of 1950, Grace's busy TV schedule effectively (and to her enormous relief) ended her modeling career. Edith Van Cleve continued to send her out to theatrical auditions, but in June a momentous development suspended those appointments, too.

Sol C. Siegel, a powerhouse producer at Twentieth Century-Fox, had seen Grace in *The Father* and contacted director Henry Hathaway, who was in New York that spring, preparing a picture called *Fourteen Hours*. After a brief reading and wardrobe and makeup tests, Grace was offered a very small role. She accepted, simply for the chance to see a movie made in a Hollywood studio. "I had my heart set on a career in the theatre, but I accepted because it meant only two days of work—I would be back in New York before the end of the summer. I really thought this would be a one-shot experience." She agreed to the offer of a $500 fee, and on June 15 the *New York Times* noted that Grace had joined the cast of *Fourteen Hours*.

DURING THE MORNING of July 26, 1938, a young man named John William Warde opened a window on the seventeenth floor of the Hotel Gotham in New York City and climbed onto the ledge, threatening suicide. His sister, a few friends, two doctors and the police tried to persuade him to come back into the room. Firemen stretched a cargo net across a lower wall to break his fall, but the ropes became hopelessly tangled during their effort. Late that evening, as thousands watched in horror and news cameras rolled, Warde leaped to his death after an eleven-hour ordeal.

Hollywood knew a good story when it happened in real life, however morbid and however much of it would have to be changed to preserve the family's privacy. A 1949 *New Yorker* account of the incident was called "The Man on the Ledge," but Fox changed that and expanded the time to *Fourteen Hours*. In addition, no studio at that time could release a picture concluding with a suicide—hence in John Paxton's screenplay, the young man is finally saved by a net and brought to safety (and the ministrations of a psychiatrist). With edgy sensitivity, Richard Basehart played the leading role as someone unhappy in all his personal relations and without hope for any success in life; his costar is Paul Douglas, as a patrolman trying to save the man's life.

When Fox sent Grace her work schedule for August, she was at the family home in Philadelphia. Her mother (in Lizanne's words) "foresaw God knows what dangers in that city full of movie people, and suggested, 'The presence of your sister would be very well received by the family.'" The Queen of England could not have adopted more formal diction than that, and at once the sisters obeyed the maternal fiat. Peggy was negotiating the shoals of a difficult marriage and motherhood, and so seventeen-year-old Lizanne went to Hollywood as Grace's unlikely chaperone.

Thanks to Edith Van Cleve and her colleagues, the Kelly sisters were installed in an expensive suite (courtesy of the studio) at the Beverly Hills Hotel on Sunset Boulevard. Next day, they arrived at the gates of Twentieth Century-Fox on Pico Boulevard. Grace was whisked off to a makeup caravan and then to wardrobe, where she put on her costume: an expensive dress, gloves, a white hat with veil and a capacious fur coat.

Her character was obviously a woman of means, and Grace was meant to be noticed in a crowd scene.

She was then escorted by an assistant director to the "New York street" on the Fox back lot, where Hathaway was ready to direct her first appearance—in a taxicab caught in a traffic jam caused by the drama of the man on the ledge. The cameras rolled, and Grace lowered the taxi's windows to tell the policeman (Douglas) that she was on her way "to an important appointment—and I'm late now." He advises her to leave the cab and walk, which she does. Hathaway called, "Cut it!" as the several angles were completed. Grace Kelly's first scene in a Hollywood movie lasted precisely thirty-one seconds in the final version. A studio driver then returned her and Lizanne to the hotel, where they called home to report on the day's excitement. Their father was unimpressed: "Those movie people can be pretty shallow," he muttered, as if he knew this from experience.

Grace's second and final scene was filmed the following day, on the set of a lawyer's office. Listening to attorneys read the complicated terms of her divorce and the formalities regarding custody of her children, she speaks only one word: "Yes." Then the actor cast as her husband (played by James Warren) was brought to the set, and we learn her character's full name—Louise Anne Fuller. She has been watching the drama of the man on the ledge from the attorney's window, and now she seems to have second thoughts about a divorce. "If you'd been on time here today," Louise says to her husband, "it would have been all right. I wanted to do it [i.e., go through with the divorce], but I got tired of waiting—and thinking." It's clear that the couple will attempt a reconciliation; the scene closes with Louise in her husband's embrace as she gazes out once more at the young man on the ledge. The point of the scene was meant to be ambiguous: Does she feel as confused and hopeless as he—or does she suddenly realize how important her own life and relationships are—or both?

The sequence required only three takes—each time because Hathaway asked Grace to bring her voice down to a lower register. The office sequence was timed at one minute and forty-three seconds, and with that, Grace's two days of work were complete. Given tenth billing in the released film, she appears in her movie debut for a total of two minutes and fourteen seconds.

Siegel, Hathaway and Fox had no further roles for Grace, and when the picture was released in March 1951, producers and agents did not race to their telephones to call her agent with offers. Decades later, it's clear that this small role could have been as well performed by any one of a score of available young actresses. Nevertheless, this is a polished and complete little performance, precisely because of her understanding of the role and the allusive structure of her lines.

Fourteen Hours was mostly ignored for a half-century, until Fox decided to rerelease it as a so-called film noir. Although most of the action occurs at night, it's certainly not in that vague genre. There are no crimes or violence, and no bad girls, but it is an effective ninety-two-minute suspense drama, marred only by the facile psychology then in common currency. Grace, who tried to learn everything she could during those two days, was an adaptable, willing and pliant collaborator as well as extraordinarily photogenic. As Cary Grant memorably said, "In two senses, she didn't have a bad side—you could film her from any angle, and she was one of the most untemperamental, cooperative people in the business."

There was one unforeseen consequence of Grace's movie debut. An Oregon teenager named Gene Gilbert saw *Fourteen Hours* and founded a Grace Kelly Fan Club that within a year had spread like the proverbial wildfire across the country. Gene kept Grace informed of new local chapters and members, and Grace responded politely. Privately, she thought this was terrifically amusing, as if she had entered a political race. After she had opened the letters from Oregon, she would announce to friends, "We've got a new girl in Washington [or wherever]. I think she's ours!"

Back in New York, Grace moved into the newly completed Manhattan House, a nineteen-story luxury rental apartment building with 581 units, at 200 East 66th Street, which occupied the entire block between Second and Third Avenues and 65th and 66th Streets—a former site for storing hansom carriages and the electric streetcars of the Third Avenue Railway System. The opening of Manhattan House to tenants in 1950 and 1951 marked the start of a new architectural style in postwar New York, its light-gray brick façade a severe contrast to the prevailing art deco designs of earlier decades.

The Third Avenue elevated train still rumbled by, but Grace's apartment did not overlook it. Her apartment had a large living room, a bedroom, a kitchen, an entry hall and a small balcony. Although she could easily have afforded the modest rent for Apartment 9A (less than $100 a month), Grace was essentially frugal—and she liked company. Hence she invited Sally Parrish, a friend from the Barbizon, to share the apartment; like Rita Gam and Judith Quine, Sally became a lifelong friend and was a bridesmaid at Grace's wedding in 1956. "The living room [at Manhattan House] was without charm, character or gender," according to Judith. "It wasn't ugly; it was utterly bland. Furniture, fabrics and colors alike were all resolutely practical. Everything seemed brown. Only the bedroom and bath revealed that its tenants were female." She may not have known that Margaret Majer Kelly had decorated the apartment, mostly with unused family pieces taken from storage and shipped to New York.

PART II

Action

(1951—1956)

THREE

Less Is More, or Not

There's got to be some better way for people to live.
—Grace (as Amy Fowler Kane) in *High Noon*

During Christmas week 1950, Grace had a telephone call from Edith Van Cleve, who told her to ring their mutual friend Gant Gaither. He had first met Grace in February 1947 at the Broadway revival of Uncle George's play *Craig's Wife,* which Gaither had produced. Now he was producing a comedy called *Alexander,* by actor-director Lexford Richards, and the rehearsals and pre-Broadway try-outs were about to begin at the Albany Playhouse, a modest but highly respected theatre owned by actor Malcolm Atterbury, a wealthy Philadelphian who knew the Kellys.

Alexander would be like a family gathering, said Gant. Would Grace come up right after New Year's Day and prepare for the role of a well-bred society girl who becomes a torch singer in a Manhattan nightclub? She would and she did, feeling (as Gant revealed) "that it would develop her ability to play another type of personality," different from those she had already played.*

Grace arrived in New York's capital amid a ferocious snowstorm on January 2 and began rehearsals even as the play, troubled from day one, was being rewritten every night. "Grace learned a lot," according to Gant. "She knew instinctively how to train for the job." She also befriended her costar, Leatrice Joy, who had appeared in films since 1915 and was once married to the actor John Gilbert. But any chance of bringing *Alexander* to Broadway was doomed by the weather and the failure of the play to attract audiences, critics or interested New York theatre owners.

After two weeks of rehearsals and two weeks of performances, the play closed. Gant hosted a farewell party, at which Grace all but frightened the horses. Aware that some of her Albany colleagues regarded her as too cool to be successful, she leaped onto a table and danced to the music of an electric guitar, throwing off her shoes and letting her hair fall from its moorings. "If she had been raven-haired instead of platinum," said Gant, "she could have been a gypsy." And with that, the party guests realized that she was "cool" only in another sense of the word.

Grace returned to New York and set about arranging her calendar for 1951, which, as it turned out, would have to be revised several times. Her first job was in a TV play called "A Kiss for Mr. Lincoln," for which she wore magnificent (and hurriedly fitted) Civil War–era costumes. David Pressman directed this comedy of manners, and Grace played the role of Mrs. Delight Kennitt, a lively young bride determined to turn her husband's attention from the boardroom to the bedroom. This idea, of course, was conveyed with the utmost delicacy re-

---

* Further details about *Alexander* seem to have vanished into oblivion.

quired of television at the time. During the evening of the action, Delight and her husband, Henry, host a dinner party for a business associate and his wife on their way to Washington, to meet President Lincoln.

When Delight appears wearing a shiny modern lip gloss, her husband calls her "indecorous" in front of the guests, and later she further shocks him by kissing the business associate. When they are alone, Delight tells Henry the reason for her makeup: "I love being kissed the way a man *should* kiss a woman—not the way a bank president kisses one of his liquid assets. I love being kissed by a man, not stroked by a beard!" In one speech, Grace's voice rises dramatically: initially she sounds like a wounded doe, then she cries and shouts like an outraged wife; finally she defends her farewell gesture: "It was a kiss for Mr. Lincoln."

Henry says that he worships and reveres her, but is afraid to take her in his arms. "I don't want reverence from you, Henry," she says more calmly. "I want love. I don't mind being a liquid asset, but you're freezing me out." In a final shot, remarkable for live TV in 1951, the couple climbs the stairs to share the same bedroom at last.

Even at this early stage of her career, Grace's elegance was exploited by the director to suggest that men want to worship rather than love her precisely because she seems to have the cool beauty of a marble statue or the distant bearing of a goddess. But that judgment is revealed to be a fault in perception: her good posture, marmoreal beauty and refined diction should not be equated with remoteness and inaccessibility. This idea—that Grace was one to be revered rather than loved— became a recurring motif in all her films, straight through to *High Society:* "I want to place you on a pedestal and adore you," says her fiancé, played by John Lund. "I don't want to be adored—I want to be loved," she replies plaintively. "That goes without saying," is his response. But of course it does not, and her expression reveals her disappointment.

A variation on the same theme occurred in her next TV assignment. Another Philadelphia native, the playwright and screenwriter John L. Balderston, had agreed to adapt his successful 1929 romantic fantasy play *Berkeley Square,* which was broadcast on February 13.*

Based on Henry James's unfinished tale "The Sense of the Past," the story tells of a modern man named Peter Standish (played on TV by Richard Greene), who is the descendant of a man with the same name. Standish comes to London to marry his fiancée, Kate Pettigrew (Mary Scott), but he has read his ancestor's diaries and correspondence and believes he could exchange places with him and go backward in time—which, miraculously, he promptly does. But things do not go so well in the eighteenth century, where he falls in love with Kate's ancestor Helen, played by Grace.

Her performance was ethereal without being unrealistic, her line readings poignant without sounding arch. In period costume, she again seems to glide across the rooms of the set—all the more remarkable because she had to take meticulously prearranged steps as the moving camera followed. In *Berkeley Square,* Grace portrayed Helen as a kind of chaste Diana, the Roman goddess—ever desired yet ever remote, revered and unloved.

EARLY THAT SPRING, Grace demonstrated that in real life she was not at all ethereal or detached from everyday reality. The African-American singer and dancer Josephine Baker had re-

---

* On June 5, 1951, Grace also appeared in "Lover's Leap," a half-hour drama broadcast on *Armstrong Circle Theatre.*

turned to the United States after years of European triumph, and she promptly became involved in the struggle for desegregation and the fight against racism in America, which was typified by the refusal of Washington's National Theatre to sell tickets to nonwhites until that year. During her American tour, Baker refused to play to segregated audiences or to register at segregated hotels. She successfully made a citizen's arrest of a racist in Los Angeles, and her nationwide fight against prejudice earned her a citation as Outstanding Woman of the Year by the National Association for the Advancement of Colored People.

Josephine Baker then came to New York and took some friends to dine at the famous Stork Club, where they were denied a table. Grace was at the club that same evening, and she was so outraged by this rank display of racism that she rushed over to Baker—whom she had never met—took her by the arm and stormed out with her own entire group of friends, telling the press she would never return to the Stork Club; she never did. Grace Kelly and Josephine Baker became friends on the spot.

From her earliest days, Grace had never understood prejudice. She and her siblings had grown up with and remained grateful for the devotion of Fordie, and during her entire life, Grace always remained color-blind. She was also completely indifferent to the sexual orientation of friends and colleagues, many of whom (like Uncle George) were gay and, at that time, constantly risked ridicule and ostracism.

Years later, an American television crew came to document scenes of palace life in Monaco. While filming a sequence of the staff's children in the royal playground, the director noticed three nonwhite children in the group, and he approached Princess Grace. "The film is to be shown in the American South," he said, "and it won't do to see black children playing with white children. At least while we're filming, we don't want them here."

"Oh, but we do," Grace replied with a smile.

The incident at the Stork Club earned her some unpleasant epithets then widely used in America for those who befriended nonwhite people. But Grace proudly accompanied Josephine Baker on her return to Europe that season, stopping in London on the way home to see the opening-night performance of N. C. Hunter's comedy *Waters of the Moon* at the Theatre Royal, Haymarket, on April 19. She kept the printed playbill and never forgot the legendary performances by two great ladies of the English stage, Edith Evans and Wendy Hiller, whose talents confirmed Grace's desire for a serious career in the theatre.

BACK HOME, there was a letter waiting from Edith Van Cleve, reporting that Grace was being considered for the role of a scheming playgirl in a Joan Crawford film, *Sudden Fear,* scheduled to begin production in San Francisco and Hollywood early in 1952. Grace rang Edith to say that she would leap at the chance to undertake something so utterly different, but Edith had disappointing news. Gloria Grahame, already cornering the market as Hollywood's conniving bad girl, had won the part. Anyone familiar with *Sudden Fear*—a crisp thriller that won Crawford her third Oscar nomination—may be tempted to imagine Grace in the role of the murderous Irene Neves. At this stage of her career, she would perhaps have been either memorably terrific or embarrassingly terrible. A deeply evil character, which she never played, may have been beyond her capacity.

But Grace was kept busy with other good projects on offer that spring and summer of 1951. In late May she went to Michigan, where she played Isabelle in the Ann Arbor Drama

Festival's production of Jean Anouilh's *Ring Around the Moon*. Following that, for the week beginning Sunday, June 24, she appeared at the Elitch Theatre, Denver, in a comedy by F. Hugh Herbert and in several other plays in repertory until the end of August.

The Elitch family, who founded what became the oldest summer stock theatre company in America, mounted its first production in 1897, starring James (father of Eugene) O'Neill. Sarah Bernhardt was on the Elitch stage as Camille in 1906, and among its many other stars over the next seven decades were Douglas Fairbanks, José Ferrer, Julie Harris, Kim Hunter, Fredric March, Antoinette Perry (for whom the Tony Awards were named), Walter Pidgeon, Vincent Price, Robert Redford, Ginger Rogers, Gloria Swanson and Shelley Winters.

Grace consistently deflected questions about her summer in Denver. This may have been because her time offstage was spent almost exclusively with another actor in the company, Gene Lyons. Eight years her senior, he had appeared on Broadway and television and seemed poised for further success. With his angular features, seductive voice and intelligent approach to the craft of acting, he at once impressed Grace, and they began an eighteen-month romance. Alas, like Don Richardson, Lyons was married, although his annulment was being processed; he had also recently ended his affair with the actress Lee Grant. More to the inauspicious point, Lyons could not control his drinking; eventually, alcoholism destroyed his career and caused his death at the age of fifty-three.

But that summer, Lyons captivated Grace as much as did the variety of plays and the genial atmosphere of the Elitch repertory company. Like many women in her amorous circumstances, Grace seems to have told herself that Lyons needed only true love in order to put down the bottle. In this she was very much misguided, but enlightenment took time. In addition, perhaps because she was only an occasional drinker and always a temperate one, she did not understand Gene's problem.

In addition, there was a general ignorance about heavy drinking. "In the 1950s, we would not have recognized an alcoholic unless we tripped over him for ten nights running in a Bowery doorway," Judith Quine recalled accurately. "Alcoholics came from places we didn't even know existed. The boys we dated or fell in love with had, at worst, 'a little drinking problem.' They 'drank like a fish' or 'couldn't hold their liquor.' "

In the United States there had been a national ban against the manufacture, sale or consumption of all alcoholic beverages by the enactment of the Eighteenth Amendment to the Constitution, which went into effect in January 1920 and lasted until the enactment of the Twenty-first Amendment, in December 1933. From Christmas of that year, drinking excessive amounts of alcohol crashed into vogue in American culture: it was a sign of wealth, and it was stylish and adult to drink (and to smoke); it was a mark of naïveté and inelegance not to. Drunkards of both sexes were considered hilariously funny in movies (and later on TV), and very few people seemed to know that alcoholism was a serious, potentially fatal condition. In this regard, Grace was a daughter of her time, and she apparently thought that Gene's little problem could eventually be solved. There was, however, an interlude in this quixotic affair.

In June, Edith Van Cleve had sent photos of Grace to the MCA talent agency, where Jay Kanter now represented Edith's former client, Marlon Brando. Based on those prints alone, MCA offered Grace a contract whereby they would represent her exclusively for movies and TV employment. At first, Grace would not sign it: she did not want to sabotage her hopes for a career on the stage, nor did she wish to be "owned" by any agency.

Kanter, meanwhile, forwarded the photos of Grace to Stanley Kramer, a producer who had recently enjoyed enormous success with *Champion* (1949), *Home of the Brave* (1949) and *The Men* (1950; Brando's first film). "I was producing half a dozen or more movies every year," Kramer said years later. "Because of that schedule, I needed actors—lots of them—and I needed them cheaply, too. I was just starting out, and the whole enterprise could have collapsed for lack of cash or a foolish use of cash." Thrifty to the point of frugality, Kramer signed up gifted directors who would soon be unavailable at the bargain prices he paid for them in the late 1940s and early 1950s—among them Richard Fleischer, Mark Robson and Fred Zinnemann (who had directed *The Men*). Carl Foreman was Kramer's business partner and primary screenwriter.

Kramer and Foreman were already at work on an untitled western, to be directed by Zinnemann. They had their title: *High Noon,* which had been temporarily used for *Home of the Brave.* The inspiration for the western was an eight-page short story by John W. Cunningham—"The Tin Star," published in *Collier's* magazine on December 6, 1947. Foreman bought the rights to it because, as Kramer said, "if I had negotiated the deal as a Hollywood producer, we would have had to pay a whole lot more. So Carl purchased it for something ridiculous."

By the time Zinnemann joined them for preproduction in early July, the screenplay was essentially complete. "We had all the supporting players lined up," Kramer continued, "but we lacked the leading man and woman." After a number of actors declined (among them Gregory Peck, Kirk Douglas, Charlton Heston, Marlon Brando and Montgomery Clift), Gary Cooper agreed to play Marshal Will Kane. A veteran of more than eighty movies, he had read the screenplay and agreed to forgo his usual high fee. As is customary in moviemaking, there were various delays in beginning the film, and during the interval, Cooper began to suffer from ulcers, a double hernia and a painful back condition. Suddenly he looked older than his fifty years.

"We still needed an attractive young woman to play Kane's wife," Fred Zinnemann recalled. "We had expected to have a much younger actor than Cooper, but it was much to our advantage to have him with us. The role of his wife was not demanding, but for some reason we had difficulty finding the right actress at a price Stanley wanted to pay. Then he showed me a photo of Grace Kelly and told me that she had done nothing [in the movies] except a small bit for Henry Hathaway. I said, 'Well, let's meet her.' "* Zinnemann did not know at the time that Kramer had already signed Grace for the movie without a meeting, after seeing her photograph. Kanter negotiated the deal for his client to play Amy Fowler Kane, Will's bride, for which Grace was paid $750 a week for a guarantee of six weeks of work. Among the opening credits, her name was to appear fifth, after those of Gary Cooper, Thomas Mitchell, Lloyd Bridges and Katy Jurado.

After her first week of performances onstage in Denver, Grace flew to Los Angeles in early July to meet Kramer's team. "She arrived, very well dressed and wearing white gloves,"

---

* Kramer always maintained that he alone interviewed Grace in Manhattan, "backstage, after her appearance in an Off-Broadway show, where I signed her up on the spot." But she never appeared in an Off-Broadway show; furthermore, his account is contradicted by the written production history and by my interviews with Grace and Zinnemann. Kramer's memory of production histories was always interesting, but his facts could be wildly inaccurate.

Zinnemann recalled. "Our conversation was brief, because she answered most of my questions with a simple yes or no. But I thought she fitted the part [of Amy] admirably, perhaps because she seemed so shy and because technically she was not quite prepared for it. This made her sometimes tense and remote—ideal, in other words, to play this role. The age difference between her and Cooper, almost thirty years, bothered me, but the die was cast. Kramer got her at a low price, and we went forward—with very happy results, I think." Kramer was more critical: "She was miscast," he said flatly. "She was just too young for Cooper. She didn't believe she did well in the role, and I didn't think so, either."

On Thursday, July 19, the *New York Times* announced that Stanley Kramer Productions would begin filming *High Noon* with Gary Cooper and Grace Kelly in late August or early September, adding, "Miss Kelly is a comparative newcomer." She could not resist the opportunity to make a film with Cooper, and this was to be a twenty-eight-day shooting schedule—hence, she could be back in New York in early autumn.

Grace read the Cunningham short story along with the script of *High Noon*. To begin with, she found no Amy Fowler Kane in "The Tin Star," which is a straightforward story about a small-town Western sheriff named Doane, whom the mayor urges to retire. Doane is past middle age, a widower with severe arthritis. A notorious criminal named Jordan is coming back to town on the 4:10 train, seeking revenge for Doane's capture of him on a murder charge five years earlier—and Jordan's gang is ready to join the violence.

Doane visits his wife's grave every Sunday. On this day, Jordan's younger brother follows him. As the sheriff sets flowers at his wife's tombstone, the man unties Doane's horse and sets it off—forcing Doane to walk back to town. There he finds that Toby, one of his deputies, has killed young Jordan, believing that the returning horse meant Doane was dead. One of Jordan's gang then shoots Toby in the leg, and the older Jordan shoots Doane several times. Throwing himself on young Toby's body to prevent him from taking a fatal bullet, Doane is shot dead by the avenging Jordan. Toby kills the murderer and takes over the role of sheriff from his dead friend.

In the screenplay and the finished film of *High Noon,* very little seems to happen until the final shoot-out. But much is implied and very much indeed is at stake. Will Kane (Cooper) is about to retire from his job in Hadleyville (population four hundred), an arid, no-account patch of land somewhere out west. As the movie begins, he and Amy Fowler (Grace) pronounce wedding vows before the local judge (Otto Kruger). Will looks forward to a quiet life with Amy, a Quaker who deplores violence and condemns killing. As the newlyweds prepare to leave town, Will learns that Frank Miller (Ian MacDonald) is returning to Hadleyville. Kane had arrested him five years earlier for murder, but the sentence was commuted, and now Miller and his gang—who once controlled and terrorized the town—want revenge.

At first, heeding everyone's advice, Kane leaves with his bride. But he returns, for the gang would have pursued them in any case, and the people of Hadleyville once again would have come under the deadly control of the Miller gang, three of whom are already in place, gloating and awaiting Frank's arrival on the noon train. Kane turns to the people for help, and to his former deputies for support. But everybody abandons him, and each man has an excuse. Harvey, the youngest deputy (Lloyd Bridges), turns away, jealous of Will; others believe that any open trouble with Miller will end only in tragedy for everyone; and others flee out of simple cowardice. At first, even Amy does not remain with Will; she is unable, by virtue of her strong pacifist principles, to understand his conduct.

High noon approaches. After writing his last will and testament, Kane meets the gang alone. In the final shoot-out, he is the only man to survive—and is in fact helped by Amy, who has returned out of loyalty. She has also been sternly counseled by saloon owner Helen Ramirez (Katy Jurado), who was once Frank Miller's mistress, then Will's, and is now Harvey's. (Wise in the ways of men and the world, Helen has certainly lived mighty fully in a town of only four hundred.) At the wordless conclusion to the picture, the four villains lie dead, and Will and Amy leave Hadleyville. Contemptuous of the townspeople's cowardice and their disregard for their own solidarity as a community, Will removes his tin star and throws it onto the dusty street.

AFTER RETURNING to the Elitch Theatre for her final performances, Grace left Denver on August 27 for wardrobe fittings and makeup tests in Los Angeles. *High Noon* was filmed from Wednesday, September 5, to Saturday, October 6—an extremely rapid schedule requiring meticulous preparation, a tirelessly efficient crew, a highly professional cast and a first-rate director, all of them working long hours with the production designer and cameraman. Exteriors were shot mostly on the back lot of the Columbia Studios ranch, and at locations in Northern California; the few interior sets were constructed at studios in Burbank.

Six days of labor is the norm in Hollywood, and twelve to fourteen hours a day is standard for all but the most famous and powerful stars and directors. According to call sheets, Grace worked on the picture twenty-two of its twenty-eight days. The summer of 1951 was unusually torrid in Southern California, and the vast bowl of the San Fernando Valley was, typically, ten to fifteen degrees hotter than the West Side of Los Angeles, closer to the Pacific. Thermometers read over 100 degrees before nine o'clock on most mornings, as smog settled into the valley; often it seemed as if there was no air to breathe. The cast of *High Noon* had to work mostly outside, and the women, dressed in heavy nineteenth-century costumes, were especially uncomfortable.

The Kelly family knew nothing about Gene and Grace, but not long after filming began in September, the gossips began to whisper about Grace and Gary Cooper, and later about Grace and Fred Zinnemann. There is not a shred of evidence to support either rumor, or a single reliable source.*

When the murmurings from Hollywood drifted eastward, there was disquiet at 3901 Henry Avenue. Lizanne was once again dispatched to live with her sister, and this time they stayed at the Chateau Marmont Hotel, a few steps north of the noisy "Sunset Strip" with its profusion of nightclubs, diners and restaurants. After almost two months, Lizanne had nothing to report to Philadelphia except what she already knew (and what Grace's letters and postcards confirm). On Sundays, Grace's only day off from work, Uncle George (then living near Palm Springs) collected them at the hotel; they went to Mass in Beverly Hills; and then he drove his nieces north to Santa Barbara or south to a beach town for lunch. "He and Grace talked constantly about the theatre," Lizanne recalled. "Usually, I fell asleep on the backseat."

High Noon is a remarkably quiet film that focuses much of its screen time on the weathered, anxious features of Gary Cooper,

---

* In a rehearsal for the scene following the marriage of Amy and Will, Zinnemann asked Grace to sit on Cooper's lap; both were out of costume and wearing their own casual clothes. They all agreed that this gesture was inappropriate for the shot, and the scene was filmed otherwise. But a stills photographer captured the moment, and soon some news editors decided that the two stars were more than colleagues.

who conveyed an anguished fear, atypical of the western hero, with subtle glances and restrained gestures. Here the actor found new resources within himself, and his "acting"—always minimal—virtually vanished. His plain angularity, the lines of gravity and premature old age, seemed more deeply etched. Members of the Academy of Motion Picture Arts and Sciences voted him Best Actor (his second Oscar in that category, following his performance as the eponymous hero in *Sergeant York* in 1941).

The story takes place in one morning, from approximately 10:40 to noon, and the action lasts little longer than those eighty minutes. Working with his cameraman and editor, Zinnemann created suspense by rhythmic cuts to close-ups of pendulums, clock hands closing like scissor blades on noon, and the railroad tracks "stretching to the horizon and symbolizing the menace," as Zinnemann said. "The restless figure of the marshal moving about the town in his search for help and letting the action slow down by degrees were all logically constructed."

The picture is remarkable for a single theme, relevant to every time and place; for the filmmakers, it was especially significant that year, when Communist witch-hunts were turning the United States into a place of hysterical paranoia where lives were routinely ruined. In Hollywood, careers were destroyed and reputations lost because, ten or twenty or thirty years earlier, a person may or may not have questioned the course of American politics and may or may not have joined informal meetings of the Communist Party—words and deeds protected by their constitutional rights, which were now all but ignored.

The movie's theme—the necessity of taking and maintaining a moral stance—is contained in an extraordinary crane shot, pulling back from a close-up of Cooper to a high overhead view of him, alone in a bleak town. The streets are dusty paths seeming to lead nowhere; the sky is washed out of clouds; there are no spacious skies, no amber waves of grain; no vast panoramas in which men and animals move in an epic journey; no sense of spectacle, or of colorful, unspoiled nature. Perhaps never before this had the technique of black-and-white movie-making found a fuller justification in a western. In *High Noon* there is only a dying town, empty of courage, hope and insight. The street is deserted, the stores and houses gray and empty; just so, the repetition of the (Oscar-winning) song in the picture, "Do Not Forsake Me, Oh My Darling," becomes both ironic and minatory, for everyone abandons the marshal.

Hadleyville is thus no romanticized western refuge from the evils of encroaching civilization. The saloon is not the community meeting place, but the locus of petty jealousies and prejudices. The marshal is not heroic by conscious choice or logical decision; he sees his position as the only possibility, and he is not above weeping with fear. As played by Cooper with a moving sense of accidental heroism, Will Kane emerges as a man whose options have dwindled like his list of friends. He confronts his enemies with the kind of stoic acceptance of the likely outcome that his life is almost over. *High Noon* is not, then, a western about sheepherders against cattlemen, ranchers against oilmen, white settlers against natives. It concerns the point at which courage is the logical and sometimes the only possible outcome of integrity.

Nor are there any pious pioneers in this movie. The towns-folk are, as Zinnemann said, "examples of human nature in every time and place . . . [of people] who abandon their loyalties, and one another, with apparently good reasons." Hence the marshal becomes the prototype of all who find themselves alone, facing an issue while others rationalize themselves out of it. Those who had crowded in to be present at Will's marriage to Amy and had praised him for once saving the town now find handy reasons for refusing to help him, one another and their community.

Grace arrived for the filming, as she later said, in a state of scarcely concealed anxiety. *Fourteen Hours* had not prepared her to play a leading role opposite a movie legend like Gary Cooper. At first their mutual shyness and reticence to engage in mere small talk augured a tense collaboration. But when he overheard her laugh at a crewman's risqué joke, he knew she was nothing like her image, or Kramer's image of her—and Cooper promptly invited her to lunch. "He was a gentle, shy person," Grace recalled, "and he greatly underestimated himself as an actor."

Just as Grace underestimated herself.

"I was very young when I made *High Noon,*" she continued, referring to that season when she was twenty-one. "Zinnemann was wonderful with people who knew their job and their métier as screen actors. But I wasn't one of those who did. Early during filming, he said to me, 'Grace, I'm sorry, I can't help you the way I should be able to.' It wasn't that he didn't take an interest—he just didn't know how to instruct me, and of course there was the problem of time. I couldn't get the kind of direction from him that I needed as a neophyte, and I wasn't equipped enough for moviemaking at that time to do it for myself. After I saw the finished picture, I was horrified! I remember thinking, 'Well, this poor girl may never make it unless she does something very quickly.' I rushed back to New York and started taking classes again, with Sandy Meisner."

Even before filming began, Kramer made no secret of his unhappiness with Grace. "She was too young, too inexperienced, too nervous." She was certainly young and inexperienced. But as Zinnemann insisted, her anxiety was entirely appropriate for the role, especially in the opening wedding scene. The virginal, innocent Quaker Amy is a girl who would indeed be nervous at her wedding to any man, especially to a respected marshal very much her senior. In Will's crowded office moments after the brief ceremony, she smiles, laughs girlishly and creates the only moment of light amid the gathering gloom.

The problem was actually not in Grace's performance, but in the fact that her character was underwritten. It's true that many actresses could have portrayed Amy Fowler equally well—but many would have been less satisfactory. Perhaps what remains most in the memory is the alarming and exquisitely appropriate contrast between the giggling bride of the opening sequence and the fearful, worried, perplexed woman she soon becomes. Grace understood this contrast not intellectually, but by imagining "how I would feel if my brand-new husband seemed to abandon me for his duty. Amy had to learn that, because he did his duty—because he did not shrink from it, as she first begged him to do—he could be a wonderful husband. So she learns something. I thought that was very interesting."

Blond Amy, all in white, exists only as a counterpoint to dark Helen, all in black. Grace's most dramatic scene is her exchange with Katy Jurado, which Grace performed with complete conviction and a sense that innocence does not mean inanity.

HELEN. How can you leave [Will] like this? Does the sound of guns frighten you that much?
AMY. I've heard guns. My father and my brother were killed by guns. They were on the right side, but that didn't help them when the shooting started. My brother was nineteen. I watched him die. That's when I became a Quaker. I don't care who's right or who's wrong. There's got to be some better way for people to live. Will knows how I feel about it.

Grace spoke the words with the terrible memories in her voice: there is a slight quiver of emotion, and an almost imperceptible tremor in her chin, as if she might weep at any moment.

"This movie was her first big break," said Katy Jurado, who was appearing in her second American film after acting in her native Mexico. "Grace and I were very different and couldn't be very close, but I saw a girl with a lot of dignity and character who wanted to be somebody. She looked weak and tiny, but she was a very strong person—one of the strongest I worked with. She knew what she wanted, and she worked hard for it." As Stanley Kramer had to admit years later, "Grace *was* determined, and she wasn't overwhelmed in her scenes with the dynamic Katy Jurado, who really chewed up the scenery."

"When I watched the film with her at home," recalled Grace's son, Prince Albert of Monaco, in 2007, "I could see how uncomfortable she was sitting there and seeing it again. She wasn't at all satisfied with her performance." But perhaps no serious, conscientious actor is ever satisfied with a performance—and a "neophyte," as she knew she was, would have been extremely sensitive about what she gave the picture.

In this regard, Grace Kelly was never content with her achievements. "My time in Hollywood was so brief," she said, "and everything happened so quickly, that I don't think I accomplished anything to be proud of. I needed good teachers and directors; I needed understanding actors to work with me. I was grateful for my theatre experience, and for the work I did in television—but none of that really prepares you for movie acting. Scenes are filmed out of context and continuity—the first day's work can be the last sequence of the picture, and what you're acting, in which scene and with which actor, is all determined by a set of complicated scheduling mechanisms. This means that a film actor has to have an understanding director who doesn't mind being a teacher. And it means that the actor has to come prepared for all kinds of variables. You wait for hours, then a shot is filmed, then something goes wrong and you wait again and it's filmed again. Then you wait some more, and another scene is shot—which may actually occur a half-hour later in the finished picture, or a half-hour earlier, at a completely different stage of the character's development. Movie acting is more challenging than most people think, and you have to be extremely clever or a seasoned veteran to carry off a credible performance. I wasn't a seasoned veteran, and I don't think I was extremely clever." (According to Zinnemann, "Grace was not self-confident at all—certainly not at this stage.")

In the final moments of the movie, when Amy takes up a gun and shoots the man who is about to kill her husband, *High Noon* is not making a statement about Amy's abandonment of her pacifist principles; on the contrary, it is asserting that sometimes violence occurs as a tragic, unwilled necessity. Amy shoots the man not to kill him, but to save her husband; it's a classic example of the double-effect principle: she wants to save a life, not to destroy one. Unlike the gang and the townsfolk, but very much like her husband, she does not take up arms to seek revenge. All this may be read on Grace's features in the last moments of the picture.

In *High Noon,* she did precisely what the role called for: she expressed youth's callow first blush and its first encounter with the wickedness that is always present and ready to annihilate. She conveys the sense that Amy is enduring a kind of moral education, just like the people of Hadleyville.

Zinnemann and Foreman were nominated by the Academy as best director and screenwriter of 1952 (the year of *High Noon*'s release), and several Oscar statuettes were distributed— for best performance by an actor (Cooper); for film editing (Elmo Williams and Harry Gerstad); for best song (Dimitri Tiomkin and Ned Washington); and for best score (Tiomkin).

In later years, awards worldwide were added to the list. These honors were unusual for a movie in the western genre.

As Zinnemann said years later, *High Noon* "seems to mean different things to different people. Kramer, who had worked closely with Foreman on the script, said it was 'about a town that died because no one there had the guts to defend it' . . . [and] Foreman saw it as an allegory about his own experience of political persecution in the McCarthy era. With due respect, I felt this to be a narrow point of view. First of all, I saw it simply as a great movie yarn, full of enormously interesting people. I vaguely sensed deeper meanings in it; but only later did it dawn on me that this was not a regular Western myth. To me, it was the story of a man who must make a decision according to his conscience. His town—symbol of a democracy gone soft—faces a horrendous threat to its people's way of life. It is a story that still happens everywhere, every day."* Grace was mostly ignored by reviewers; when her name appeared, it was mentioned with other cast members who were "the best of many in key roles," as the *New York Times* noted.

GRACE HAD no reason to remain in Hollywood after the completion of *High Noon:* the picture was not released until the summer of 1952, and no offers of further movie work were forthcoming—and so, as she later said, she hurried to New York, where she resumed private studies.

Sanford Meisner, then forty-six, was one of the most influential acting teachers of the twentieth century. Since 1940 he had taught in the acting program at the Neighborhood Playhouse

---

* Issues of conscience often dictated Zinnemann's choice of subject matter, perhaps most memorably in his films of *The Nun's Story, A Man for All Seasons* and *Julia*.

School of the Theatre in Manhattan and then, as director of it, he continued to develop a technique until his retirement in 1990. Whereas Lee Strasberg emphasized "emotion memory" exercises, Meisner encouraged actors to imagine *the character's* history, thoughts and feelings in the text (rather than *one's own* history, thoughts and feelings, à la Strasberg). When Elia Kazan and Robert Lewis founded the Actors Studio in 1947, Meisner (not, at first, Strasberg) was invited to teach there. When Strasberg became director of the Actors Studio in 1951, Meisner returned to the Neighborhood Playhouse.

"Less is more" was one of Meisner's mantras. "Silence has myriad meanings. In the theater, silence is an absence of words, but never an absence of meaning." Most of all, Meisner urged his students to think of acting a role as "living truthfully under given imaginary circumstances."

For a year beginning in the autumn of 1951, Grace studied several times weekly with Meisner. Training in voice and body movement had been part of the curriculum at the American Academy of Dramatic Arts, but now Grace was exposed to a different technique, aimed (as Meisner insisted) on "seeing into, understanding and breathing life into a stage character. The thing about acting that moves audiences is the emphatic sense of the reality of the human being who is portrayed, greatly enhanced but not dependent on the excellent diction with which the lines are spoken. Students need a body as flexible as a gymnast's, a voice as malleable and responsive as a singer's, and a director who understands and can communicate the way of life which gave birth to the play in the first place."

Meisner's technique also asked an actor to sit quietly, waiting until a flash of imagination impelled a fresh understanding before reciting dialogue. This was no bogus mysticism, much less was it merely subjective comprehension without guidelines. There were specific exercises developed for each student, no

matter the text assigned. Over time, the Meisner Technique in-
fluenced three generations of successful actors, writers and
directors—among them Bob Fosse, Diane Keaton, Sidney
Lumet, David Mamet, Steve McQueen, Arthur Miller, Gregory
Peck, Sydney Pollack, Marian Seldes and Joanne Woodward.

But Grace's life was not all work. Gene Lyons had followed
her to New York at the end of the Elitch season, and there the
romance continued. When her friend Prudy Wise wrote to ask,
"Are you still in love with old Gene?" Grace replied emphati-
cally that autumn, "YES! We had our first fight last night, but
all is alright again."

Nor was her life all work plus the vicissitudes of passion.
Grace's television career resumed at full speed in New York
that autumn. On November 21, she appeared in a teleplay
called "Brand for the Burning," and on December 10, in "Smith
Serves." Somerset Maugham introduced the latter on the television series that bore his name.

In "Smith Serves," Grace was listed third in a cast featuring
Eddie Albert and Joan Chandler. Set in New York in 1895, the
story tells of a man who wants to marry an old flame—but
when she learns that he has become a South Dakota farmer instead of a glamorous entrepreneur, she declines the offer. He
then meets the woman's housemaid, who was once a farm girl.
They are mutually attracted, but she does not want to go back
to a rural life: she is studying to be a secretary in New York.
Enter Grace, as a sophisticated city girl who says that she loves
her family's farm north of New York City, and that she loves to
ride horses there—thus implying that she might be the answer
to the man's search. But she is actually the farmer's longtime
platonic friend, about to be married; she had gladly agreed to
be a ploy to arouse the housemaid's jealousy. The ruse works,
and the maid will marry the gentleman farmer.

"Smith Serves" is a slight but effective play, convincingly

performed by Eddie Albert with a wry combination of the "gosh-darn" country boy and the savvy, successful business-man. Joan Chandler as the housemaid—dark-haired, poised and quick with a mordant observation—is the perfect foil for Grace, who enters the cluttered, claustrophobic house like a fresh breeze. She gave an agreeably amusing performance that indicated an inchoate gift for high comedy.

THE NEW year 1952 was a rush of activity. Classes with Meisner continued four days a week during that year, and Grace re-hearsed and performed in no fewer than fifteen live television programs, eleven of them before the summer.* In "The Big Build Up," she portrayed Claire Conroy, a classy New York star who has come to Hollywood to be promoted, or "built up," so we are led to believe, by an old boyfriend, now a powerful press agent (played by Richard Derr). But in fact he is her estranged husband. The story then flashes back to happier days, when they encouraged each other's professional aspirations. Back in the present, the story concludes with touching ambiguity.

Most remarkable about Grace's performance here, as so often in her dozens of TV roles, is her complete artlessness, the lack of pretension and the naturalness of her gestures and her

---

* In addition to the four programs for which commentary is provided here, Grace was seen on TV during 1952 as Dulcinea to Boris Karloff's Don Quixote. She was also in "Prelude to Death," with Carmen Mathews; in "Life, Liberty and Orrin Dudley," with Jackie Cooper; in "The Borgia Lamp," with Hugh Griffith and Robert Sterling; in "Candles for Theresa," "The Small House," and "The Cricket on the Hearth." She assumed the role of a dance-hall girl threatened by a serial killer in "Fifty Beautiful Girls," and was seen with Shepperd Strudwick in "City Editor." Grace was also in a new production of "Leaf Out of a Book," originally presented on the *Goodyear Television Playhouse* in 1950, and she appeared in "A Message for Janice," again with Jackie Cooper.

diction. These qualities, critics have complained in recent years, were sometimes absent during key moments of *High Noon* and her subsequent movies. If this was occasionally the case in her first three pictures, there is an easy explanation: "To tell the truth, I was intimidated at first, working with directors like Zinnemann, Ford and Hitchcock—they were among the big guns of the movies in those days, and they were my first directors [after her brief appearance in *Fourteen Hours*]."

In addition, Zinnemann, Ford and Hitchcock frequently asked their casts for multiple takes of a shot, and Grace—convinced that these were her fault and not, for example, owing to problems with lighting or sound recording—became, for a while, ever more self-conscious, which in turn sometimes made her performance less spontaneous and credible. Zinnemann's admitted inability to help a newcomer, Ford's grumpy machismo and Hitchcock's lifelong failure to compliment an actor on a job well done—even when he liked what he saw—were qualities that worried the inexperienced Grace. As it happened, it was precisely her trio of roles for Hitchcock that erased every bit of artifice, but that took time.

After a week of rehearsals, television plays were presented live, and there was no time to correct accidents. "It was like living on the edge of a volcano or in the midst of a hurricane," Grace recalled. "We didn't even think about mistakes, we just muddled along with them. Most of the time it was quite funny, and our biggest problem was not to burst out laughing. Once I had a scene in bed. I had to wear all my clothes beneath the covers, so I could leap out and run to the next scene on a nearby set. But the TV camera didn't cut away—so there I was, leaping out of bed with all my clothes on and dashing off-camera to the next room. The viewers at home must have wondered what the hell was going on.

"The same year I did 'The Big Build Up,' I was in 'The

Cricket on the Hearth.' In one scene, a wonderful old English character actor and I were coming to bring a steaming hot pie to an orphan on Christmas Day. We were told to wave at the boy through a window, but the pie was too hot to hold in one hand, so I set it down for a moment—and the old actor stepped right into it. He came limping into the door of the 'cottage' with his left shoe stuck in a pie—and simply said to the other actors, as if everything was perfectly natural, 'Here's a lovely hot pie for all of you—Merry Christmas!' "

THREE WEEKS after "The Big Build Up," on February 10, Grace appeared in Walter Bernstein's hour-long TV version of F. Scott Fitzgerald's story "The Rich Boy." She had much anticipated this job: she would again be directed by Delbert Mann (of "Bethel Merriday"); the role of Paula Legendre was both challenging and appealing; and, perhaps most of all, her leading man was none other than Gene Lyons, in the role of Anson Hunter.

Set in New York during the Roaring Twenties, "The Rich Boy" opens in the autumn, at one of Anson's chic Manhattan parties, where he meets Paula and her mother, who are visiting New York "for the season" from their home in California. Paula quickly falls in love with Anson, but soon she has to hurry back to the West Coast. Before her departure, Grace speaks with great warmth and understanding:

PAULA (GRACE). You drink a lot, don't you?
ANSON (LYONS). I suppose so.

The dialogue could have been spoken between them in real life.

Anson. We're both rich.
Paula. It's nice, isn't it?

There are very long kisses between them in "The Rich Boy"—unusual for TV in 1952—and home viewers may have wondered why those moments seemed so convincing.

In subsequent scenes with Paula, Anson is always polite and courtly, but he is gross, indecent, and drunk with others—a pathetically louche character ruined by privilege, an absence of value and a failure of purpose. Each time Paula and Anson are together, she sees more drunken sprees, and she is warned by her disapproving mother (as Margaret Kelly would have sternly advised Grace).

Paula. You have one idea about life and I have another.
    Maybe we're too far apart. Why do you have to drink so
    much?
Anson. Because I want to!

Time passes, and they have been engaged for eight months, but he is in no hurry to set a wedding date. Soon Paula fully sees the danger, and she breaks their engagement. Later he learns that she is engaged to marry in Florida. Anson finds her there, and the old spark is reignited in him. But Paula has been "worn away inside" after the long wait for Anson to reform himself, and she won't accept him. He returns to New York and begins an affair with another young woman, but he breaks this off: "I don't love you one bit," he tells her cruelly. "You better wait for someone who does."

Anson then learns that Paula has married. He becomes richer than ever, but he cannot control his drinking. In time, Paula divorces her husband and happily remarries, while Anson has not been able to have one enduring relationship. By chance, he meets Paula, her new husband and her three children in New York. In a moment of privacy, she gently reminds Anson that their romance was nothing more than an infatuation—that it wasn't good for either of them and never could be. Then the stock market collapses in 1929, signaling more disaster for Anson Hunter. Thus the story ends.

Considering the lives of the real-life leading duo, the teleplay of "The Rich Boy" is astonishingly autobiographical—as much about Grace and Gene as it was about Fitzgerald himself—and it is tempting to imagine their conversations when they rehearsed privately. Indeed, the script is a virtual template for the doomed romance of these two actors.

On March 22, the New York press carried a small item, announcing that Grace was joining rehearsals for a new Broadway play by William Marchant, starring Neil Hamilton, John Drew Devereaux and Dorothy Stickney. This rather wan comedy, *To Be Continued,* opened at the Booth Theatre on April 23 and closed, after thirteen performances, on May 2. Grace knew the play was troubled when she accepted the role of Janet ("a very dignified, attractive young lady," according to the text), the daughter of a philanderer. But every theatre credit was important toward her goal—even a part that kept her onstage for less than three minutes. Her only function in the play was to dissuade her father's mistress of twenty-five years from accepting her mother's invitation to meet:

JANET (GRACE). My mother wants to prove to herself that her husband has never cared one iota for her. She wants to hear it from your lips. She wants to see it in your eyes.
DOLLY (DOROTHY STICKNEY). I didn't know that.

JANET. I'm afraid it will turn her into one of those lonely, unloved women you see everywhere nowadays. Her foundations are terribly shaky—really shaky. I'm afraid she might go to pieces. Before you see my mother, will you please think of the consequences?

Thinking of the consequences might have prevented the playwright from trying to make a drawing-room comedy out of a painful marital situation. The New York critics (who did not mention Grace in their reviews) noted that there were too many solemn moments for a fey treatment of infidelity, and an excess of virtuous looks instead of mocking glances.

That summer, after working in several more TV dramas, Grace hastened to the Playhouse in the Park, Philadelphia, where she appeared in two comedies. In mid-August she returned to the Bucks County Playhouse, playing the plucky young secretary in love with a depressed, middle-aged playwright in Samson Raphaelson's 1934 comedy, *Accent on Youth*. There seem to have been no reviews of or news items about these productions.

She then returned to New York, where she received a call from her agent. An English movie executive named Sidney Bernstein, then in partnership with Alfred Hitchcock, wanted to meet her, for they could not find the right leading lady for a picture called *I Confess,* soon to begin filming in Quebec. "I met Mr. Bernstein for lunch at his hotel," Grace recalled, "but I guess I didn't make a very good impression." A fine Swedish actress named Anita Björk was soon engaged for the leading role in *I Confess,* but she arrived with an illegitimate child in her arms and a lover at her side, and was forthwith turned away by Jack Warner. Instead, the part went to Anne Baxter.

Grace then began rehearsals for one of her most successful TV appearances, again demonstrating her superb gift for a special kind of romantic comedy of mistaken identities. Convoluted and improbable but engaging and lively, the show was called "Recapture," and in it Grace received top billing on TV for the first time—perhaps because of the recent release of *High Noon*.

As director Ted Post recalled, "I thought Grace's voice was not yet blended with her stately posture—it was still high, a little girlish and breathless. But I said nothing, certain that things would improve during rehearsals. Then one day her mother came to the studio and took her aside: 'Darling, your speech sounds a little affected.' And Grace replied, 'I know, Mother—I'm working on it.' And work on it she did. By the time of the broadcast, everything was much more natural." For the moment, the problem, one might say, was Grace's immersion in a variety of forms. She needed to find a palette of modulated expressions for films and an unforced projection for stage plays. But on live TV she had to lower her register while maintaining complete clarity. At first, therefore, her efforts produced what her mother heard as a certain fastidious affectation.

The tendency to exaggeratedly polite speech was soon erased, thanks mostly to Sandy Meisner's exercises. By the time of "The Kill," a western broadcast on September 22, Grace's performance was entirely credible, and the character was nothing like Amy Fowler Kane. The director, Franklin Schaffner, was swiftly extending the effects possible with a moving camera on live TV, for which he directed more than two hundred shows before going on to Hollywood, where he directed *Planet of the Apes* (1968) and *Patton* (1970).

In "The Kill," Grace plays a woman married to a man with a frightful temper. They go to a local saloon, where he meets an old flame, now married, and then he starts a fight with men who are stealing from his irrigation system. A young man is killed in the mêlée, and the husband flees. When the men approach the wife in search of him, she scares them off with a rifle—a strong scene by Grace, who liked playing such a different woman. "She seemed much more at home with a firearm than Amy Fowler did!" Grace recalled. "I had fun with 'The Kill.' " In her role as a frontier heroine, Grace became a kind of Minnie (in Belasco's play and Puccini's opera *The Girl of the Golden West*), and her portrait of an anxious wife, attempting to keep men at bay with a heavy rifle, is both moving and suspenseful.

MEANWHILE, EXECUTIVES at Metro-Goldwyn-Mayer were arguing over the casting of a film they wanted to rush before the cameras that autumn—in Africa. *King Solomon's Mines* (1950), produced by Sam Zimbalist, had been successful for Metro, as *The Snows of Kilimanjaro* (1952) had been for Fox; both pictures were among the kinds of colorful adventure stories that were being created to lure people away from their television sets.

Zimbalist had approached Dore Schary, who had recently replaced Louis B. Mayer as head of Metro, with the idea of remaking a film the studio had made in 1932 called *Red Dust,* which had starred Clark Gable. Although set in Southeast Asia, it had been made entirely at the studio in Culver City. At first Schary waved off Zimbalist's suggestion. But fifty-one-year-old Gable, after a number of indifferent movies indifferently received, was nevertheless still vigorous, still popular—and available. So was Ava Gardner, one of Metro's bankable leading ladies who (apart from her dark sultriness) had the kind of image once projected by Jean Harlow, the blond star of *Red Dust.* Zimbalist pushed his case: for a remake of the original, the studio needed only a third actress—one with evident elegance and covert passion, like Mary Astor in the original. To clinch his argument, the producer told Schary that the director

John Ford was interested: he already had three Oscars and was soon to win a fourth.

They sought among their contract players for the right actress to play opposite Gable. Deborah Kerr had been appealing in *King Solomon's Mines,* but Ford growled his displeasure at that idea. Zimbalist judged that Metro's Greer Garson was too affected—and so the ideas rose and sank. Ben Thau, a vice president at Metro, then suggested that they look for someone new. They sat for days looking at tests made by aspiring actresses and at reels submitted by agents' models. No one impressed them.

In 1952 it was common for studios to exchange screen tests made by actors they subsequently rejected. At Metro they sifted through tests sent over by Columbia, RKO and Warner Bros. Then, one day in October, they saw a test made for a Fox film called *Taxi,* with an unknown girl who had an ordinary appearance and an unconvincing Irish accent. Sighs of disappointment came from the Metro executives as they prepared to order up the next test from the archives—until John Ford interrupted. "This dame has breeding, quality and class," he said. "I want to make a color test of her—I'll bet she'll knock us on our ass!"

Next day, Jay Kanter rang Grace in New York with the news that Metro wanted to test her for a major role. She was lukewarm to the idea until she heard two words: "Africa" and "Gable." Departing early the following morning, she was, by nightfall, enjoying a moonlight swim in the pool at the Bel-Air Hotel, Los Angeles.

FOUR

L'Affaire Gable

When I was younger, I was always falling in love.
— GRACE KELLY GRIMALDI

DURING THE EARLY DAYS OF THE MOVIE INDUSTRY — FOR about twenty years, beginning in the early 1890s—very few actors were identified in the films that unspooled in penny arcades, nickelodeons and music halls. People worked anonymously in these "flicker" movies, which were considered a form of entertainment for the lower classes, on a par with carnival sideshows. Performers with stage experience feared they would lose future theatrical employment if it became known that they were in these mere fake pantomimes. In addition, the first film theatre owners were hesitant to promote the names of their employees, worried that they would demand higher salaries.

But things changed. The first name credited in a movie was that of Florence Lawrence, a stage actress since childhood who worked for Thomas Edison's company from 1907 and later appeared in films under the direction of D. W. Griffith. Sarah Bernhardt and Geraldine Farrar were among many renowned actors and singers who were immortalized in silent films, and by the time of the World War, movies became more respectable fare. Audiences gradually recognized their favorite performers from picture to picture and wanted to know more about them; soon producers began to see financial advantages in creating and promoting certain players, called "stars"—perhaps because they illuminated the darkness of movie theatres.

The era of the great studios coincided with the fame, fortune and power of these movie actors, who became essential in promoting the products. Directors, on the other hand, were mostly ignored, and for a long time, few of them had any real clout and all were regarded as secondary to a movie's success. The conventional wisdom was that only the stars and producers turned films into hits, and so studio executives selected young hopefuls they liked and essentially created identities for them, even to the point of changing their names and insisting on certain patterns of conduct even in their private lives. Archibald Leach, an acrobat from England, became Cary Grant. A flapper-era dancer named Lucille Le Sueur became Joan Crawford. Spangler Brough was renamed Robert Taylor, and Roy Scherer was rechristened Rock Hudson. Thousands received new identities, and backgrounds were created for them that sounded more interesting, more exotic or more acceptable than the truth.

Thanks to powerful studio publicists and "talent handlers," the public never knew that so-and-so might be socially objectionable according to the standards of the day. Under threat of dismissal or permanent demotion to minor, stereotyped roles, for example, lesbian and gay actors were usually forced to marry for the sake of their careers. Non-Caucasian actors were rarely cast as anything but servants, criminals or people of doubtful morality. Even on their own time, women could not appear in public without makeup and a fashionable outfit. Men had to be seen as unimpeachable gentlemen, and any studio player could be dismissed for failing to adhere to certain moral standards, often defined in their contracts and even sometimes invented in a moment of whimsy by a movie mogul. Public appearances and provocative romantic rendezvous were arranged for the sake of image, and the press was duly alerted in advance; in this regard, the situation remains largely unchanged in the twenty-first century.

If a movie star was alcoholic, a drug abuser, unfaithful to a spouse or even found guilty of a crime—well, the studios could take care of that. They routinely paid for media silence, bribed the police and negotiated with newspapers and gossip columnists. In the so-called glory days of Hollywood, the studios thus essentially directed the lives of countless thousands. All this control was taken for granted as a part of American big business.

The year 1924 was perhaps a watershed in which merely profitable entertainment became a huge corporate industry. New York theatre owner Marcus Loew, who had already bought Metro Pictures and Goldwyn Pictures, added Mayer Pictures to his list—with the aim of placing Louis B. Mayer as head of Los Angeles studio operations and Irving Thalberg as production chief. For decades afterward, the legal name of the holding company was Loews, Inc., while corporate power, as with all the Hollywood studios, was wielded by New York executives, with their proximity to Wall Street financiers. In the fullness of time, Mayer added his name to the studio's—and so was born Metro-Goldwyn-Mayer.

Thanks to Mayer's creation of what his publicists called "more stars than there are in the heavens," the studio boasted an impressive roster of popular players—among them Lionel Barrymore, Wallace Beery, Jean Harlow, Jeanette MacDonald, Norma Shearer, Joan Crawford, Clark Gable, Myrna Loy and Greta Garbo. Later, Metro placed under contract Gene Kelly, Jane Powell, Lana Turner, Judy Garland, Ava Gardner, Fred Astaire, Mickey Rooney, Katharine Hepburn, Spencer Tracy, Ann Miller, Esther Williams, June Allyson and Elizabeth Taylor. More than any other Hollywood studio, Metro was deeply involved in the personal lives of its contract players; for Mayer and his colleagues, that was simply a matter of protecting their investments.

From the late 1920s to the mid-1940s, Metro was the most successful studio in Hollywood: it never lost money during the Depression and released a feature film every week—along with animated cartoons and short subjects. Then the United States Supreme Court, ruling against corporate monopolies, ordered the studios to divest themselves of theatre chains, and Loews, Inc., had to yield control of Metro; thus began the studio's decline, for they could not survive without guaranteed showcases.

In the early 1950s, with Dore Schary as Louis B. Mayer's replacement, the studio continued to dominate the musical genre. This brought a new generation of talent, many of them young singers and dancers like Howard Keel, Debbie Reynolds, Cyd Charisse and Leslie Caron. From 1939 to 1955 the studio released six or seven musicals a year,* and in 1951, the Oscar for best picture went to the musical *An American in Paris*. But by then Metro could not depend on its musicals alone to woo the shrinking audience away from television. Despite the need to remedy the situation, Schary (like Mayer) had no great regard for strong directors, and only once did a Metro contract director receive an Oscar for directing a Metro picture (Vincente Minnelli, for *Gigi,* in 1958).†

---

* Among the memorable MGM musicals: *Annie Get Your Gun, The Band Wagon, Brigadoon, Easter Parade, The Harvey Girls, Love Me or Leave Me, Meet Me in St. Louis, On the Town, Royal Wedding, Seven Brides for Seven Brothers, Show Boat, Singin' in the Rain* and *The Wizard of Oz*.
† Victor Fleming's Oscar for directing *Gone With the Wind* (1939) was awarded for a David O. Selznick production released by MGM, and William Wyler was an independent director when he won for MGM's *Mrs. Miniver* (1942).

~

By the autumn of 1952, when Grace was invited to test for a movie the studio hoped would be a blockbuster, the Culver City complex had grown from 40 to 187 acres. On them were six back lots, more than fifteen huge stages, a lake with a harbor, a jungle, a railway station and parks, squares and streets from different eras and in a variety of styles. However, this turned out to be intemperate expansion, because Metro's glory days, as the most successful studio of the 1930s, were numbered. They had a shortage of great directors, and their glossy star vehicles were becoming old-fashioned and predictable—in 1953, for example, *Knights of the Round Table* followed *Ivanhoe.* "It was a lush and gaudy period," as Dore Schary said. The studio was reluctant to use color for anything but musicals, costume dramas or period spectacles, and the number of productions was dropping each year: Metro was making less than a sixth of Hollywood's output. "We had trouble finding roles for all of our contract players," added Schary. In light of all this, but reluctantly joining the effort to do anything to attract audiences, Metro decided that, after the success of *King Solomon's Mines,* they should produce another epic—the remake of *Red Dust,* updated to be called *Mogambo.*

John Ford directed Grace's color test, which pleased him, Schary and the executive board. A seven-year contract was drawn up for her and sent to Jay Kanter at MCA, where he and his superior, the formidable Lew Wasserman, tinkered with a few clauses. By late October it was ready for Grace's signature. But when she read it, she hesitated and asked for some important alterations, which astonished everyone, for this was considered willful and autonomous behavior. Metro's offer gave them the right to her services on three pictures a year for seven years, during which time they could dismiss her after every six months and loan her out to other studios at their pleasure. Her salary was to begin at $750 a week, with escalation clauses to be negotiated in good faith depending on her success, and a $20,000 bonus if she completed three pictures in any year. She may have smiled at the salary, for she had made far more money as a model.

Grace wanted every other year off from movie work, so that she could return to the theatre, and she insisted on the right to retain her primary residence in New York. These concessions Metro granted—again, to Hollywood's astonishment. It was immediately clear that Grace Kelly was not to be controlled easily.

"I signed with MGM," she recalled in 1975, "because *Mogambo* offered the opportunity to work with John Ford and Clark Gable, and to make the picture in Africa. If the production had been scheduled in Arizona, I wouldn't have signed the contract. But I did—at the departure desk of the airport, on my way out of the country."

Filming took from autumn 1952 through late winter 1953, first in Uganda, Tanganyika and Kenya, and then in London. On November 2, Grace arrived at the New Stanley Hotel, Nairobi. That evening at dinner, she met Gable and the British actor Donald Sinden, who was cast as her husband. "Grace proceeded to astonish Clark and me by ordering the entire meal for the three of us—in Swahili," Sinden recalled. From the moment in Hollywood when she had learned the precise African location, Grace had taught herself the rudiments of the local dialect. *"Lete ndizi, tafadhali,"* she told an astounded native waiter at the end of the meal—"Please bring me a banana."

In his fifties, Clark Gable—the self-styled "King of Hollywood"—had lost little of his renowned virile charm tempered by a kind of protective, paternal warmth. Far from the familiar comforts of home and friends, Grace formed an intense affection for Gable that lasted throughout their time in

Africa. But it is impossible to say unequivocally if theirs was a fully realized affair. A strong attraction is not invariably expressed sexually, no matter how randy the principals. At various times Gable and Grace were asked directly about rumors. Perhaps it was not surprising that each of them smiled and dismissed the topic, but nobody connected to the production ever asserted that there was a clandestine romance, and no one claimed to have held the lamp.

There was definitely a passionate friendship, however. Grace undertook to knit Clark a pair of socks for Christmas (which she never finished), and they spent much of their free time together. "Clark's eyes were quite definitely on Gracie," said Ava Gardner, "and hers, for that matter, were on him. They were both single at the time, and it's very normal for any woman to be in love with Clark." There was Grace, Ava added, "in Africa, with exotic flora and fauna all over the place—and Clark, strong and smiling and completely at home, made her love him more."

Both Grace and Gable were long deceased when Ava made this statement, which is highly ambiguous: "in love" may (but does not necessarily) mean "in bed." Ava was always bluntly straightforward about herself and others, and if there had indeed been an affair, one would have expected her to say so plainly.

"When I was younger, I was always falling in love with someone who gave more to me than I gave back," Grace said years later. "I knew I was immature and incomplete as a person, that I was really taking and absorbing more than I was giving. I think that's true of all young people. In the selfishness of youth, we need to feed our psyches and our souls by taking from others."

But her relationship with Gable was not only about taking, for she had a great deal to offer him. In his way, Gable was as lonely as Grace, and more than a little fretful. His career had been stymied in recent years by various ailments and the inevitable shifts in movie styles and movie-star popularity. He found the physical demands of *Mogambo* extremely challenging, and he was in the process of a divorce from his fourth wife (Lady Sylvia Ashley, the English model and socialite who had once been Mrs. Douglas Fairbanks). Romantic though Grace was, and smitten with her legendary costar, she was also sympathetic to his anxieties, and she made every effort to bolster his spirits during this difficult time in his life. As she wrote to her friend Prudy Wise, Grace and Clark dined together every night while working in Africa, which was not unusual for two single costars. In addition, Clark was of course enormously flattered to have the attention of a beautiful, playful and proficient young woman who clearly adored him.

On November 8 the company welcomed the fourth major player in the movie when Ava Gardner breezed in lustily with her husband, Frank Sinatra. As usual throughout their marriage, this couple argued constantly when they were not making loud intimate merriment; alternately, they drank excessively, shouted and threw things at each other whenever they had a few spare moments—until Frank left Africa to take a role in Zinnemann's *From Here to Eternity,* which jump-started his stalled movie career.

On November 12, the cast and director drank champagne and toasted Grace's twenty-third birthday, repeating the festivities on Ava's birthday, Christmas Eve. "After that," Ava recalled, "no matter where in the world I was, every year a birthday present arrived from Grace. She never forgot, and she sent a handwritten card—it wasn't left for a secretary to do. She was a great lady, and also great fun." But unlike others in the cast, Grace did not drink much. "Her little nose would get pink, she'd get sick, and we'd have to rescue her." Different though they were, the two American actresses became fast and lifelong friends. Ava attended Grace's wedding, and she often visited the palace in Monaco. She admired Grace's relaxed elegance, and Grace appreciated Ava's lack of inhibitions and the candid displays of emotions that Grace usually kept in check.

During the first week of production, which began on November 17, scenes were shot at an animal preserve. Jungle sequences were then filmed in Tanganyika, where Metro built a village with elaborate tents for the cast and crew, as well as kitchens and offices.

Every contingency was foreseen. The production company comprised hundreds—the usual array of technicians along with pilots, translators, native guides and guards, cooks, servants, a physician and nurses. But life was not luxurious. Water had to be boiled; foods were limited to what could be shipped from London or inspected by company monitors; and baths were limited, even in torrid and humid weather. Constant vigilance had to be maintained, for danger lurked everywhere: one location—on the banks of the Kagera River—was very near the habitat of scores of crocodiles not well inclined to a human invasion. Despite all the precautions, several crew members died in auto accidents or from tropical diseases, and scores contracted intestinal parasites or pathogens difficult to treat. Wherever the company of *Mogambo* went, an infirmary was established, and it was always occupied by employees ill with infections from insects, reptiles, tainted water and a variety of jungle maladies. By monitoring what she ate and drank, and where she went, Grace sailed through the production with nothing more serious than a heavy cold.

On his side, John Ford was a gifted director but an infuriating bully. Donald Sinden recalled the "appalling treatment" Ford meted out to various crew members—something often seen by such as Henry Fonda, who appeared in no fewer than nine Ford pictures. "He had by instinct a beautiful eye for the camera," Fonda said of the director. "But he was also an egomaniac. He never rehearsed and didn't want to talk about a part. If an actor asked questions about dialogue, he responded with insults or tore the pages out of the script"—thus reducing the actor's role. Ava Gardner described Ford as "the meanest man on earth—thoroughly evil." But she respected him.

Gable was silent about his dealings with Ford, but their relationship was no more than civil. At the time, the actor suffered from a tremor—a benign condition that caused his left hand to tremble occasionally, but this was not a symptom of either nervous tension or anything serious. Ford, who hated retakes of a shot and always felt that what was real could be captured the first time, lost his patience over the necessity to reshoot several of Gable's scenes. But he gave in to the star's male vanity. As Donald Sinden recalled, "Clark, whose chest was completely devoid of hair, insisted that no other actor should appear on film [in *Mogambo*] exposing a hirsute breast." And so, once a week, a makeup man came to Sinden with electric clippers.

As for Grace, she, too, felt the director's wrath. "I was awfully anxious about this part," she said. "I knew how much was on the line after *High Noon,* and I desperately wanted to do well—especially since Jack Ford had liked my test and apparently saw something in me that no one else had before him. Well, one day during filming, he shouted at me, 'Kelly—what the hell are you doing over there?'

"I replied, 'In the script, it says that Linda walks over here—then turns around and—'

"And he shouted back, 'Well, Kelly, we are shooting a *movie*—not a *script*!'

"You see, he shot a picture in such a way that the editor had very little—almost nothing—to work with. He very rarely shot close-ups, and then he did so only when something was very dramatic and important. Many directors filmed long shots, medium shots, close-ups and so forth. John Ford preferred to do one long shot; he moved in for a medium shot, did the rest of the scene in two or three takes maximum, and that was all. No one ever did more than four takes with John Ford! In my case, he knew how he wanted to photograph me, and to hell with the script.

"But no one ever told me about this in advance—I had to hear it from the assistant director. If Ford had said something at the outset, I would not have had to figure out where I was going to stand and why, and all the rest. But he really gave me no direction, no hint."

BASING *MOGAMBO* on his original screenplay for *Red Dust,* writer John Lee Mahin changed the names of all the earlier characters and transposed the action from Southeast Asia to Africa. Victor Marswell (Gable) is a safari guide in Africa. Into his wild but uncomplicated world come two women—the uninhibited, worldly-wise, single but experienced Eloise "Honeybear" Kelly (Ava Gardner), who immediately has a passionate week with Victor; soon after, anthropologist Donald Nordley (Donald Sinden) and his very prim wife Linda (Grace) arrive. *Mogambo* then becomes the story of a romantic triangle. In true Hollywood fashion, the jungle is the setting for the release of wild passions, and Linda finds Victor seductive in ways her scholarly husband is not. But the blond Grace and the brunette Ava are not the two Isoldes. Because the film was made in 1953, the conclusion is achingly proper: the Nordleys rediscover true love, and Victor realizes that "Honeybear"—always called "Kelly" in the film—is the right gal for him.

Grace's experience of working with John Ford repeated the

situation that had prevailed with Zinnemann, who had neither the time nor the desire to provide Grace with any direction, much less to discuss her character in the story. Ford was not interested in conversation or in entertaining any questions except with his technicians—and he was far less courteous than Zinnemann. At their first meeting, Grace mentioned to Ford that she was the second Kelly to be working for him—that her uncle Walter had appeared in Ford's film *Seas Beneath,* made in 1930. "Yeah?" Ford grunted, and chomped his cigar.

Sinden remembered an incident that perfectly represents Ford's directorial method that winter. Sinden and Grace were to make their entrance into the story from a river steamer. Without rehearsal or instructions, the actors were sent aboard and the boat moved toward shore. Suddenly they heard Ford's voice over a loudspeaker: "Grace—Donald—get below deck. OK. Donald—come on deck. Look around at the scenery. Call Grace. Put your arm around her. Point out a giraffe over on your right. Get your camera out—quickly. Photograph it—the giraffe. Smile at him, Grace. Grace—look at that hippopotamus on your left. Get Donald to photograph it. A crocodile slides into the water. You're scared, Grace—you're scared! OK. You're coming onto the pier. Look around. What's in store for you? Natives run down to meet you. OK! OK! Cut! Print it!"

And that, Sinden said, was their first day of being directed by John Ford—exactly as if he were still directing silent films.

Gable conveyed real poignancy in the role of the aging macho hero, a character frightened not of wild animals but of loneliness, a man who has to reconsider his lifetime of bachelorhood when he falls in love with two very different women. Ava Gardner contributed an exquisitely calibrated performance in the picture, in the smartly written role originally played by Jean Harlow. With Gardner's smoky baritone voice, her balance of sarcasm with tenderness, her flawless timing and subtle expressions, she created a memorable character who transcended every cliché normally associated with a woman of easy virtue whose generous spirit finally earns her true love—in this case, Clark Gable.

During her acting career, Gardner was usually regarded as a sexy dame and not much more; indeed, she represented precisely the opposite of what Grace, all too briefly, epitomized on the screen. Sadly, Gardner believed the conventional, shallow assessment of her talent and never thought much of her achievements. But she was a fine actress, and toward the end of her career, even the critics had to take note of her exquisite performance in John Huston's 1964 film of Tennessee Williams's play *The Night of the Iguana.*

As screenwriter Mahin admitted, Grace's role was disappointingly two-dimensional, and *Mogambo* offers the audience no reason to empathize with Linda Nordley. As the wealthy, beautiful wife of a wealthy, handsome husband with the time and money to indulge his academic interests, Grace portrays a woman who allows herself the luxury of a reckless dalliance, oblivious to and careless of her husband's feelings. She did her best to temper Linda's cardboard primness with a fear of the jungle and anxiety over an illicit passion, but she could not supply sufficient dialogue (nor could she demand close-ups) to win the audience's sympathy. The critical consensus was that "Grace Kelly's blond beauty remains intact, despite the remarkably silly lines she is made to say," such as (Grace to Gable, in the jungle): "I didn't know monkeys could climb trees!"

"I really wasn't very good in *Mogambo,*" she said years later, "because I was so new in the business and I needed to learn so much." But she was perhaps judging the character, not her performance; she did what was required, and she could not exploit what was not provided. Depending on which sources are consulted, *mogambo* is the Swahili word for *passion* or for *danger*. Linda Nordley demonstrates little of the former, and the latter is provided in only one scene, involving a giant python that turns out to be implausibly friendly.

In fact, *Mogambo* is as tedious as the dreadfully polite Nordleys; it has none of the rapid, wisecracking humor and tight narrative line of *Red Dust*. An incessantly talky yarn set in an exotic wilderness, with a few animal roars thrown in, *Mogambo* is the sort of movie that could only have been saved by cutting about forty minutes and re-editing the rest. John Ford, ill and losing his sight, was a "tyrant" from day one (as producer Zimbalist said), interested only in the lush tropical scenery and the wild beasts, and the cast had to cope with a legion of logistical problems.

But audiences loved it, and the picture grossed a healthy $5 million on its first release. The Academy justly nominated Ava Gardner as best actress of 1953, and, for reasons that defy comprehension, Grace Kelly as best supporting actress; in that category she won a Golden Globe from the Hollywood Foreign Press Association. But when they mentioned her at all, the critics were not passionate: "Grace Kelly is all right," sniffed the *New York Times*. Clark Gable perhaps fared best of all: *Mogambo* revived his career, and he remained in demand until his death at the age of fifty-nine, in 1961.

Grace and her colleagues were glad when the African sojourn was ending, for they were exhausted. "Ava and I are now great friends," Grace wrote from Africa to Prudy. "The times we have been through! Frank [Sinatra] left Friday, so maybe things will be easier. It's been a strain on all of us. The old man [Grace's nickname for John Ford] is very anxious to leave Africa, and everyone is terribly nervy and on edge. I think the picture is going to be awfully good, but right now not many people give a damn."

∼

IN FEBRUARY 1953, the production company moved from Africa to England, where interior scenes were photographed at Metro's Borehamwood Studios, Hertfordshire. Immediately, Clark Gable turned a chilly shoulder to Grace, refusing to date or dine with her, or even to speak more than a few words except about work—a sudden, severe shift in behavior that left her baffled and hurt. At the time, rumors of a romance were trumpeted in the press—stories perhaps planted by Metro, for publicity purposes. Some biographers, therefore, have jumped to the conclusion that Gable rejected Grace's proposal of marriage or her insistence on continuing the affair in London (and later, in Hollywood). But the truth was more prosaic: he did not want to jeopardize the decree absolute of his divorce (scheduled for April in an English court) by providing grounds for a charge of improper conduct. For all that, Grace was disheartened at the way he ignored her, and she was, for once, glad for a visit from her mother, who was eager to meet the King of Hollywood.

The leading players were lodged at the Savoy Hotel, London. One day, in the foyer, Grace was greeted by Morgan Hudgins, the studio's unit publicist on the picture, who had been with the production from the start. Hudgins was having a drink with a tall, courtly gentleman, forty-year-old Rupert Allan. Born in St. Louis and educated at Oxford, Rupert was at the time working for *Look* magazine and had been assigned to cover the coronation of Queen Elizabeth II in June. He later worked with the publicist Arthur P. Jacobs and compiled an impressive client list of his own. Very quickly, Grace and Rupert became friends, and he was often her escort in London, Hollywood and New York. He also became her personal publicist and, as princess, she asked him to be Monaco's consul general in Los Angeles.

That Rupert was gay was a matter of profound indifference to Grace, who loved him like a brother, and for the rest of her life he was her close confidant. In Beverly Hills, Grace often visited Rupert at his home on Seabright Place, where he lived with the love of his life, Frank McCarthy. A World War II hero and a retired brigadier general in the U.S. Army, McCarthy eventually produced the Oscar-winning *Patton*. Whenever anyone uttered a word against gay men or women, Grace was outspoken. "You shouldn't criticize people who are homosexual," she told her friend Prudy Wise. "It can be very destructive, and it is so easy to become mean without realizing it."

Mogambo finally wrapped production in March 1953 and was listed for release in October. Back in America, Grace visited her family in Philadelphia before returning to Manhattan. "You know, the girl must have had a lot of fascinating experiences," her father told a reporter, "but she just won't talk!"

But there was neither theatrical nor movie work on offer. "She was pretty much in the same place she had been after the unsuccessful test for *Taxi*," recalled Dore Schary, "and although she was available for other roles, none appeared."

The fact is that Metro, Schary and company simply did not know what to do with her at the studio. They were producing costume dramas such as *The Prisoner of Zenda, Plymouth Adventure, Young Bess* and *Beau Brummell*—and none of these had roles they considered right for her. After several conferences that spring, her bosses quietly let it be known around town that Grace was available for loan-out to other studios, as her contract permitted. This would raise money for Metro, which would charge a hefty fee for Grace's services elsewhere and, in turn, pay her only the fee her contract stipulated. The loan-out, an old Hollywood tradition, was an easy moneymaking proposition for studios. Still, nothing happened until very late that spring of 1953.

But Grace kept busy. Jay Kanter invited her to his wedding on April 15, in New York. His bride was Judith Balaban (later Quine), daughter of the president of Paramount Pictures. Grace and the Kanters became close friends, and three years later, Judy was one of her bridesmaids. A few days after the Kanters' wedding, Grace had a less pleasant appointment: the funeral of her first love, Harper Davis, who had succumbed to multiple sclerosis at the age of twenty-six.

In May and June, Grace appeared in three live TV dramas: "The Betrayer," with Robert Preston; "Boy of Mine," with Henry Jones; and "The Way of the Eagle," in which she and Jean-Pierre Aumont costarred as Mr. and Mrs. John James Audubon. Then forty-two, Aumont had been widowed since the death of his wife, the actress Maria Montez, in 1951. As a popular, handsome actor much in demand both in his native France and in America, he was also a prime target of aspiring brides on both continents. Aumont found twenty-three-year-old Grace far more interesting and mature than many women he met, and he asked her to be his guest for lunch on the day after the broadcast of "The Way of the Eagle," scheduled for June 7.

Although she found Jean-Pierre enormously attractive and sophisticated and very much liked his Gallic charm and wit, Grace declined the invitation. Some of the gossips believed that an affair between Grace and Jean-Pierre began at once—a canard that, alas, has taken on the authority of fact. Others claimed that, no, Grace turned him down because she was awaiting a resumption of *l'affaire Gable*. Once again they were all wide of the mark. The fact is that Grace could not accept

Aumont's offer of a lunch date because Jay Kanter had telephoned her during TV rehearsals for "The Way of the Eagle." She was to leave for Los Angeles on June 8. An appointment had been made for her to meet Alfred Hitchcock, who was looking for a new leading lady.

FIVE

Over the Moon

The best way to do it is with scissors.
— ALFRED HITCHCOCK

THE TEST I MADE FOR THE ROLE OF THE IRISH GIRL IN *Taxi*—a part I didn't get—turned out to be very important in my career," Grace recalled. "John Ford saw that test and cast me in *Mogambo,* and then Hitchcock saw the same test and wanted to see if I would be right for his next picture. I was very nervous and self-conscious at my first meeting with him [in June 1953], but he was very dear and put me at my ease. We talked about travel, food and wine, music, fashions— everything, it seemed, except the character of Margot Wendice in the movie."*

Grace's initial anxiety was reasonable. Alfred Hitchcock, who marked his fifty-fourth birthday that summer, was unquestionably one of the world's most popular and successful

---

* Hitchcock told me that when he first met Grace he had not seen *Mogambo* or a rough cut of it: he knew only her black-and-white test for *Taxi* and (he thought on reflection) perhaps a scene or two from *High Noon*. He did not need any more than that to make the right decision.

filmmakers; later he would justly be hailed as one of the cinema's artists, a man whose movies were frequently profound as well as enormously entertaining. From his earliest days in England, he was also his own best publicist, and he made certain that his name and presence were known and remembered—hence the cameo appearances in his movies, among other publicity stunts over a half-century. "Actors come and go," Hitchcock said repeatedly in the 1920s, "but the name of the director should stay clearly in the mind of the audiences." Until the 1960s, the average moviegoer in England and America could name only three directors: Cecil B. DeMille, Charlie Chaplin and Alfred Hitchcock.

As a great visual storyteller, Hitchcock had a vivid fantasy life, as his writers, designers, crew and actors attested. He frequently shared fabulous ideas for movies he made and never made, and told the bawdiest jokes about sex and the most horrific tales about murder—simply to monitor his listeners' reactions. As a mastermind of the movies, Hitchcock deserved all the respect he commanded and which was invariably rendered; but he was also a lonely, complex man, "frightened of everything," as he said. Gregory Peck, who starred in two of the director's movies, said that "something was ailing Hitchcock—throughout his entire life, I think." That "something" had at least partially to do with deeply repressed desires and emotions and a feeling that he was doomed to isolation and romantic abnegation.* Those elements are the common currency of his most deeply felt films.

---

* On Hitchcock's life and art, there have been books and articles past counting, in many dozens of languages. He is unquestionably the director most often considered by biographers, academics, historians and appreciative moviegoers. Detailed but necessarily partial lists of volumes and essays about Hitchcock are included in my three books about him, which are listed here in the bibliography.

Hitchcock was born in the East End of London and felt himself to be a marginal person from the beginning. As a Catholic and a Cockney, he did not hail from polite, acceptable society; and although his father was a prosperous greengrocer and fishmonger, that occupation meant Joseph Hitchcock was "in trade" and therefore not a gentleman. In addition, young Alfred was creative, clever, and gifted with a prodigious memory; he was also restricted by a lifelong tendency to morbid obesity. "Hitch" (as he called himself) had mastered the art of film as a storyteller, designer and assistant director before he was permitted to direct his first silent picture, in 1925; from then to 1953, he directed more than three dozen movies that made him both celebrated and wealthy.

After leaving England in 1939, he directed, during his first dozen years in America, some of the finest movies ever to come from the old Hollywood studio system—among them *Rebecca, Foreign Correspondent, Shadow of a Doubt, Notorious* and *Strangers on a Train.* He then continued to produce and direct movie masterworks until a few years before his death in 1980. That June morning in Burbank, Hitchcock told Grace that he had a multi-picture deal with Warners, and after rummaging for a year in search of the right subject or property for his next movie, at last he had found one he could make in fulfillment of his contractual obligation.

Dial "M" for Murder, by the English writer Frederick Knott, had originated as a BBC television thriller early in 1952. On June 19 that year, it was staged as a full-length play in London, and on October 29 it opened on Broadway, where it was still selling tickets for every seat, every night. Even before the West End premiere, the Hungarian-British filmmaker Alexander Korda had snapped up worldwide film rights to the play for a modest £1,000. Hitchcock saw *Dial "M"* and believed that, in the absence of any obvious alternative, he could make a film of it for the brothers Warner, who then had to come up with Korda's asking price of £30,000. With its single set and few characters, it seemed an easy task to transfer the play to celluloid: Hitch was, as he later said, "running for cover."

There was, however, a major condition in the sale of movie rights: any motion picture of *Dial "M"* could not be released as long as the play was running. (Indeed, it had 552 Broadway performances, from October 29, 1952, to February 27, 1954. The movie was finally released three months later.) In addition, for Hitchcock, there was another, more troublesome condition: Warners required him to make the movie in the three-dimensional format.

By 1953 there were 25 million TV sets in America. To entice audiences out of their living rooms and into theatres, Hollywood came up with a variety of gimmicks that television could not offer: the wide screens of Cinerama and Cinemascope, huge historic epics, flimsy costumes and sexual innuendo, stereophonic sound, and even a mercifully short-lived contraption called Smell-O-Vision. Flashiest of all were 3-D movies: *Bwana Devil* and *House of Wax* had already roped in audiences, and Warners wanted to continue the technique with *Dial "M"*—even though Hitchcock accurately predicted that 3-D was an unwieldy fad that would quickly die. The process did not interest him at all: "It was essentially anti-cinematic," he told me during one of our many conversations. "3-D constantly reminded the audience that they were 'out there' and not drawn visually and emotionally into the story. Until I met Grace, I just wanted to get through with this thing as quickly and unceremoniously as I could. Then I realized that here was a girl I could really do something with, despite the problems of the 3-D camera."

As the title character in the TV drama *Ann Rutledge,* February 1950.

As a New York fashion model, age 18, spring 1948.

As Amy Kane in *High Noon,* September 1951.

As Louise Fuller in *Fourteen Hours* (with James Warren), August 1950.

As Margot Wendice in *Dial "M" for Murder* (with Ray Milland), July 1953.

With director Alfred Hitchcock while filming *Dial "M" for Murder,* August 1953.

With Clark Gable, at the premiere of *Mogambo,* October 1953.

As Lisa Fremont in *Rear Window* (with James Stewart and Alfred Hitchcock), December 1953.

As Nancy Brubaker in *The Bridges at Toko-Ri* (with director Mark Robson), January 1954.

OPPOSITE:
As Georgie Elgin in
The Country Girl
(with Gene Reynolds,
Bing Crosby and
William Holden),
February 1954.
*Danish Film
Institute/Stills and
Posters Archive*

With costar John Ericson, during the production of *Green Fire,*
April 1954. *Danish Film Institute/Stills and Posters Archive*

Working on
To Catch a Thief,
on the French
Riviera in June
1954.

In the studio
with Alfred
Hitchcock:
To Catch a Thief,
August 1954.

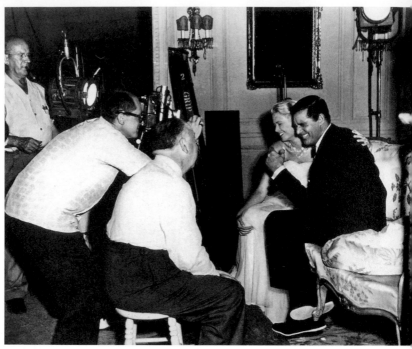

During the filming of *To Catch a Thief* (with Alfred Hitchcock and Cary Grant), August 1954.

At the Los Angeles premiere of *Rear Window* (with Alfred Hitchcock and Oleg Cassini), August 1954.

Age twenty-five, November 1954.

Moments after receiving her Academy Award as Best Actress, for *The Country Girl,* March 30, 1955.

The first meeting with Prince Rainier—in the palace gardens, Monaco, May 6, 1955.

Departing from New York for Los Angeles, autumn 1955.

As Princess Alexandra in
The Swan (with Louis
Jourdan), December 1955.
*Danish Film Institute/Stills and
Posters Archive*

As Tracy Lord in
High Society,
January 1956.

1690-2

In *High Society* (with John Lund), February 1956.
Danish Film Institute/Stills and Posters Archive

Age forty, 1969.

At the Lincoln Center Film Society tribute to Alfred Hitchcock, April 1974. *Ron Galella*

In her office at the palace, Monaco. *Prince's Palace Archives, Monaco*

Grace Kelly Grimaldi, HSH the Princess of Monaco, age 50.
Prince's Palace Archives, Monaco

On July 22, 1953, the Hollywood trade papers announced that Grace Kelly had been borrowed from MGM for the role of Margot Wendice in Alfred Hitchcock's 3-D movie version of *Dial "M" for Murder,* scheduled to begin filming on July 30. Frederick Knott had written the scenario after making one or two minor cuts in his play, and Hitch was ready to go. "I was determined not to do the usual pranks with 3-D," he said, "because I felt that it was a trick that was already on the wane. Therefore, I told Bob Burks [the cinematographer] that we would not have knives or fists flying out at the audience, and no one would fall from a great height into their laps. In other words, I made it as if it were a normal movie."

The complicated plot concerns a retired tennis champion, Tony Wendice (played by Ray Milland) who concocts a plan to murder his wife (Grace) in order to get his hands on her fortune. Resentful of her affair with an American crime novelist named Mark Halliday (Robert Cummings), Wendice arranges what appears to be the perfect crime. To commit the murder, he blackmails a man named Swann (Anthony Dawson), a former classmate with a criminal record. However, the plan goes wrong when Margot resists the killer, reaches for a pair of scissors and stabs him to death. Tony then decides to take his scheme in a different direction, trying to convince Chief Inspector Hubbard (John Williams) that his wife killed Swann because he was blackmailing her. The inspector, however, reasons otherwise, and with the help of Mark and Margot, a situation is set up that reveals Tony as the villain.

As much as possible, Hitchcock filmed the play chronologically, and the opening sequences reveal his background in silent film. At breakfast in their London flat, Tony kisses Margot—no dialogue. Then we see her glance at the morning paper reporting Mark's arrival on the *Queen Mary*—still no dialogue. Cut to Mark's arrival by ship—no dialogue. Then Hitch cuts to another kiss, between Mark and Margot. All this occurs in silence (but for the Dimitri Tiomkin score). The story proceeds smoothly and the plot is set in motion calmly—until the violence of the attempted murder by strangulation, ending with Margot's stabbing of Swann. The would-be killer then leaps up and around in his death agony, and the scissors become lethally embedded in his back as he collapses on the floor.

The murder scene remains one of Hitchcock's most violent sequences, even more shocking because it was filmed like an attempted rape. The director inserted shots of Grace's legs, pushing against Dawson as he falls on her in a parody of sexual writhing as attempted strangulation. There is a kind of frenzy in the scene, requiring the intricate editing of many separate shots for the final effect, which, decades later, has lost none of its power to terrify and to repel. Eventually, Hitchcock had to trim the sequence and reduce the violence in order to satisfy the Motion Picture Association of America and Joseph Breen, vice president and director of the Production Code Administration. As Hitchcock said with witty ambiguity, "The best way to do it is with scissors."

"That sequence took an entire week to shoot," Grace said, "and it was very, very difficult for Anthony Dawson and me. Each of the shots had to be carefully set up, because Hitch wanted it to look as if the only light source was the blaze from the fireplace. That was especially complicated—everything had to be shot brighter because the lenses on the 3-D cameras tended to pick up colors oddly. So we had to stop, the lights had to be fixed, then we started again. Then Tony Dawson wrapped the scarf around my neck and we had to make it look as if he was really strangling me. Then I had to twist around on the desk—I remember the assistant director warning me that I had to fall just so, or I would have broken my back.

"Then Tony Dawson had to fall on top of me on the desk,

and we stopped again—and then the shot was set up with my feet kicking against him. Then we stopped, because something went wrong with the 3-D camera—and then we began again, and Hitch told me to reach out for the scissors, behind me on the desk. Then we had to stop again—and that's the way it was, for a week. We tried to keep everything cheerful during the breaks, but frankly, it was all awkward and difficult. This was my first leading role in a movie, and I tried to give Hitch what he wanted. But after three or four days of work on this sequence, from seven in the morning to seven at night, I went back to my hotel covered with bruises.

"Hitch wanted the costume department to make a velvet robe for me—he said he wanted the effect of light and shadow on the velvet during the murder. I had a fitting for it—and it seemed right for Lady Macbeth in her sleepwalking scene, but not for me in this sequence. So I told Hitch I didn't feel the robe was right for the part. I said that if Margot gets up in the middle of the night to answer the phone and there was no one in the apartment, she would not put on this great velvet robe. Hitch's face went slightly red—it always did if he was upset—and he asked me, 'Well, what would you put on to answer the phone?' and I told him, 'I wouldn't put on anything at all—I would just get up and answer the phone in my nightgown!' And Hitch replied, 'Maybe you're right.' And that's the way we shot it. After that, I had his confidence as far as wardrobe was concerned, and he gave me a very great deal of liberty in what I wore in his next two pictures."

With impeccable manners, Grace continued to disagree with her colleagues when she thought they were wrong. "I got into quite a fight with the makeup man, who wanted to keep putting more and more rouge on me—even in the scene that takes place after Margot has spent a long time in prison. When I objected, he said that Mr. Warner likes a lot of rouge on his actresses. I told him, 'Well, let me call Mr. Warner,' and he replied that Mr. Warner was in the South of France. 'Well,' I said, 'you tell Mr. Warner that I refuse to wear all this rouge, and if he's angry with you, tell him I threw a fit and wouldn't wear it!' " When the makeup staff reported the incident to Hitchcock, he knew that his new leading lady had a mind of her own and was not to be prevented from using it.

This was indeed Grace's first leading role in a movie; she was the only woman in the cast; and she was acting under the direction of the legendary Alfred Hitchcock, who disliked and rejected interference from mere actors ("cattle," as he puckishly termed them) and only rarely took their suggestions. But with Grace, he had found his muse, and he told everyone that she was the best leading lady he had since Ingrid Bergman, who had appeared in a trio of films for him (*Spellbound, Notorious* and *Under Capricorn*); Grace would match that record.

"The subtlety of Grace's sexuality—her elegant sexiness—appealed to me," Hitch said. "That may sound strange, but I think that Grace conveyed much more sex than the average movie sexpot. With Grace, you had to find it out—you had to discover it."

Which he did—not only the sexiness, but also the vulnerability and the strain of melancholy that existed alongside the passion in Grace Kelly's image, as it did in her own authentic character. In this regard, it was surprising that few critics, in 1953 or since, noted the deeply affecting and fragile portrait she created for the last sequences of *Dial "M."* As Margot, she returns to her flat after her stay in prison—a day before her scheduled execution—and is, to her surprise, drawn into a scheme to unmask her husband as her intended killer. Grace conveyed a heartbreaking directness here, her voice thin, her manner that of a woman who has lost touch with her innocence and who now gazes, resistless and uncomprehending, at death.

Even Hitchcock was astonished at her performance, for he did not request repeated takes. "From the *Taxi* test," he said, "you could see Grace's potential for restraint. I always tell actors not to use their face for nothing. Don't start scribbling on the paper until you have something to write."

THE DIRECTOR and cast had to have complicated rehearsals because of the enormous 3-D camera in a single set.* "Hitch felt very encumbered and frustrated by having to do the picture in 3-D," Grace maintained. "But it was the policy of Warner Bros. at the time, because Hollywood had been hit by television. This was the first picture shot at the studio after a six-month hiatus, and here we were—this small cast, rattling around on this big stage. Hitch told us the picture would never be shown in 3-D, that it would be released 'flat,' that 3-D was just a passing fancy that wouldn't last. And he was right. The machine was the size of a room—it was enormous—and when Cary Grant visited us one day, he pointed to the camera and said, 'Well, Hitch—is that your dressing room?' It was just gigantic, and Hitch had a terrible time with it."

The technical challenges angered Hitchcock. He could not vent his wrath against his male actors, who had years of experience and would have responded appropriately. Therefore, as filming continued that summer, Hitchcock took out his irritation on his leading lady. "We were blocking a scene," Grace recalled, "and I was standing there, a little bewildered. Then I heard a voice calling me, 'Miss Kelly, what do you think you are doing?' I called back to him, 'I'm trying to figure out where

---

* There are a few very brief shots outside the set of the Wendices' London flat—quick cuts to the local police station, to a men's club, and to Tony and Mark riding in taxis.

Margot would glance, and where she would go at this moment.' And Hitch said, 'Well, Miss Kelly, if you had read your script properly, you would know that she is to look in this direction and go over here. Don't you ever read stage directions?' So I was called down on that." She had been embarrassed in front of the cast and crew, and Hitchcock had successfully exerted control over someone in lieu of something on the production.

Grace remembered another incident when he tried to tease her. "Hitch always had a fund of naughty stories," she recalled. "One time he turned to me after telling Ray Milland a very raw joke, and he said, 'Are you shocked, Miss Kelly?' I smiled and replied, 'Oh no, Mr. Hitchcock, I went to a girls' convent school—I heard all those things when I was thirteen.' He loved that answer."

Hitchcock was always a good mentor—until he became emotionally involved, and then he demanded too much private time with his young trainee and turned into a benighted lover *manqué*. However, Grace kept the tone light, appreciating the time Hitchcock took to help her develop precisely the right accent for the role—that of a young English wife, wealthy, stylish and refined but sufficiently amorous to engage in an extramarital affair. John Ford had told Grace that he didn't care "what the hell you do" when she had played Linda Nordley, and Grace's voice and tone were often inappropriately strident in *Mogambo*. "With Hitch, it was different," she recalled. "He had endless patience with me."

Hitchcock's coaching required no intensity. "All I had to do was encourage her to lower the voice," he said. "Once she had it down, it was no trick for a girl as clever as Grace to keep it there." His technical frustrations during production were much relieved by the cooperation and good humor of his leading lady, and soon it was evident to everyone on the production that Hitchcock had developed a schoolboy crush. He instructed and rehearsed Grace, teaching her the elements of acting and moviemaking for which Zinnemann and Ford had neither time nor inclination.

Halfway through production, Grace and her costar, Ray Milland, were thrown into turmoil by gossip-column innuendoes that their occasional dinners *à deux* were more than friendly encounters during his wife's visit to England. How much was true and how much not is impossible to establish, but Ray's wife Malvina was sufficiently sensitive about the matter to take with absolute gravity the buzz about her forty-eight-year-old husband and the actress less than half his age. Then and later, there were various tales: (1) that Mal threatened divorce because of Ray's affair with Grace; (2) that Milland told Grace he would divorce his wife to marry her; and (3) that a torrid affair continued until the end of filming, when they calmly agreed to terminate the relationship.

Just as with the Gable "affair" (if such it was), no one connected to *Dial "M" for Murder* was aware of or spoke about any intrigue; neither of the principals ever alluded to a romance; and the stories emerged only later—fueled by the gossips but not seriously regarded except by Mrs. Milland. Hitchcock, who loved to gossip about his leading ladies, never had a word to say about it. If there was indeed more than a flirtation, it was conducted with the utmost discretion and secrecy—not a simple achievement in Hollywood. In any case, Ray Milland was never separated (much less divorced) from his wife. When he died in 1986, he had been married to her for fifty-four years.

The rumor that Grace very nearly destroyed the Milland marriage is based on the sexist notion that a beautiful young woman can easily reduce a man to nerveless idiocy, hypnotizing him, annihilating his will and poisoning a solid twenty-one-year marriage. The real Grace was neither an ice maiden nor a scheming profligate.

Contrary to later tales that Grace spent time on the set of *Dial "M"* flirting with everyone, Robert Cummings recalled that "she disappeared into her dressing room the moment a scene was over," and there she studied her lines for the next sequence. "I kissed her a lot in the movie," Cummings added, "but I don't think she said more than fifty words to me outside the script. She was very private."

"ALL THROUGH the making of *'Dial 'M,'* " Grace recalled, "the only way for Hitch to preserve his sanity in the midst of 3-D chaos was by preparing for his next picture. He talked to me about it even before I knew I was going to be in it. He discussed the plans he was making—he was going to build the biggest indoor set in the history of movies, which was going to be an entire four-story apartment building, with people in each unit, and he described them and what they would be doing. I could see him thinking—thinking all the time while we waited for that enormous 3-D camera to be pushed around. He didn't tell me I was going to be one of the leading characters in the story. I was just an interested listener, and because I was under contract to MGM, I didn't even think about whether there was a role for me in it. Anyway, he was going to direct it at Paramount. At this point, I still didn't know if I was pleasing Hitch or not. During that summer, we filmed *Dial 'M' for Murder*—but talking about *Rear Window* was his real delight."*

When Hitchcock completed the picture, on September 30,

---

* That summer, Hitchcock's agent, Lew Wasserman, arranged a multi-picture deal for him at Paramount Pictures, by which Hitch would produce, direct and eventually own the rights to five films (which turned out to be *Rear Window, The Trouble with Harry, The Man Who Knew Too Much, Vertigo* and *Psycho*) and for Paramount to produce and own four—but the studio got only one (*To Catch a Thief*).

Grace hurried to New York. "Working with Hitch was wonderful for me," she recalled, "but there was very little about Hollywood that I liked. The only value out there seemed to be money, and it seemed to me that many friendships and even marriages were often based on wealth and how relationships could benefit someone's career. I saw so many unhappy people—miserable people, really—and so many alcoholics and [those who had] nervous breakdowns. In addition, I didn't like the eternal sunshine of Los Angeles and being dependent on a car to go all those long distances from one part of town to another. I preferred to live in New York, where it rained sometimes, and where you could take a walk down the street without being stopped by the police or being thought dangerous or crazy not to be in a car."

She had a good professional reason for hurrying home. José Ferrer was preparing to direct and star in a November revival of *Cyrano de Bergerac* at the City Center of Music and Drama, and, on the recommendation of Raymond Massey, Ferrer and producer Jean Dalrymple invited Grace to audition for the role of Roxane. Grace was eager to return to the theatre in a play she knew well, and in a romantic role she had coveted for several years.

On October 15 she read with Ferrer onstage, but she had a severe cold that day, and her voice was not heard beyond the third row of the cavernous theatre on West 55th Street. She had not improved after a second audition, and Ferrer—pressed for time and unimpressed by Grace—engaged another actress. Her failure to land the role of Roxane disappointed her as no other rejection had, and there was no word from her agent about work at Metro or anywhere else. Her weekly salary from the studio continued to arrive, but, as always, she wanted and needed much more than a paycheck.

Grace had missed out on a great theatrical romance, but she

was soon to gain a real-life one. Not long after the New York premiere of *Mogambo,* she had met Oleg Cassini, an internationally renowned clothes and costume designer, recently divorced from his second wife, the actress Gene Tierney (for whom he had designed dozens of movie costumes). Sixteen years older than Grace, Oleg was born and educated in Europe, where his roots were in both the Russian and Italian aristocracy.*

Strikingly handsome, slim, dark-haired and mustached, with an almost princely demeanor and a courtly manner that usually left women breathless and men intimidated, Oleg was multilingual, highly refined and much in demand socially and professionally. He was also in the front ranks of American clothes designers, and eventually he became the primary stylist for First Lady Jacqueline Kennedy, for whom he created a look that was imitated worldwide. Oleg spoke proudly of his reputation as a notorious roué; now, at forty, he had the kind of mature but not weathered good looks that deepened his European allure. As she said, Grace was quickly "over the moon" in love.

For the time being in 1953, the bond between them remained platonic. They were frequent dinner companions, but Grace was entirely devoted to her career and he was devoted to the art of conquering other attractive women, a trait she would not tolerate if they were to embark on a serious intimacy. Still, he was in ardent pursuit of her and assailed her with flowers, cards and invitations. "On November 12 [he wrote in a telegram on her twenty-fourth birthday], the Earth became alive for me and created the loveliest thing in the world—you. I love you, my darling—will call you tonight."

---

* The Cassini-Kelly affair was no rumor. It was detailed in thirty-seven pages of his autobiography and was well known to Grace's family. Her children included letters, photos and *billets doux* exchanged between their mother and Oleg Cassini among the items in the 2007 tribute to Grace at the Forum Grimaldi.

"I saw her only in profile," recalled Oleg of their first meeting. "I saw the utter perfection of her nose . . . the long, elegant neck . . . the silky, diaphanous blonde hair. She wore a black velvet two-piece [outfit], very demure, with a full skirt and a little white Peter Pan collar. Later, when she stood, I noticed that she had a pleasing figure: tall, about five foot eight [!], good, broad shoulders, subtle curves and long legs—a very aristocratic-looking girl . . . not the sort you simply called for a date."

Then Grace had a call from Jay Kanter. "Hitchcock wanted me for *Rear Window,*" she recalled. "Paramount had negotiated with MGM to loan me out, and, if I liked the script, I would have to be in Hollywood for wardrobe fittings in late November. But I wanted to stay in New York for personal reasons"—by which she meant Oleg.

Next day, it seemed she could have both a splendid role and continue the dance of possibility with Oleg—without going to Hollywood. Grace received the script of *On the Waterfront,* with an offer to play the role of Marlon Brando's girlfriend in a film directed by Elia Kazan in New York.

"So I sat in my apartment, with two screenplays—one was going to be filmed in New York, with Marlon Brando, and the other was going to be filmed in Hollywood, with James Stewart. Making a picture in New York suited my plans better—but working again with Hitch . . . well, it was a dilemma. Finally my agent called me and said, 'I have to have your answer by four o'clock this afternoon. Which part do you want?' I told him, 'I don't know what to do! I want to stay in New York, but I love working with Hitchcock.' My agent told me he would give me exactly an hour to make my decision."

On the Waterfront was already in production, and Grace would have to join a seasoned cast and director already familiar with the exterior locations in Brooklyn and New Jersey. The story contained unusual and violent material—and she would have to learn about characters in a crude setting foreign to her. *Rear Window,* on the other hand, was scheduled to start studio filming in December and to be completed in early January. She would, Grace reasoned, be working with a director she trusted, and playing a sophisticated high-fashion buyer, a wealthy former model at the top of Manhattan society—in other words, a character and milieu she knew and understood. On November 23, Paramount Pictures issued a press announcement confirming her forthcoming participation in *Rear Window.** With her recent Oscar nomination for *Mogambo* and a Hitchcock picture behind her, MCA could negotiate favorable terms for Grace's loan-out to Paramount from Metro: she was paid $20,000, prorated over seven weeks from preproduction to the film's completion, at $2,857.15 per week (before agent's fees, union dues and taxes were withheld).†

She returned to Los Angeles on November 21 and stood for wardrobe fittings two days later. Hitchcock had already instructed costume designer Edith Head about the colors and styles of the five outfits for his leading lady. As usual, Hitchcock left no detail of color or line unconsidered, and no costume was completed without his approval. In this case, Grace worked closely with Edith on the final designs for her wardrobe.

Hitchcock told Edith that Grace's outfits had to advance the conflict in the story and still, as the designer recalled, "make her look like a piece of Dresden china, something slightly untouchable."

---

* In her first movie role, TV actress Eva Marie Saint won an Oscar as best supporting actress for *On the Waterfront* and began a long and busy career.
† Audrey Hepburn and Marilyn Monroe had long-term deals with, respectively, Paramount and Fox; each was paid about $15,000 per picture for the run of the contract, although occasionally a bonus was added. Grace's base pay was a bit higher.

Edith learned that Grace had been a model and that she knew how to wear clothes. "Grace was delightful to work with because she was very well educated and we could talk about anything together—art, music, literature. She enjoyed museums. She would get excited about classical music. . . . Sometimes she would come into my salon [at Paramount] with her lunch and the two of us would talk and laugh for hours. It was always a pleasure to see her kick off her shoes and relax.

"Off screen, she was not the best-dressed actress in Hollywood, but she was always very fastidious about the way she looked. She wore white gloves and very sheer hose. . . . People today would call her manner 'uptight,' but she wasn't. Grace had a very cool, reserved demeanor, which tended to put off people who didn't know her. Actually, she was quite shy. Since she was so beautiful, men were always flirting with her, and she wasn't especially comfortable with such superficiality."

As Edith and others observed, people on a production often mistook Grace's manner for aloofness—"but in fact she couldn't see anybody who was standing more than six feet away from her" unless she wore her glasses, recalled Judy Quine.

As Grace said, "Hitch told Edith that she had to design a peignoir that could fit in a small handbag. Well, the trouble we had with that peignoir, getting it into that travel case and out and in again! Then we went for a rehearsal, and I wore the peignoir onto the set. Hitch called for Edith—'The bosom is not right on this,' he said. 'We'll have to put something in there.' He didn't want to upset me, so he said this to Edith—and everything had to stop. Edith came to my dressing room and said, 'Grace, there's a pleat here, and Mr. Hitchcock wants me to put in falsies.' I told her I wouldn't wear them, and Edith said she didn't know what to do—he was the boss. Finally she said, 'I'll try to take it in here and pull it up there.' So I pulled the peignoir down, and I stood up as straight as I could and walked back to the set without falsies. Hitch took one look and smiled. 'There now, Grace—that's more like it! See what a difference they make?' We never told him that we changed nothing."

Hitchcock respected Grace's opinions as he did few other actors' notions about their characters. "There's a moment in *Rear Window* when I went over and sat on the window seat of Jeff's room during the dialogue rehearsal. [Assistant director] Herbie Coleman said, 'Look, Hitch, this will cost us a fortune—we'll have to light up all the apartments in the courtyard in back of her if she does the scene this way. Can't she sit somewhere else?' And Hitch replied, 'Herbie, if that's where Grace wants to sit, that's where she will sit.' I hadn't even thought of the technical problem involved, and I told Hitch, 'Oh, don't bother with that—I'll sit somewhere else!' But Hitch said, 'No, Grace, it's better your way.' " As it happened, Hitch used an angle and close-up that did not require the full background.

Grace established a lifelong friendship with Edith Head, a formidable talent but a somewhat peculiar woman who had eight Oscar statuettes on her shelf. She created the costumes for more than five hundred movies from 1927 to 1980, but she never shared the credit with her army of assistant stylists, cutters and seamstresses, who did a great deal of the designing and all of the manual labor. While she was working with Grace and Hitchcock on *Rear Window*, Edith walked to and from an adjacent Paramount sound stage, consulting with director Billy Wilder on the costumes for *Sabrina*.* For that picture, Edith designed some clothes—but she was not responsible for one single item for the star, Audrey Hepburn, who had gone to Paris before filming began and, with the help of Hubert de

---

* Work on the two movies overlapped. *Rear Window* was in production from November 29, 1953, to January 14, 1954, and *Sabrina* from September 29 to December 5, 1953.

Givenchy, had selected all her outfits from his workroom. When the Oscar for best costume design of 1954 was handed to Edith Head for *Sabrina,* she accepted it happily, without ever mentioning Givenchy's name—nor did Paramount list him in the movie's credits.

IT IS interesting to compare the careers of Audrey Hepburn and Grace Kelly, who were born in the same year and were high on the list of audience favorites in 1953. Both had appeared twice on Broadway, where they had received Theatre World Awards, and they had both worked as models. Like Grace, Audrey was working with first-rate directors: William Wyler, on her Oscar-winning role in *Roman Holiday;* now with Billy Wilder; and later with King Vidor, Fred Zinnemann and John Huston. Grace and Audrey both had a rare, classic elegance, photogenic beauty and high public esteem. And, contrary to popular expectations, each woman became disillusioned with mere fame and gave up everything for a different life.

Paramount producers like Wyler and Wilder were not as judicious with Audrey's presentation as Hitchcock was with Grace's—especially with regard to makeup. Audrey's eye liner and mascara, for example, were almost comically exaggerated in *Roman Holiday, Sabrina* and *Love in the Afternoon,* while Grace's makeup was far more natural in all four of her Paramount Pictures (a lesson Metro had learned when it came to their productions of *Green Fire, The Swan* and *High Society*). Until her appearance without the semblance of any makeup at all (in *The Nun's Story,* filmed in 1958), Audrey was painted with elongated eyebrows and excessive, over-the-lip lipstick. But Grace simply would not go along with the prevailing embellishment of the time: she knew what was right for her look and she prepared it herself. After her Oscar for *The Country*

Girl, Metro was in no position to insist on the cosmetics Grace wore in her last two pictures for them.*

REAR WINDOW reveals a great deal about Alfred Hitchcock — and as much about Grace Kelly; indeed, it presents all the evidence needed to cite him as a majestic talent and her as an icon of her time.

"I was feeling highly creative at the time," Hitchcock said. "I remember thinking that my batteries were fully charged." So fully charged, in fact, that he was able to produce and direct a movie to satisfy even the most bored, cynical and detached spectator — someone just like the character played by James Stewart.

Based on a story by Cornell Woolrich and a film treatment by Joshua Logan, the sparkling script was written by John Michael Hayes — the first of four he wrote for Hitchcock — and it remains a model of construction, of suspense interlaced with humor, and of a thriller that also has important things to say about life, relationships and moviemaking. The Woolrich story has no female character; Logan had invented one, but the full development of all the roles must be credited to Hayes.

The rear window looks out from a cramped two-room apartment in Greenwich Village, New York. There, a free-lance traveling photographer named L. B. Jefferies (Stewart, who was twenty-one years older than Kelly) is confined to a wheelchair, his left leg encased in a plaster cast after a serious injury sustained while on assignment. With little to distract

---

* Grace also refused to smoke cigarettes in any of her pictures. When Hitchcock instructed her to light up in *Rear Window,* the camera cuts away — from the cigarette, unlighted, between her lips, then to Stewart, and finally to the lighted cigarette held for a few seconds and then stubbed out. As the saying goes, she never inhaled.

him from boredom and the emotional predicament he faces in his troubled relationship with his blond girlfriend, Lisa Fremont (Grace), "Jeff" takes to spying on the neighbors in a building across the courtyard. He soon suspects that a traveling salesman named Lars Thorwald (Raymond Burr) has murdered his blond invalid wife Anna (Irene Winston). In an effort to persuade his detective friend Tom Doyle (Wendell Corey) that Thorwald is a killer, the chair-bound Jeff accepts the help of Lisa and of his visiting nurse Stella (Thelma Ritter), who become his "legs." Jeff is enormously impressed by Lisa's pluck and daring, but they are both nearly killed when Thorwald learns about the spying.

While the characters are completely absorbed in proving the guilt of the killer, Hitchcock was not: the crime was only another example of his so-called MacGuffin, the pretext for a story that is really more concerned with the difficulties of a romantic relationship. The audience does not see the crime in *Rear Window,* nor do we know anything about the Thorwalds other than his occupation and her bedridden state. Throughout the picture, Hitchcock is more concerned with the reactions of the watchers than with the private life of killer and victim. And he very much liked what he called the "symmetry" of the picture: "On one side of the yard, you have the Stewart-Kelly couple, with him immobilized by his leg in a cast, while she can move about freely. And on the other side there is a sick woman who's confined to her bed, while the husband comes and goes."

The opening credits appear over a bamboo shade, which slowly rises to reveal the array of apartments in the building opposite Jeff's—the largest specially built indoor set in movie history, for which Hitch furnished and lighted no fewer than thirty-eight individual apartments. He also had studio researchers do their homework: according to the script, Thorwald's apartment is said to be at "125 West Ninth Street." But

West Ninth Street ends farther east, at Avenue of the Americas (Sixth Avenue); thereafter, West Ninth is called Christopher Street. For legal reasons, moviemakers do not use authentic addresses—hence Paramount used 125 Christopher Street as a geographic basis but had to rename it 125 West Ninth, which does not exist as a postal address.

In fact, 125 Christopher Street, on the northeast corner of Hudson Street, was the model for the design of the movie's apartment complex. A courtyard separates it from Jeff's residence, on West Tenth. This explains why, when the police are summoned in the movie, they arrive after just a few seconds: Manhattan's Sixth Precinct is just across from Jeff's flat, also on West Tenth. It also explains the plot point about the short distance to the Hotel Albert, then at Tenth Street and University Place.

The first third of the picture explores Jeff's dissatisfaction with his girlfriend Lisa—a woman whose life he sees as completely incompatible with his own. He travels to dangerous locations around the world for his work as a freelance photographer; she is a glamorous Manhattanite, her world that of high fashion, top-end stores, the theatre and all the trappings of urban sophistication. If Jeff may be regarded as a surrogate for Hitchcock, Lisa is certainly a kind of stand-in for Grace herself. Indeed, the script specifies that Lisa resides on East 63rd Street—the site of the Barbizon Plaza Hotel for Women.

Far from establishing the murder as its central concern, *Rear Window* focuses on other issues—specifically, whether Jeff will take Lisa more seriously than as an occasional girlfriend, and whether he will trust her desire, as she says, "to be part of your life." The focus of this movie is on the romantic efforts of Lisa, who tries and tries again to get through to a man she loves. Jeff remains a cool, independent, detached observer of life, while Lisa is involved in it and places herself at risk to help in trapping

Thorwald. Throughout the picture, what the audience *feels* depends entirely on the performance of a *secondary character:* Lisa. When *Rear Window* was released, Grace was still not given before-the-title credit, but there was no doubt where the emotional focus was—and no doubt about Grace's extraordinarily poignant, funny, stylish yet deeply human portrait.

CHAIR-BOUND JEFF gazes at a series of rectangles (the neighbors' windows) and sees people, turns them into characters, gives them names ("Miss Lonelyhearts" and "Miss Torso," for example), and makes up stories about them. Finally he sends a blonde into danger. He is, in other words, just like the director, Alfred Hitchcock—who, as usual, worked closely with his screenwriter.

At the same time, each of the neighbors offers a possibility for Jeff's future. In the opening sequence, Jeff speaks with his editor on the telephone: "Can't you just see me, coming home from work to a nagging wife?" As he says this, he gazes across at Thorwald, arriving home from work to a nagging blond wife (who, in long shot, bears a disturbing resemblance to Grace). Each of the female neighbors he subsequently sees becomes a variation on what Lisa could become. She might turn into the blond wife of a befuddled, balding husband who lavishes all her affection on their small dog. She could become a shapely blond dancer entertaining a small platoon of men but faithfully awaiting the return of her true love from the army. She might mature into a middle-aged sculptress with obviously dyed hair, working on an abstraction called *Hunger.* Alternatively, perhaps more tantalizingly, she could be the sexually insatiable young bride who has just moved in nearby. But most clearly linked to Lisa is the pathetic "Miss Lonelyhearts."

The role of this desperately lonely spinster was assumed by

Judith Evelyn, among the most intense actresses of her day and a specialist in neurotics and destructive characters. She had first met Grace in 1947, through George Kelly, when Evelyn played the title role in the Broadway revival of *Craig's Wife*. Their reunion now was a reason to celebrate, which they did by sharing a split of champagne in Grace's dressing room one afternoon.

There seems to be no hope for Jeff in his relationship with Lisa precisely because he prefers to watch her: he likes her to model clothes for him, but he is patently afraid of going further (as Stewart is similarly afraid to do in *Vertigo*). In this regard, the movie's signature tune has enormous significance. Bing Crosby croons "To See You Is to Love You" (from the Paramount picture *The Road to Bali*). These words are literally true for Jeff, who is satisfied with merely gazing at an image—"To see you is to love you, and you're never out of sight, and I love you and I'll see you in the same old dream tonight." Indeed, there seems to be no hope for Jeff, who uses his physical disability as an excuse to avoid any kind of intimacy unless initiated by Lisa—and then he talks his way out of it. Early on, he complains to Stella that Lisa is the kind of girl who loves things like a new dress or a lobster dinner—and moments later she arrives with a new dress and a lobster dinner. However, even the realization of this little bit of imagination is too much for him, and at the end of the evening he rejects her cruelly and precipitates her abrupt departure from his apartment.

When Lisa gamely climbs the fire ladder into Thorwald's apartment, she finds the wife's wedding ring and slips it on her finger, proudly displaying it to Jeff as he watches across the courtyard. But this gesture gives her away to Thorwald, who glances from her finger to Jeff watching him (and to us). At this moment Hitchcock closes the circle of his intention: Lisa has used the adventure as a way of showing Jeff how brave and resourceful she could be as his wife—thus she points to the wedding ring on her finger.

"*REAR WINDOW,*" Hitchcock said years later, "was structurally satisfactory because it is the epitome of the subjective treatment. A man looks, he sees, he reacts—thus you construct a mental process. *Rear Window* is entirely about a mental process, done by use of the visual." Regarding Grace, Hitchcock added, "Everybody wants a new leading lady, but there aren't many of them around. There are a lot of leading *women,* but not enough leading *ladies.* An actress like Grace, who's also a lady, gives a director certain advantages. He can afford to be more colorful with a love scene played by a lady than with one played by a 'hussy.' With a hussy, such a scene can be vulgar, but if you put a lady in the same circumstances, she's exciting and glamorous."

Everyone working on *Rear Window* could see Hitch's fascination for Grace. "Of course he fell in love with her," assistant director Herbert Coleman said in 1981. "But who didn't? Nothing happened, nothing came of this fantasy romance— he often had to fall in love with his leading ladies." The fantasy romance was a pattern that had begun with Madeleine Carroll in 1935, was repeated with Ingrid Bergman from 1944 through 1948, and would recur later, with disastrous consequences. Hitch had a preference for blondes: they photographed better against dark backgrounds, and he viewed their apparent icy remoteness to be like snow on top of a volcano. Hence, Hitchcock regarded Grace's sophisticated beauty as hiding an inner passion, blended with her obvious wit. She became his latest obsession—his last had been with Ingrid Bergman, who had left America five years earlier. Now, with Grace, he imagined that he would never need any other actress in his future films; this was one of the most futile prospects he ever entertained.

Grace's first appearance in *Rear Window* has the distinctive look and feeling of a dream. With the camera holding to the face of the sleeping James Stewart, we hear the sound of someone entering Jeff's apartment. Then we see Grace, approaching the camera slowly, as if to embrace the lens (and thus the viewer). Cut to the profiles of the two heads, as Grace bends over to kiss Stewart. Hitchcock said he shook the camera for the final shimmering effect of this shot, but the fact is that he double-printed several frames of film, to give a more dreamlike, romantic feeling to the scene.

Holding to the two profiles, Hitch told Grace to whisper her first words to Stewart:

LISA. How's your leg?
JEFF. Hurts a little.
LISA. And your stomach?
JEFF. Empty as a football.
LISA. And your love life?
JEFF. Not too active.
LISA. Anything else bothering you?
JEFF. Yes—who are you?

She moves away with a smile and turns on three lamps as she answers, "Reading from top to bottom: Lisa—Carol—Fremont."

Hitch worked with John Michael Hayes on a later scene that perhaps no other director could then create, remarkable in its erotic frankness and yet completely inoffensive. Kisses had time limits in Hollywood films, but Hitchcock finessed that requirement here, just as he had with Ingrid Bergman and Cary Grant in *Notorious:* he interrupted the kissing—but not the embrace—with whispers and small talk, turning up the heat while moving his plot forward. Lisa returns to Jeff after a clash of wills over their future together. The scene, loaded with innuendo and sexy double entendres, opens with a close-up of them in a tight clinch in his wheelchair, as she sprawls over his lap:

LISA. How far does a girl have to go before you notice her?

JEFF. Well, if she's pretty enough, she doesn't have to go anywhere. She just has to be.

LISA. Well, I am—pay attention to me.

(More kisses.)

JEFF. I'm not exactly on the other side of the room.

LISA. Your mind is. When I want a man, I want all of you.

JEFF. Don't you ever have any problems?

LISA. I have one now.

JEFF. So do I.

(More nibbling on lips and ears.)

LISA. Tell me about it.

JEFF. Why would a man leave his apartment three times on a rainy night with a suitcase and come back three times?

LISA. He likes the way his wife welcomes him home.

(More kisses by the passionate Lisa.)

JEFF. No, not this salesman's wife. Why didn't he go to work today?

LISA. Homework—it's more interesting.

JEFF. What's interesting about a butcher knife and a small saw wrapped in newspaper?

LISA. Nothing, thank heaven.

(Closer embracing, more kisses.)

JEFF. Why hasn't he been in his wife's bedroom all day?

LISA. I wouldn't dare answer that.

JEFF. Well, listen—I'll answer it. Lisa, there's something terribly wrong.

LISA (*as she rises from his embrace*). And with me, I'm afraid.

JEFF. What do you think?

LISA. Something too frightful to utter.

Speaking in whispered, passionate murmurs, Grace created an authentic portrait of a woman aroused by the mere proximity of her lover, frustrated by his physical incapacity and anxious about his preoccupation with the possibility of a local murder. As Hitchcock intended, this was a side of Grace Kelly that had never before been seen. "I didn't discover Grace," he said, "but I saved her from a fate worse than death. I prevented her from being eternally cast as a cold woman."

The stated consensus about her slowly improved, although audiences were far more enthusiastic than media critics. She was "fascinating," according to the *New York Times,* whose reviewer gauged the picture as "insignificant, superficial and glib, [and] the purpose of it is sensation." But a year later, both the National Board of Review and the New York Film Critics Circle honored Grace as best actress of the year 1954 for her performances in a trio of pictures released that year—*Dial "M" for Murder, Rear Window* and *The Country Girl.* BAFTA, the British Academy of Film and Television Arts, climbed aboard the Kelly bandwagon, too, nominating her as best actress for *Dial "M"* and *The Country Girl.*

When *Rear Window* wrapped on January 13, 1954,* Hitchcock told Grace she would soon be working for him again; he did not inquire about her plans, or Metro's. He had decided that she would soon be back in the Hitchcock fold, and that was that.

---

* Several sources state that Grace made her final appearance in a live TV play on the *Kraft Television Playhouse* episode "The Thankful Heart," broadcast live from New York on January 6, 1954. I have been unable to reconcile this assertion with the Paramount production files, which indicate that she worked on that date on *Rear Window,* which occupied her on nine of the first twelve days of that year.

~

IN CULVER City, meanwhile, the men at Metro still had no idea what to do with Grace. "I don't understand all the excitement about this girl," said an uncomprehending publicist at that studio, speaking on the record to a journalist. His opinion was obviously that of his bosses, for—even before *Rear Window* was completed—they renewed the loan-out deal with Paramount. Beginning January 4, 1954—"or on any day following completion of principal photography of *Rear Window*"—Grace was to appear in Paramount's *The Bridges at Toko-Ri*.

Metro contract player Van Johnson understood the reason for Grace's popularity with moviegoers, studio bosses to the contrary notwithstanding: "There hasn't been a newcomer of her thoroughbred type [for many years], as contrasted with the cuties who've flung themselves up any old way. The public has had so much sex pitched into its face recently that it's gone for Kelly in rebellion against a broadside of broads."

Hitchcock and Johnson may well have been alluding (perhaps rather unfairly) to another blonde—Marilyn Monroe, whom Twentieth Century-Fox was presenting as the epitome of the new, bold sexiness in movies, exploiting her with breathless, almost desperate speed: in 1953, Fox released three Monroe pictures—*Niagara, Gentlemen Prefer Blondes* and *How to Marry a Millionaire*. Talented beyond the material she was given, Monroe was a phenomenon, presented as the antithesis of everything Grace stood for.

Film roles were one way to keep a studio's actors in the public eye and mind. Another way to maintain their fame was through interviews and articles discreetly arranged and then published in fan magazines and national newspapers. Movie stars were commodities, after all, and they had to be properly advertised, presented and celebrated for the sake of the studio's financial success. Stars, as one movie historian has written, "had to be accepted by the public in terms of a certain set of personality traits which permeate all his or her film roles. The successful stars have been those whose appeal can be catalogued into a series of such traits, associations and mannerisms." The unofficial syllabus of developing stars was the same everywhere in Hollywood: there was an initial construction of an image, a series of photographs sent to the print media, a careful presentation of the star's background—and even a rumor of romance, as indication that the star was no bloodless mannequin. When an actor was cast in a major film, a "unit publicist" attended the entire production, supervising publicity and interviews and planting harmless and helpful tidbits in the press.

Metro exploited the fact of Grace's wealthy family, her education and her theatrical apprenticeship, in order to suggest that she was the perfect lady of the 1950s, an era that idolized and idealized the amalgamation of prosperity, family ties and hard work to achieve the American dream. Although Grace's image was carefully molded to appeal to a male audience, she was also presented as a respectable, white-gloved girl who could be admired by women—hence she was featured in magazines like *McCall's, Ladies Home Journal* and *Mademoiselle.* "There's Grace Kelly," commented an anonymous columnist at *Vogue*. "Her gentle, fine-bred prettiness is rapidly reversing Hollywood's idea of what's box office." A Metro publicist wrote that line and successfully slipped it to a *Vogue* editor.

Grace's image was based on the generally truthful contours of her family background—her father's achievements in business and sport, for example—and on favorable comments from colleagues. But remarks from Grace herself were rare, and when forced by the studio to give an interview, she did not divulge intimacies. Marilyn Monroe was once asked what she wore to bed, and she replied, "Chanel Number 5." When the same question was put to Grace, she said, "I think it's nobody's business what I wear to bed. A person has to keep something to herself, or your life is just a layout in a magazine." And so it went.

There was nothing patronizing in Grace's personality, and the aloofness that went along with her ice-maiden image was something that none of her friends and colleagues ever saw. "She was anything but cold," said James Stewart. "Everything about Grace was appealing. She had those big warm eyes, and if you ever played a love scene with her, you'd know she wasn't cold." As for her professional skills, Stewart spoke for many of her leading men when he said, "You can see her thinking the way she's supposed to think in the role. You know she's listening, and not just for cues. Some actresses don't think and don't listen. You can tell they're just counting the words."

Terms like "lady," "genteel," "elegant," "patrician" and "reserved" were most often used to describe Grace—along with puns and plays on her first name. It's almost impossible to keep count of the number of articles, over thirty years, that were titled "Amazing Grace."

At exactly the same time, Paramount's publicists helped journalists with their descriptions of Audrey Hepburn, who was routinely termed "elfin" (although elves are spiteful, malignant dwarves), "gazelle-like" (despite the fact that gazelles are spotted antelopes); "coltish" (although colts are male horses); and, most often, "gamine" (which means a street urchin or a homeless waif). With Audrey and Grace, new vocabularies were needed for new styles, and the publicists pored over their dictionaries. In "real life," if Grace or Audrey was seen in a restaurant or at a public event, there was quite literally a collective, audible intake of breath: it was the appearance of a goddess to mere mortals.

Neither Audrey Hepburn nor Grace Kelly ever acquired the sort of image that Marilyn Monroe had as the ultimately desirable playmate, available if only a guy had the chance.

Just as the public was told of Audrey's European aristocratic background—her mother was a Dutch baroness—so Grace was presented as a kind of American noblewoman, from a "good family" that worked hard to achieve social primacy (which, in fact, they never enjoyed). Monroe, on the other hand, came from a hardscrabble background: she had been married for the first time at sixteen, and she had toiled her way to independence and fame as she became the supreme sex symbol of the decade. Suggestive remarks were composed not only for her movies, but for her to say during interviews, too.

Never mind that Marilyn Monroe was actually a woman of keen intelligence and serious purpose: she had to serve the studio's manufactured image of her if she wanted to maintain her popularity and position. And never mind that Audrey and Grace were both healthy young women who dated, had love affairs, wore jeans, occasionally used a four-letter word and liked to balance hard work with a good time and laughter. They both exhibited a natural refinement and were unfailingly courteous to colleagues and strangers, but these qualities were presented as the sum total of their personalities. They were nothing like goddesses in person, although they were certainly beautiful, stylish and always considerate. They were women to respect, but they could never be fully defined as merely respectable—a term that alternately amused and annoyed them both.

"I never really liked Hollywood," Grace admitted. "Oh, I liked some of the people I worked with and some friends I made there, and I was thankful for the chance to do some good work. But I found it unreal—unreal and full of men and women whose lives were confused and full of pain. To outsiders, it looked like a glamorous life, but it really was not."

friends and Lovers

Nothing is quite so mysterious and silent as a dark theater.
— GRACE (AS GEORGIE ELGIN) IN
THE COUNTRY GIRL

OVER THE COURSE OF FOURTEEN MONTHS — FROM July 1953 through August 1954—Grace Kelly completed six of the eleven films that constitute the sum of her movie career: *Dial "M" for Murder, Rear Window, The Bridges at Toko-Ri, The Country Girl, Green Fire* and *To Catch a Thief.* That was a remarkable achievement by any standard. She was energetic, ambitious and admired by her colleagues, but moving immediately from one production to the next often left her exhausted. "I realized much, much later that I had no time for myself—no time to reflect, to think about what I was doing and where I was going. I thought I had the best intentions, but of course, one always does. The pictures were made in Hollywood, South America and the South of France, but except for Sundays, I didn't have much time off in the first eight months of 1954. Looking back, I'm not sure how I survived."

When the columnist Hedda Hopper asked, in May of that

year, how old Grace was, she replied truthfully, "Twenty-four—
and aging much too quickly." Did Grace think an actor would
make a good husband? "No, but I don't think someone outside
the business would make a good husband, either." Would Grace
be willing to give up her career for marriage? "I don't know. I'd
like to keep my career. I'll have to wait and make that choice
when the time comes. Of course I think about marriage, but
my career is still the most important thing for me. If I interrupt
it now to get married—because I don't believe in a part-time
family life—I would risk passing the rest of my existence wondering whether or not I would have been able to become a great
actress."

For the public, 1954 was "a year of Grace," as journalists repeatedly asserted, and audiences agreed. She was invariably
counted among the most fashionable women in America, and
before the year's end, she was on several best-dressed lists. But
the public had no idea of the wide streak of melancholic dissatisfaction within her, caused by her desire for a husband and
children. "I suddenly noticed that I was an aunt several times,
and a godmother many times, and that I was receiving invitations to one wedding after another. For a while I was the only
unmarried woman I could name! I was going to be twenty-five
that year, and as each month passed and each film was finished,
I was more and more confused. I had no time for myself, and
when a magazine asked me, 'Who is the real Grace Kelly?' I
replied, 'There isn't any real Grace Kelly yet! Come back in ten
years and I'll tell you—I'm still trying to find out.' "

BEFORE *REAR WINDOW* was completed in January, Grace
gained a new and valuable friend. She had known Rita Gam in
New York when they were both working as models and acting
in TV dramas, and Rita, too, had come to Hollywood. While

Grace was working on *Rear Window,* Rita was at Universal, filming the historical epic *Sign of the Pagan.* They both knew the producer and former agent John Foreman, who suggested that the two young women might become friends.

"Grace had taken an apartment on Sweetzer Avenue in West Hollywood," Rita recalled, "and she had shared it with her friend and secretary, Prudy Wise. When Prudy left Los Angeles, Grace rang me and invited me to come over for a cup of coffee. We clicked immediately—the friendship was virtually instantaneous—and Grace, who didn't like living alone, invited me to share her apartment. I was lonely living at a hotel, and I accepted at once." Like Judith Balaban Kanter, Rita was a bridesmaid at Grace's wedding and a lifelong friend.

Grace's rented West Hollywood apartment was a simple place in a nondescript building, but Rita remembered that Grace had made it her own. "It was feminine and sentimental, filled with snapshots, sketches and souvenirs from her films, and everywhere there were pictures of her family. As she poured the coffee at our first meeting, we compared notes about our separate African adventures—she having filmed *Mogambo* in central Africa, and I just back from North Africa, where I appeared in *Saadia* for MGM.

"She was generous, open, tolerant, fun and completely down to earth—and she was always working. She had huge ambitions to become one of the fine stage actresses in America—that's what she wanted more than anything else. Her film work became just a detour. I think that's why she never owned a home in Los Angeles—New York was always her home, and she was never in Hollywood with all her heart. She just saw it as a temporary opportunity, and she had other plans for her future—on the stage."

That year, as Rita remembered, Grace "was often very tired, but she enjoyed the work. Occasionally on Sunday, she went to lunch and spent the day with her uncle George, and she always spoke about him with great warmth and affection. He was extremely important in her career, and he seemed to understand everything she resented about Hollywood—especially the whole publicity machine. There she was, the envy of every woman in Hollywood—but she disliked being turned into this great romantic image. Only her sense of humor got her through all this—her humor and the conviction that once she got too tired of it all, she would settle down and have a family."

Grace was protective of her siblings and loyal to her parents, Rita added. "She admired her father, although she thought he was too tough on her and she knew that he didn't approve of her acting. It was always 'Peggy this' and 'Peggy that' for her father. And her mother wasn't a warm person at all. But Grace wouldn't hear a word against them. She was a good-hearted gal. She had an understanding about people, and compassion—she didn't talk about it, but you heard how she spoke and saw how she behaved."

Grace's agent, Jay Kanter, and his wife, Judy, recalled an afternoon with Grace and her parents that year, after Grace received her Academy Award nomination for *Mogambo*. Jay told John and Margaret Kelly about their daughter's impressive accomplishments and the offers MCA was receiving for her every day. "She was a weak little thing," interrupted Grace's father, changing the subject to Grace's childhood. "I don't understand why she wanted to be an actress—never did—but I told her she could go to New York when she asked because I couldn't think of anything else she could do. Oh, well, I'm glad she's making a living." In the eyes of her father, as Judy recalled, "Grace was a write-off."

As for the men in Grace's life, Rita "made it a rule never to ask about her boyfriends, and she was the same with me. That served us both well and kept our friendship. Her beaux came and went, but they weren't the focus of her life, and in Hollywood there was never that one special person who could fulfill her idea of the perfect mate for her. Her focus was on her career. Although we never pried into one another's life, Grace was very kind and especially caring when I broke up with Sidney [Lumet, her first husband]. No one could have been a more attentive friend."

AT THE COMPLETION of *Rear Window,* Grace was full of anecdotes about Hitchcock. "She told me he was a great director," Rita recalled, "and they had a great working relationship laced with jokes and good humor. But he never went out of his way for anybody. Hitchcock, Zinnemann and Ford were all like benevolent tyrants. None of them really liked women. They were male chauvinists, and they treated Grace like a cutout. But she made sure she had a good time, and she did what she was told on the set. Grace was tough and strong—mentally, emotionally and physically—and she cut through a lot of the nonsense. Hollywood was like a game for her. She was also a good businesswoman, and this allowed her to win in her struggles with MGM. She knew how to play the corporate game, and she played it so that it worked for her."

Between Rita and Grace there was no competition—only a mutual understanding and a certain touching protectiveness. "Over the years, I found that people didn't think of Grace as very bright, but she was—all her acting talent and her success came through her intelligence."

As attractive, unattached young movie stars, Rita and Grace were frequently invited to Hollywood parties and suppers, and producers and studio executives said they would send a car to collect them. "I often said OK to that," Rita recalled. "But then Grace interrupted me: 'Don't you dare let them send a car! We may want to get out of there. I'll drive us.' She knew the ways of the world and didn't want to be trapped in an uncomfortable situation. So although she never liked to drive, she did if we went to a party."

The day after Grace concluded work on *Rear Window,* she moved over to another sound stage at Paramount, to begin filming her scenes in *The Bridges at Toko-Ri.* The role of Nancy Brubaker was a brief but affecting one, mostly in support of William Holden, who played her husband, Harry, a navy hero during the Korean War.

Born in 1918 into a prosperous Illinois family, William Beedle had been noticed by a Paramount scout when he was a college student in Pasadena. Rechristened William Holden by the studio, he had made two minor pictures until 1939, when the leading role in *Golden Boy* raised him to instant stardom.

In 1941, Holden married actress Brenda Marshall, but nothing about that union seemed authentic, despite its thirty-year length—for the most part, it veered between pathetic soap opera and low comedy. They both engaged in a dizzying array of extramarital romances, usually with each other's full awareness, and these intrigues ended with tearful acts of contrition—just before the next paramour came into view. To prevent the complication of illegitimate paternity, Holden decided—with his wife's encouragement—to undergo a vasectomy in 1947, after the births of his two sons by Brenda. This decreased neither his libido nor the number of his conquests, who, for obvious reasons, were delighted with the medical news.

By the 1950s, the Holdens lived mostly separate lives—but unofficially, as Paramount executives and publicists demanded. Bill's good looks and charm were the main features of his seduction technique; for much of his life he had a reputation that made Casanova seem like a Trappist monk. But as he approached forty, he was also an alcoholic.

That January, when Bill met Grace, he had just come out of a brief but torrid affair with Audrey Hepburn, with whom he had costarred in *Sabrina*. Now he turned his charms full throttle on his new costar, and his efforts were immediately rewarded—not only because of his humor and courtesy toward her, but also perhaps because (like Gene Lyons) his problematic drinking aroused Grace's sympathy. "She had an ability to turn men on," said her sister Lizanne, "and most men who dated her fell in love with her." So it was with William Holden.

Their liaison lasted only about three weeks. Years after her death, Grace's children acknowledged the affair by including photos of her and Bill in the 2007 tribute to Grace, and by official approval of a book with a brief account of the matter: "She succumbed to the charms of the actor, who was twelve years her senior and married. The friendship rapidly turned into a fiery passion."* In any case, Grace's prior experience with Lyons had taught her the perils of life with a heavy drinker. A sudden attack of reality cooled her feelings and enabled her, with the utmost delicacy, to end the intrigue when she left the picture. Within days, Holden was finding consolation in the arms of another.

GRACE HAD neither sought nor fought for the small role of Nancy Brubaker in *The Bridges at Toko-Ri;* she was forced into it by MGM, which continued to realize a healthy profit on another loan-out. Again, the deal was made with Paramount, where producer William Perlberg and director George Seaton had a better sense of her worth.

The screenplay for *Bridges,* based on a long story by James

---

* Indeed, the 2006 book by Dherbier and Verlhac (see bibliography) contains a complimentary foreword by Prince Albert of Monaco, Grace's son.

Michener that had appeared in *Life* magazine, was written by Valentine Davies and directed by Mark Robson. Set in 1952 during the Korean War, the story concerns navy pilot Harry Brubaker, assigned to bomb a string of strategic bridges. His wife, Nancy, brings their two children to see him during a short leave in Japan, where she must accept the possibility that her husband's dangerous assignment may leave her a widow. In an ending unusual for war movies of the time, that is precisely what happens.

Grace, who had second billing after Holden, appears for no more than fifteen minutes, and she is last seen waving farewell as he leaves for his fateful mission. The half-hour sequences opening the picture, showing navy heroics, and the forced humor of the dialogue combined with ultrapatriotic observations, make for an unsatisfactory movie. The audience is invited to care about the wife and children of a doomed pilot, but we leave them at the dock and never see how they are affected by his death or begin to cope with it. In the Michener story, a straightforward but affecting prose style makes for a more emotionally satisfying experience than the movie, which focuses far too long on the battles at sea and on land. Together with another 1954 movie, *Green Fire, Bridges* was a film Grace did not rate highly.

At the time, Perlberg and Seaton were not so indifferent, and they saw *Bridges* as a kind of trial run for her possible appearance in their next Paramount picture—for which, by a kind of bitter irony, William Holden had already signed up. "Grace doesn't throw everything at you in the first five seconds," Seaton said later of her role in *Bridges*. "Some [actors] give you everything they've got at once, and there it is—there is no more. But Grace is like a kaleidoscope: one twist, and you get a whole new facet." There were not many twists to the character of lovely, normal Nancy Brubaker, but at least (in the chaste bedroom scene) she had an opportunity to show that she could portray both love for her husband and fear for herself. As in the Michener story, the role of Nancy Brubaker exists for the sake of exposition—she's there only to ask why the war is necessary and to be brave at her husband's departure. Still smarting from the ravages of World War II and Korea, American audiences loved the role and the actress.

For over two months, Grace had been inundated with long, loving letters and cards from Oleg, who also telephoned almost every evening when she returned home from the studio. When *The Bridges at Toko-Ri* was completed at the end of January, she planned a return to New York, in order to determine precisely what was happening in this odd relationship with Cassini— odd because it had all the characteristics of a love affair except the obvious one. Grace needed to know more about him, to determine her feelings for him; at the same time she was wary because of his widely known amorous activities.

But, for a good reason, her trip to New York had to be postponed. William Perlberg and George Seaton had obtained film rights to the Clifford Odets play *The Country Girl,* an enormous success of the 1950–51 Broadway season. Perlberg was to produce and Seaton to adapt the play and direct it for Paramount. For her achievement as Georgie Elgin, the prematurely aged wife of an alcoholic actor, Uta Hagen had earned the Tony Award as best actress of the year; now, however, Paramount wanted a movie star to help sell an intense drama that was not automatically expected to be a crowd-pleaser. Georgie is a challenging part—a once vibrant and attractive woman who has become weary and cheerless in support of her irresponsible, alcoholic husband. Many women in Hollywood coveted the role, and Perlberg, Seaton and Paramount had first settled on

Jennifer Jones—perhaps because of her recent superb performance in the title role of the film *Carrie* (also for Paramount), based on Theodore Dreiser's novel *Sister Carrie*. But that idea for casting was scotched when Jennifer's husband, the producer David O. Selznick, announced that she was pregnant.

Georgie could not have been more different from the roles Grace had played so far. The innocent, idealistic Amy Kane of *High Noon;* the genteel Linda Nordley of *Mogambo;* the wealthy, discreet Margot Wendice in *Dial "M" for Murder;* the sophisticated, stylish Lisa Fremont of *Rear Window;* and the anxious navy wife of *The Bridges at Toko-Ri:* these women did not bear the remotest resemblance to the wan, tired and impoverished Georgie. But this difference was precisely what attracted Grace to the role, and when Perlberg surreptitiously handed her the script (which by all rights he should have submitted to her through MCA), she knew this was the part that would both challenge and establish her as a serious dramatic actress.

The primary obstacle in her way was her Metro contract. Dore Schary had decided it was time to bring her back to Culver City, this time for another jungle adventure, to be filmed partly in South America. The project was *Green Fire,* and they had a script, a director, a leading man and a stalwart supporting player ready to go; Grace would be the glamorous complement, glamorizing a story of uncommon languor. The screenplay, riddled with clichés, had been doomed from the start. Metro's contract star Eleanor Parker had simply walked out on it, and Robert Taylor said he would rather retire than act in such nonsense. Eager to get the film in production and to bring Grace back to the studio, Metro flatly turned down Perlberg-Seaton's request to loan her to Paramount for *The Country Girl*.

But Schary and company had not foreseen that at this stage of her career she was not prepared to behave like a compliant tool in corporate hands. "I asked my agents to give my New

York address to all the MGM executives, so they would know where they could send their Christmas cards. It took a moment for them to realize what I meant, and I *did* mean it—I was prepared to leave Hollywood forever if they denied me the chance to play in *The Country Girl.* And I was more than willing to tell the press *why* I was retiring."

As Judith Quine recalled, Dore Schary and his colleagues were "rocked to the core. So was the rest of Hollywood as the story spread." At that time, Grace's challenge to a powerful studio was shocking: a young actress with only a few films to her name (and nothing released since *Mogambo,* the previous October) was now brazenly confronting—even threatening—a major company and, it seemed, jeopardizing her future. Indeed, careers were forever destroyed by what the moguls considered rank insubordination. If the studio suspended her, she would be out of work, and her period of inactivity would be tacked onto the term of her contract. But Grace could be neither intimidated nor bribed, and money made no impression on her. She had never been a starlet, had never worked in "B" pictures, had never posed in a bathing suit, had never liked any sort of publicity; she cherished her privacy and refused to go around Los Angeles dressed as if she were always on her way to a cocktail party. She wanted only good roles in good pictures, and in her mind *Rear Window* and Hitchcock had more than demonstrated her competency.

It's easy to imagine corporate chairs being knocked over and multiple midday martinis being downed for false courage as Metro's executives rushed to interoffice meetings and to their telephones, in order to prevent a major industry embarrassment. "This is blackmail!" bellowed one studio operative to Jay Kanter's boss at MCA, Lew Wasserman. Well, of course it was—after all, this was Hollywood. Prudent heads prevailed in Culver City, and soon the studio was unwilling to play the villain in a case against a beautiful actress who had two Hitchcock pictures soon to be released. And so, just as Grace was about to go through with her plan, to call Metro's bluff and book an airline ticket to New York, things happened with a speed she may have anticipated. On January 29, a press release from Culver City announced that Metro had agreed to loan Grace Kelly to Paramount for their forthcoming production of *The Country Girl*—in exchange for a fee of $50,000 and the guarantee that Grace would appear in *Green Fire* immediately after the Perlberg-Seaton movie wrapped. Signatures were affixed to contracts on February 8.

"The men at MGM couldn't have cared less about me until these other offers came in, first from Hitchcock and then from Perlberg and Seaton," Grace recalled. "I always thought that if a studio had someone under contract—an actor who was wanted elsewhere for good roles—that the home studio would try to do something for that actor. I just never understood them. I remember that they called me, Clark and Ava into their offices when we returned from Africa after *Mogambo,* to show us some magazine layouts. Oh, they were raving about all the publicity they planned for the picture. I remember one gentleman saying, 'It's glamour in Africa!' Clark had a few choice words about *that* statement. But then there was no work for me until Hitch got hold of my agent. Then MGM kept picking up my option every six months because they could make money by loaning me out—not because they had big plans for me, as they said season after season."

When it came to *The Country Girl,* she was quite specific. "I felt I just *had* to do this picture, because it had a really strong part—it was my chance to be more than a supporting character for the leading man. I had always worn beautiful clothes, or beautiful gowns or lingerie, or there were dramatic and colorful backgrounds. This was something completely different, and I worked very hard on it."

Grace's first love was always the theatre, and *Dial "M"* and *The Country Girl* had been successful Broadway plays, with very little changed in the transfer to the screen. The last two roles before her departure from Hollywood would also be in films based on plays—*The Swan,* by Ferenc Molnár; and *High Society,* a musical version of Philip Barry's *The Philadelphia Story.*

Two WEEKS of rehearsal preceded the filming of *The Country Girl,* and when the cast gathered for the first reading, there was considerable tension. "The first week, we all didn't pay much attention to one another," Grace remembered. "In fact, we didn't get along very well." William Holden's presence in the cast may have contributed to the atmosphere, but there was an even more delicate factor.

Bing Crosby, a hugely popular singer and actor during the 1940s, was then fifty, a perilous age in Hollywood for a crooner never associated with serious drama—not to say a role that ran against his public image. Perhaps because he longed for a change of pace, he had agreed to play Frank Elgin, a once-successful singer and stage actor who was now a pathetic drunkard, steeped in guilt, completely lacking self-confidence and entirely dependent on his wife after the accidental death of their son.

During the ten-hour rehearsal days, the three principals worked on dialogue, characterization, reactions and bits of business—where and how to include a glance, a vocal nuance or an expression that would convey a lot with a little. "Bing was so nervous about playing Frank Elgin," Grace said. "All his previous roles had been variations on Bing himself—the affable pop singer, the good guy, dear Father O'Malley in *Going My Way* [for which he had won an Oscar a decade earlier]. But now he was playing a boozer who has lost faith in himself. Some of us knew—but the public didn't—that this was very close to Bing's own life in the 1950s. He had once been at the top of the list, and he had a drinking problem that became worse after the death of his wife in 1952.

"I knew at the time—and it was no secret in Hollywood— that Bing had wanted Jennifer Jones as his leading lady, and he almost withdrew from the picture when he heard that I was going to play the part. 'She's too pretty,' he told the producers about me. 'She has no experience . . . she's too glamorous for the part of Georgie . . . she won't take direction.' Endless objections! Those first days of rehearsal were pretty rough, but Mr. Perlberg and Mr. Seaton were my champions." They did not have to defend Grace for long. Prep was concluded, the first scenes were filmed quickly and economically, and Crosby—to his credit—changed his tune. "I'll never open my big mouth about a casting problem again," he told the producers and the press. "I'm sorry I had any reservations about this girl—she's great!"

Crosby's praise for Grace became more personal over the next two months, when he tried to court her—but Grace politely discouraged his intentions. (Contrary to the later grindings of the rumor mill, nothing like a romance ever occurred, much to Bing's disappointment.) "Grace called me up one night," recalled Lizanne, "and she said, 'Bing has asked me to marry him'—but she wasn't in love with him at all. She admired and respected him, but she was not in love." The gossips, however, fueled the chatter after Crosby invited Grace, her sister Peggy and a few of his friends to his birthday celebration at a nightclub after the picture was completed. Photographers caught the group at a table and then neatly excised everyone from the picture except Bing and Grace. As Hitchcock famously said, the camera can make you believe anything.

During rehearsals, Edith Head and her staff rushed to finish Grace's wardrobe for *The Country Girl*. "I was happy until I read the script," Edith remembered. "She was to play a woman who has been married for ten years and has lost interest in clothes, herself—everything. The character had absolutely no resemblance to Grace." But Edith did what was required, putting Grace in drab housedresses, an old cardigan sweater, and skirts and blouses that would look suitably dreary in a black-and-white movie. The final touch—Grace's suggestion—was that she wear her glasses. This being Hollywood, however, Paramount insisted that George Seaton add two scenes not found in the play: a flashback in which Grace is dressed like a sophisticated fashion plate, and the finale, at a fancy Manhattan party, for which she appears in elegant finery. (She thought these two sequences were regrettable, and they were, although she acknowledged that the first sequence revealed how happy a person the younger Georgie was, once upon a time.)

Regarding her plain and dull outfits, director Seaton recalled, "A lot of actresses would say, 'Well, why don't we just put a few rhinestones here and some jewelry there. I want to look dowdy, but this woman has taste, after all,' and before you know it, the actress would look like a million dollars. But not Grace. Grace wanted to be authentic."

Crosby, on the other hand, had to be coaxed into authenticity.

On the first day of shooting, he was two hours late. Finally the head of the makeup department summoned Seaton, who arrived in Crosby's dressing room to find him wearing a wavy, twenty-year-old hairpiece. "I've just decided that this is what I'm going to wear in the picture," Crosby said defiantly. Seaton calmly replied that this was entirely inappropriate for the role, but Crosby was adamant: "I've got my audience to think of—I don't want to look like an old man on the screen!"

Seaton reminded him that he had to look the age and the character of dissipated Frank Elgin. "Bing, let's be honest—you're frightened," the director said—"and Bing almost started to cry, saying, 'I can't do it!'"

"Please have faith in me," continued Seaton. "I'm frightened, too—we're all frightened—so let's be frightened together." Director and actor then walked onto the set, and soon there were no further problems. Bing Crosby gave an astonishing, deeply felt performance that had the critics ransacking their vocabularies for superlatives. (The Academy nominated him as best actor of the year, but Marlon Brando took the honor, for *On the Waterfront*.)

Fourteen Hours, High Noon and *The Country Girl* were Grace's only three monochrome pictures; the other eight were filmed in color. In fact, she was one of the few stars of her era to be associated with the alluring gloss and polish of Technicolor. Years after the fact, she told me, "I wish I had been given the chance to do fewer pictures in color and more serious productions in black and white." But she had no control over this aspect of moviemaking, and her rise to stardom was itself concurrent with the increasing use of color. There is no doubt, however, that the gravity of *The Country Girl* absolutely required the stark contrasts of black and white.

In ways that were perhaps surprising for her, Grace sometimes found Bill and Bing unsure of themselves. "It took [director] George Seaton's considerable diplomatic skills to get us through those five weeks," Grace recalled. "I really didn't have time to be afraid or to ask myself if I was up to the task—I was too busy trying to understand each and every scene and to deliver it perfectly."

She need not have been anxious, for her performance must be

included among the finest of the 1950s. She brought a quiet, bereaved intensity to her portrait of a listless wife who fights with her last atom of energy on behalf of her weak husband. In some inchoate, unconscious way, Grace tapped in to the repressed but ever-present streak of melancholy in her own character—the sense of loneliness and longing in her since childhood that had always been sensed by her friends at quiet times, in privacy. To this, she added her art: a kind of benumbed sadness in Georgie, who comes to see that her loyalty has exacted a high price, and that she has missed very much of life.

Grace seemed not merely to speak her lines of dialogue, but to imply that beneath them were, as Wordsworth wrote, thoughts too deep for tears. Nothing seemed calculated, nothing cerebral or artificial—and there was nothing for her to rely on but her substantial talent: no color, no fine wardrobe, no flattering cosmetics and no witty, crowd-pleasing dialogue. Her understanding of Georgie Elgin is a study in the most mature kind of screen acting—a remarkable achievement for a twenty-four-year-old. She could have relied on a few histrionic tricks to win the audience's sympathy; instead she created a character rich in complexity and almost unbearable in empathetic intensity.

One scene may be taken to stand for many in this compelling picture, in which Grace had an unusual number of speeches and long, uninterrupted scenes of dialogue with the two leading men. Confronting Holden (who played her husband's director), she begins calmly and builds the emotion:

GEORGIE. Can you stand him up on his feet, Mr. Dodd? Because that's where all my prayers have gone—to see that one holy hour when he can stand alone! And I might forgive even *you,* Mr. Dodd, if you can keep him up long enough for me to get out from under! All I want is my

own name and a modest job to buy sugar for my coffee!
You can't believe it, can you—you can't believe that a
woman has to be crazy-out-of-her-mind to live alone—
in one room—by herself!

(He grips her arm, but she resists him.)

GEORGIE. Why are you holding me? I said—you are
holding me!

Her eyes are suddenly wild with rage and desire. He kisses
her "fully on the mouth," according to the stage directions, before they step apart.

GEORGIE. How could you be so cruel to me a moment ago . . .
to be so mad at someone you didn't even know . . . [She
turns away from him.] No one has looked at me as a
woman for years.

He turns to leave, and just before he reaches the door, she
speaks:

GEORGIE. You kissed me—don't let it give you any ideas,
Mr. Dodd.

This was a performance made credible not by lighting, costumes or music. Its force derives from the complete lack of calculation in Grace's impressive art—a paradox that virtually
defines every memorable acting achievement. Decades later,
we do not watch her as a movie star playing at or around a role,
nor are we conscious of her gestures, her slight raising of the
eyebrows, the sudden drop of her voice. We do not observe an
"artiste" struggling to impress. Grace Kelly, the beautiful actress, disappears when we watch Georgie Elgin in *The Country
Girl;* we see only the real weariness of a woman almost out of

strength, almost empty of feeling—except that her feeling, and ours, is indeed too deep for tears.

On the last day of production, in late March, the film crew presented Grace with an inscribed plaque: "For our Country Girl—may this hold you over until next year's Academy Awards." The critics also responded warmly, noting that Crosby and Kelly were completely successful in playing offbeat roles that were very different from the public's perception of the actors: "Miss Kelly will get her share of praise for the quality of strain and desperation she puts into the battered, patient wife," ran a typical review. Asked for his reaction to all these signal achievements, her father responded with his usual dispassionate detachment: yes, he was "pleased for her," and that was that.

"I was very young when I played in *The Country Girl,*" Grace said years later. "I was twenty-four, and I hadn't yet been married. I remember thinking at the time, 'Oh, if only I were five years older, I could do this so much better!' And then, after I'd been married five years, I thought, 'Well, I could certainly do *The Country Girl* better!' And now, years later, perhaps it would be even better."

The day after her final scene in *The Country Girl,* Grace rushed to Metro for costume and makeup tests, and then to the company physician for necessary injections. Soon she was off for ten days of location shooting in the Colombian jungle, to fulfill her obligation. "I was exhausted when *Green Fire* began," said Grace, "because *The Country Girl* had required long days of rehearsal and long hours of filming, with a great deal of concentration. So although it was a grueling schedule that spring, going right away onto *Green Fire* was in some ways a relief.

There were no politics [with her leading men] to consider—just that *awful* story that MGM pushed me into. They probably didn't allow themselves to recognize the disappointing truth that the studio was no longer the great machine it had once been. I think they were trying to repeat the success of *Mogambo,* with the South American jungle substituting for Africa, and they gave me Stewart Granger, the resident studio swashbuckler," who had been in Metro's *King Solomon's Mines.*

This time, the mines contained emeralds (thus the title), sought by prospector Rian Mitchell (Granger). He copes with a band of Colombian bandits, who claim the treasure belongs to them, and he is further blocked by a growing romance with Catherine Knowland (Grace). She and her brother Donald (John Ericson) own and manage a successful coffee plantation near the land where the emeralds are buried. Mitchell digs and digs; Catherine sighs and sighs. No one gets anywhere until shortly before the end of the movie, when (1) a flood hits the plantation, (2) the bandits attack the emerald mine, (3) a box of dynamite blows the thugs to guacamole, (4) a rockslide deflects the course of the river, (5) a tropical storm breaks, and (6) a rainbow shines through, arching over (7) the final embrace of Granger and Grace.

"*Green Fire* was not the kind of picture I became an actress to do," Grace said. "I had to accept it for the chance to make *The Country Girl,* and it taught me a lesson—never agree to a role before reading the script. They told me my pages [of the screenplay, by Ivan Goff and Ben Roberts] weren't ready, but that I had to do it, and that it would be an easy and exciting picture to make. Silly me—I believed them and agreed to do it." Later, Dore Schary admitted, "It was a dog, and we never should have made it—it was just terrible, but we thought it would do well, that it would bring some money in. It didn't."

But there were other knots in the tangle of her life and career.

First, it was precisely the intense, creative satisfaction of performing in *The Country Girl* that evoked in Grace a growing impatience with Hollywood and a desire to return to the stage, the source of her best roles. "I kept confiding in my uncle George," she said. "He was the only one who understood that my heart was not in Hollywood, but in the theatre. By [May] 1954, I just wanted to get away."

In addition, since she had left New York in November 1953, she had been bombarded with letters, calls and even a surprise visit from the zealous Oleg Cassini, and she wanted to see if this relationship was going anywhere. He had a thriving and demanding business in New York, where he was successfully climbing the social and commercial ladder—but he insisted that Grace was important in his life.

Finally she had an opportunity to "get away" and to test Cassini's earnestness—but she would have to rush through *Green Fire,* to the point of asking the director to bring forward the shooting of her final scenes in order to accommodate her as a courtesy to another director. "Hitchcock wanted her for *To Catch a Thief,*" as Granger recalled, "and if the dates fitted, she would go straight from our film to her next leading man, Cary Grant. Poor Grace was worried that she wouldn't finish [*Green Fire*] in time, because Hitchcock waits for no man or woman."

To complicate the issue further—and simultaneously to make it all the more attractive—the production schedule of *To Catch a Thief* called for location shooting on the French Riviera from May to July. Even before she completed *Green Fire*—and before Metro had signed off on yet another loan-out to Hitchcock and Paramount—Grace was making late-night calls to Edith Head about the costumes for Hitchcock's picture. "Just go ahead," she told the designer. "I'll get the picture." Her confidence was doubtless rooted in Alfred Hitchcock's insistence (which he told her on the sly) that he would not seriously consider a replacement for her. "I'm not sure what I would have done if I hadn't been able to get Grace," Hitch said many years later. "I saw her in this role ever since I bought the rights to the novel."

JOHN ERICSON, who played Grace's brother in *Green Fire,* had been a student with her at the American Academy of Dramatic Arts and was also under contract to Metro that year. Just when he and Grace began work, his previous picture was released—*Rhapsody,* in which he appeared to very good effect with Elizabeth Taylor. A strong but not brutish actor on the studio roster, John was a strikingly handsome young man, already believable in a wide variety of roles. He, too, should have been more wisely managed by Metro, as Grace recognized. "They're doing the same thing with John Ericson as they have with me," she wrote to columnist Hedda Hopper that season. "To the press, they're full of enthusiasm and generous with their promises. But then nothing comes of it, and now they are ignoring a fine actor in John, and I think it's shameful."

"Grace had always been surrounded by a group of admiring young men in our student days," Ericson recalled more than fifty years later. "And on *Green Fire,* she was as serious as she was popular, and completely professional—even though she didn't want to be in the picture. But everyone in the cast and crew grew very fond of her."

John's scenes did not require him to travel to South America with Grace and Granger, who went for ten days in April and worked in fiercely uncomfortable conditions in Barranquilla, along the Magdalena River and in the mountains surrounding Bogotá. "It wasn't too pleasant there," Grace wrote in another message to Hopper. "We worked at a pathetic village, with miserable huts and poverty-stricken people who were forced to live in awful conditions. Part of our crew got shipwrecked—it was terrible." Years later she added, "Really, it was a wretched time. Everybody at MGM knew we had a very, very bad picture on our hands, but the production just dragged on in all the heat and all the rainstorms because no one knew how to end it—and for lots of reasons, I wanted to end it!"

The remaining exteriors were shot on the slopes of Mulholland Drive in Los Angeles, and on Metro's back lot. "We were lucky to have Andrew Marton as our director," said John Ericson. "He was not temperamental, but very helpful to everyone, especially in the action sequences. I remember that Grace insisted on doing her own [horseback] riding scenes, which surprised everybody and caused us some anxiety. But she did it like a champion rider, and without any fuss or fanfare. She was the least prima-donna-like actress I ever knew."

"I had the misfortune to be in the only really bad movie Grace ever made," recalled Granger. "She was stunningly beautiful, but I thought she was lonely and agitated. One treated Grace differently. You didn't chum up with her or smack her on the bottom"—which was precisely what he did, while embracing her in the movie's concluding rainstorm. She was not pleased.

"The whole experience was unhappy for me," Grace said. "I took the role for the sake of *The Country Girl*—and because my old friend Marie Frisbee was in Colombia at the time. She and her husband had to live there for a while because of his job, and she felt lonely. I hoped to surprise Marie—but when I tried to contact her after my arrival in South America, I was told that she had gone to Washington for a vacation. That was the first disappointment, and more followed."

In the movie, Grace smiled amiably for the camera, but of course she could not rewrite the astonishingly bad dialogue. "I don't think I've ever been in love before," she had to say in one scene—"not really in love—not like this." Years later she laughed when reminded of a peculiarly apposite line in another scene: "I've had a few proposals of marriage," she says in one romantic sequence, "and I turned them down. But I'm not panicking yet. There's always the chance that Prince Charming will come down out of the mountains on his charger one day." The ordeal of *Green Fire* finally reached its term in late May, after the interior scenes were completed in Culver City.

On May 2, Metro and Paramount issued press statements that Grace Kelly was going directly from *Green Fire* to Alfred Hitchcock's next picture, *To Catch a Thief. Dial "M" for Murder* and *Rear Window* were still unreleased, but the advance word was more than encouraging. At the same time, Grace was be-having with poise and refined resolve—not to say remarkable audacity—in her dealings with Metro.

The studio announced that, after the Hitchcock picture, she would at once star in *The Cobweb,* but she refused to play its rather gloomy role of a psychiatrist. The press was then in-formed that Grace had the leading role in a western called *The Long Day,* but she turned that down, too. The public then read the news that she would be the leading lady in a historical ro-mance called *Quentin Durward,* but she also turned aside that offer. "All the men could duel and fight," she said. "But I would just wear thirty-five different costumes, look pretty and act frightened. It seemed to me that eight people were to be chasing me [in *Durward*]—an old man, robbers, gypsies—and the stage directions on every page of the script said, 'She clutches her jewel box and flees.' It read like a satire, and I knew I would be bored to tears by all that nonsense."

And so it went, as Grace refused to yield to studio pressure to perform in roles that she considered unsuitable or that would in no way deepen her talents or advance her career. She also rejected the scripts for the movies *Diane, Something of*

Value, Bannon and *Tribute to a Bad Man.* A period of the movie industry was dying, and Grace was dancing at the funeral. This was more than a simple case of individual pride, willfulness or prudent self-management of her career. Grace was quite consciously putting one of the final nails in the coffin of a moribund studio system.

THE TRADITION of the seven-year contract gave movie studios the legal right to drop a player who was not drawing crowds to the box office—but the rights of the players were limited to a guaranteed minimum wage for six months, after which they could be dismissed. Actors had no control over their own careers, and almost no share in the decision of what roles they would play and how their public image would be created, sustained, managed and altered. The seven-year system, in other words, created a kind of indentured servitude, and many competent players were blithely pushed onto the unemployment lines because studio executives disliked them.

Almost twenty years earlier, Bette Davis had challenged the control of Jack L. Warner. Convinced that her career was being irreparably damaged by a series of mediocre roles into which she was forced, Davis simply ignored her contract and accepted an offer to work in England. There, she brought her case against Warner Bros. to the English courts, confident that they would decide in her favor. Her counsel listed her complaints: that she could be suspended without pay for refusing any role; that the period of suspension could be added to the term date of her contract; that she could be required to play any part regardless of her opinions; that she could be required to support publicly any political party even against her private beliefs; and that her image could be displayed anywhere and in any context the studio thought helpful for business.

When Jack Warner was called to testify, he was asked, "Whatever part you choose to call upon her to play—even if it is distasteful and cheap—she has to play it?" Warner replied immediately and cheerfully: "Oh, yes, of course she must play it!" Bette Davis lost the case and returned to Hollywood in 1937, burdened with debts and without any prospect of income. Jack Warner, however, never doubted her star power, and she returned for several years to his studio—under the terms of the standard seven-year contract.

Later, Davis's friend Olivia de Havilland picked up the battle standard against Warner Bros. and fought her case all the way to the California Supreme Court. According to the state labor laws, personal service contracts were limited to a maximum of seven years. De Havilland had signed a standard contract with Warners in 1936, and during the ensuing years she frequently refused various roles and was put on suspension for as long as it took another actor to complete the role she had rejected. When her contract expired on August 31, 1943, she thought she was finally free of Warner's control, but de Havilland was informed that she had to continue working to compensate the studio for the times she had been suspended.

She thought this was preposterous: she had been obligated to the studio for seven years, and that, she believed, should have been the end of it. She filed a lawsuit against Warner Bros., and in 1945 the State Supreme Court decided in her favor. Seven years indeed meant seven years, with no time added for bad behavior.

But Grace Kelly carried the issue further. She flatly refused to do what the studio expected, relying on her own talents and her own perceptions of what was good for her and what was not. If she did well, she reasoned, her success would support her—hence she would force the studio to comply by sheer force of will and achievement. "I never believed in the studio system," she told me. "I signed the contract with Metro in order to do *Mogambo,* and I agreed to do *Mogambo* in order to see Africa and work with Clark Gable and John Ford. The idea of being owned by a studio was offensive to me, and the more I saw the consequences of that seven-year deal, the more determined I became to make my own way and find my own direction. For a wonderfully long time I was left to do that, but then the chickens came home to roost." In fact, they were vultures.

To Metro's annoyance, the more assertive she became, the more the public seemed to love her. Grace was in demand for newspaper interviews and magazine feature stories, and her picture was popping up all over America: the April 26 cover of *Life* magazine, for example, proclaimed, "Grace Kelly—America's Brightest and Busiest New Star." Her agents took advantage of her growing status and were able to renegotiate the deal with Paramount, whereby Metro was paid $80,000 to loan her out for ten weeks of work on the Hitchcock picture—but $50,000 of that sum was paid to her. Five thousand a week was a respectable sum for Grace in 1954; on the other hand, Cary Grant, her costar in the forthcoming Hitchcock picture, was paid $18,750 a week (in 2009, the equivalent of $150,279 a week).

"I finished *Green Fire* at eleven o'clock on the morning of May 24," Grace recalled. "I went into the dubbing room [to rerecord lines that were unclear in a few outdoor scenes] at one in the afternoon—and at six o'clock that evening I was on my way to France."

SEVEN

Climbing Over Rooftops

Palaces are for royalty. We're just common people with a bank account.

—GRACE (AS FRANCIE STEVENS) IN *TO CATCH A THIEF*

UNTIL AGE AND POOR HEALTH IMPEDED HIM, ALFRED Hitchcock loved to travel to the smartest and most luxurious venues in the world for his holidays: to the best Swiss resorts, the finest Caribbean hotels—and to lesser-known but equally expensive places. In London, New York, Paris and Rome (to mention but a few major cities he visited regularly), he and his wife were royally welcomed at five-star accommodations. Whenever possible, Hitchcock synchronized his holiday with a movie project—a concurrence ensuring that his considerable personal expenses would be borne by the production's budget.

Such was the case in May 1954, when he and his crew arrived on the French Riviera. They remained for six weeks, filming in and around Cannes, in the hills above the Mediterranean, along picturesque roads, in the flower market at Nice and on the sun-drenched tourist beaches. Hitchcock also arranged for the entire company to have plenty of time for sightseeing and sampling the best French restaurants along the Riviera.

To Catch a Thief was Hitchcock's forty-first feature. Cary Grant, appearing in his third picture for the director, was fifty years old, but Hitchcock was right when he told Paramount's executives that audiences would accept Grant as a romantic leading man opposite twenty-four-year-old Grace Kelly, also appearing in her third Hitchcock feature. Fit and tanned, Grant had an ageless, urbane charm, and his acting was on the mark for a director who preferred understatement. In a career that ultimately spanned thirty-five years, he had already performed with Mae West, Marlene Dietrich, Katharine Hepburn, Irene Dunne, Jean Arthur, Rosalind Russell, Joan Fontaine, Ingrid Bergman and Marilyn Monroe, among others. As the Hollywood cliché put it, Cary Grant was bankable.

John Michael Hayes wrote the screenplay for *To Catch a Thief,* based on David Dodge's novel. Hayes had written the script for *Rear Window* and later wrote two more for Hitchcock (*The Trouble with Harry* and *The Man Who Knew Too Much*); his work is noteworthy for a warmth of characterization often lacking even in some of Hitchcock's masterworks.

The director called *To Catch a Thief* "a lightweight story," and so it is—a rambling, relaxed comic caper, the work of a man on holiday, telling a story without the atmosphere familiar to his fans. Some critics feel that the picture's sheer visual appeal and sexy charm overwhelm the suspense, that we really don't care about the villain at all, and that the thriller aspect—the hero's need to unmask a crook in order to exonerate himself— is lost in a glamorous travelogue. The film is, to be sure, far more interesting for its ravishing shots of the French Riviera (which earned Robert Burks the Oscar for color cinematography) than for its ho-hum narrative, which is exceedingly short on Hitchcockian tension.

The plot concerns John Robie (Grant), a former jewel thief and once a collaborator with the Resistance against the Nazi occupation of France. The police now believe that he has returned to his old larcenous habits and is responsible for a series of burglaries along the Riviera. To prove his innocence, Robie embarks on his own investigation to catch the thief. He enlists an insurance agent (John Williams) and soon meets a rich young American named Frances "Francie" Stevens (Grace) and her mother (Jessie Royce Landis). Francie is fascinated—even excited—by Robie's reputation as a thief. She falls in love with him, and although at first she thinks him guilty, she finally helps him trap the real cat burglar. The culprit, Danielle Foussard (Brigitte Auber), turns out to be a woman Robie thought was a friend, the daughter of a former Resistance colleague who is involved in a ring of thieves.

"For me, this was the perfect part after the intensity of *The Country Girl* and the discomforts of *Green Fire*," Grace recalled in 1976, "and how could I turn down the chance for another Hitchcock picture? I was flattered he wanted me. It was a comedy, but it was also romantic—and rather daring for its time, too, but always with the sophisticated Hitchcock touch. Francie is eager to be a thief—she's out for kicks and thrills, and she thinks it's exciting to join up with a man she believes to be an outlaw. She was all set to climb out over the rooftops with him."

Grace had clear memories of filming several especially clever sequences. In the first, Danielle and Francie meet in the waters of the beach club, as rivals over Robie:

DANIELLE (Brigitte Auber). What has *she* got more than me—except money, and you are getting plenty of that.

ROBIE (Grant). Danielle, you are just a girl—she is a woman.

DANIELLE. Why do you want to buy an old car if you can get
a new one cheaper? It will run better and last longer.

ROBIE (scanning the horizon). Well, it looks as if my old
car just drove off.

FRANCIE (Grace—suddenly bobbing out of the water). No,
it hasn't—it's just turned amphibious. I thought I'd come
out and see what the big attraction was—and possibly
even rate an introduction.

ROBIE. Miss Foussard—Miss Stevens.

They are all treading water.

FRANCIE. How do you do, Miss Foussard—Mr. Burns
[Robie's temporarily assumed name] has told me so little
about you.

ROBIE. Well, we met only a few minutes ago.

FRANCIE. Only a few minutes ago, and you talk like old
friends. Ah, well, that's warm, friendly France for you.

ROBIE. Would you like me to teach you how to water ski?

FRANCIE. Thank you—but I was women's champion at
Sarasota, Florida, last season. Are you sure you were
talking about water skis? From where I sat, it looked as
though you were conjugating some irregular verbs.

ROBIE. Say something nice to her, Danielle.

DANIELLE. She looks a lot older up close.

ROBIE (groaning). Oh-h-h-h-h-h . . .

FRANCIE. To a mere child, anything over twenty might
seem old.

"HITCH TOLD us to improvise some of our dialogue," Grace recalled, "and so Cary and I did just that. We rehearsed it first

with Miss Auber, whose English was not so fluent. We all had terrific fun trying to see what we could get away with, because we knew Hitch wanted us to go as far as we could. Cary and I shared the same warped and sometimes risqué sense of humor, so it was just a great deal of fun for us. Only one sequence in the picture really troubled me, and it does to this day. When I see the costume ball sequence at the end, I feel very embarrassed. It seems overdone—and I did my bit in those scenes badly. Hitch should have made me do them over."

Earlier in the movie, Robie accompanies Francie to the door of her hotel suite. They have been introduced only moments before, and are not yet on a first-name basis—and so Hitchcock surprised his audience by having Francie, all in cool blue chiffon, enter her room, turn and, without a word, boldly plant a kiss square on the lips of the astonished but quite pleased Robie. This is a hint of what is to come later—some of it, too, improvised by the actors:

ROBIE. What do you expect to get out of being so nice to me?
FRANCIE. Probably a lot more than you're willing to offer.
ROBIE. Jewelry—you never wear any.
FRANCIE. I don't like cold things touching my skin.
ROBIE. Why don't you invent some *hot* diamonds?
FRANCIE. I'd rather spend my money on more tangible
    excitement.
ROBIE. Tell me—what do you get a thrill out of the most?
FRANCIE. I'm still looking for that one.
ROBIE. What you need is something I have neither the time
    nor the inclination to give you—two weeks with a good
    man at Niagara Falls.

Later, at their impromptu picnic, shared in her car at the roadside:

FRANCIE. I've never caught a jewel thief before. It's so
    stimulating! [As she offers him pieces of cold chicken:]
    Do you want a leg or a breast?
ROBIE. You make the choice.
FRANCIE. Tell me—how long has it been?
ROBIE. Since what?
FRANCIE. Since you were in America last.

From her first to last appearances in *To Catch a Thief,* Grace
reveals her gift for high comedy, demonstrating in every scene a
keen ability to match Cary Grant's established excellence in that
genre. No expression or tone is exaggerated, and her apparent
coolness—as so often with Hitchcock's female characters—
masks a simmering passion. In Francie's hotel suite that evening,
for example, as fireworks illuminate the night sky, the suggestive
dialogue continues:

FRANCIE. If you really want to see fireworks, it's better with
    the lights off. I have a feeling that tonight you're going
    to see one of the Riviera's most fascinating sights—I'm
    talking about the fireworks, of course.
ROBIE. May I have a brandy? May I fix you one?
FRANCIE. Some nights a person doesn't need to drink.

The conversation then turns to stolen gems:

ROBIE. I have about the same interest in jewelry that I have in
    politics, horse racing, modern poetry and women who need
    weird excitement—none.
        (Francie sits seductively with him on the divan, her
        diamond-and-platinum necklace glittering above the
        bodice of her white strapless gown.)

FRANCIE. Give up, John—admit who you are. Even in this light, I can tell where your eyes are looking. Look, John—hold them—diamonds! The only thing in the world you can't resist. Then tell me you don't know what I'm talking about.

    (A fireworks display can be seen in the background. She kisses his fingers one by one, then places his hand beneath her necklace. There is a close-up of raging fireworks in the harbor.)

FRANCIE. Ever had a better offer in your whole life? One with everything!

ROBIE. I've never had a crazier one.

    (Cut back to vast fireworks.)

FRANCIE. Just as long as you're satisfied.

    (Fireworks again.)

ROBIE. You know as well as I do that this necklace is imitation.

FRANCIE. Well *I'm* not!

    (They kiss—cut to fireworks—back to a long, passionate kiss—then back to the final explosion of fireworks. End of scene.)

"What I find most striking after all these years is how we got away with all that dialogue," Grace recalled. "I saw the movie on a flight from New York recently, and I thought—oh, how beautiful Cary and I were." She spoke with a kind of wistfulness.

"Because Grace commanded so much respect, there was almost total silence when she arrived on the set," recalled Cary Grant. "But she never distanced herself from others, and she was enormously friendly to everyone—no stuffy attitude, no star complex. As for her talents, Grace acted the way Johnny Weissmuller swam or Fred Astaire danced—she made it look easy. And she probably went through life being completely misunderstood, since she usually said exactly what she meant."

In an essay approved by Princess Grace's children after her death, Frédéric Mitterrand wrote that "Alfred Hitchcock fell in love with Grace Kelly." The love was strictly platonic, but on Hitch's side it was a tangle of emotions, complicated with all sorts of fantasies and phobias.

Hitchcock had scrupulously followed every rumor about Grace's private life since they met in June 1953, less than a year before the first scenes of *To Catch a Thief* were filmed. Although the accounts of her romances have been grotesquely exaggerated, it is nevertheless true that in her twenties Grace was a healthy, popular young woman who enjoyed intimacies with a few men to whom she was seriously (if only temporarily) attached. A devout Catholic, she was nevertheless sufficiently mature and independent of spirit to allow for love and its facsimiles without assuming a burden of neurotic guilt.

Grace and her parents presumed she would eventually marry—preferably a Catholic, but certainly not a divorcé. She grew up in an era when polite young women simply did not marry without their parents' approval, and it is necessary to appreciate the strength of that social and familial bond in order to understand why Grace and her friends (with very few exceptions) looked to their families to endorse potential unions.

Hitchcock was privy to her mixed feelings on this, for Grace confided in him; I do not think she thought that he would subsequently entrust those confidences to me, although apparently most of what she told him she eventually shared with me, too. These reflections may be essential toward an understanding of Alfred Hitchcock's adoration of Grace Kelly, whose eventual departure from Hollywood he saw as a personal rejection (precisely as he had regarded Ingrid Bergman's departure, in 1949). Hitchcock was, as her family later knew, in love with her—but the way a schoolboy develops a hopeless crush on an unattainable object of desire; in his case, however, the love seemed to be accompanied by a sense of futile possessiveness.

With *To Catch a Thief* nearing completion, Hitch was already planning Grace's future. As soon as her obligations to Metro were resolved, their collaborations would, he expected, resume with a film of James M. Barrie's ethereal romance *Mary Rose,* which Hitch had hoped to bring to the screen ever since he had seen it onstage in London decades earlier.

His unexpressed but clear intention was that Grace (again, like Ingrid) would forever belong to him, at least professionally, in roles created for her that were variations on how he saw her or wished her to be. Grace listened, smiled and said nothing to disillusion him. But the fact was that (in the words of Mitterrand) "her California blues" were turning her more and more away from movieland and toward a serious consideration of her future as a wife and mother—a vocation she saw as possibly fading with the rapid passage of time.

On July 6, the production company of *To Catch a Thief* moved to Hollywood for the interior scenes, and on August 13, Hitch's fifty-fifth birthday was celebrated on the set of the fancy ball sequence. He continued to supervise Grace's capacious eighteenth-century costume, the arrangement of her hairpiece, and each tilt and angle of her head. She felt stiff and awkward and, as she said, she did not like her performance in that sequence; she thought she seemed statuesque and unreal. Nevertheless, critics were pleased: "She is cool and exquisite and superior," commented the *New York Times.*

Throughout the final weeks of filming, at the end of August, Hitchcock seemed content with cosseting Grace, advancing an image of chic, refined sensuality. She was Hitchcock's willing and winsome Galatea, but she did not see her life and career as ineluctably linked to his. At the same time, although Hitchcock was both obsessive and possessive, he was not completely divorced from reality. He knew that any idea of sexual activity between them was doomed to disappointment. It was precisely this combination of elements—of longing, desire and fear—that gave the life and character of Alfred Hitchcock its enormous poignancy.* His marred, marvelous perception shared something of our common humanity; were it otherwise, we could not adequately explain his enduring worldwide popularity and the legacy of his cinematic art.

"Grace can play comedy not only sexily but elegantly," Hitchcock said as the film wrapped that August. "It's a quality most women do not have. It has already taken her a long way—it may even take her to the top. But so far, she has yet to play the character around whom a whole film is built. That will be her big test. But I am sure she will come through it with flying colors. I hope to go through it with her, to make sure that she gets a rich role, not a tintype part in a celluloid soap opera."

When a visitor to the set of *To Catch a Thief* asked Grace if anyone had told her she was as aloof in life as she was often on the screen, she replied, "Lots of people have told me that. But until I know people, I can't give much of myself. A year ago, when people asked me, 'What about you?' I froze. I'm better now, but I'm still not cured." Years later, asked just what she felt she needed to be "cured" *of,* she said she hadn't felt obliged to promote herself when she was in Hollywood—"I was hired to be an actress, not a personality for the press."

Still, word was out about the "remote" Miss Kelly. Ironically—because she neither sought publicity nor invited

---

* See *The Dark Side of Genius: The Life of Alfred Hitchcock* and *Spellbound by Beauty: Alfred Hitchcock and His Leading Ladies.*

journalists and photographers into her private life—she was reported to be unfathomable, mysterious, baffling or, worst of all, proudly aloof. She was none of these things, but because people had to speculate, and because colleagues insisted that she was a joy to work with and utterly without affectations, Grace appeared to be almost as inscrutable as Greta Garbo. And so, then as later, scandalous stories and a totally inaccurate personality had to be invented.

To MAKE the situation with Hitchcock even more byzantine, Grace had fallen deeply in love. With her consent, Oleg Cassini had followed her to the Riviera in May. "Those were the most enchanting days I ever had in my life," he said in 1998.

In April, Oleg had offered to accompany her on the trip to Colombia for *Green Fire,* but she had discouraged him: "My work is one thing. My personal life is another. They have nothing to do with each other." By way of letters and phone calls, they fenced and parried until the end of May, a period during which she was aware of his dalliance with the young actress Pier Angeli. But in France, things happened quickly. On weekends and her days off, and during the evenings when she did not have an early call on the production, Grace was constantly with Oleg—"We have lunch and dinner just about every day," she wrote to Prudy Wise.

They drove to Grasse and Vence. They packed a picnic lunch and headed for cool parks near St. Maxime and Villefranche. They dined at the finest restaurants. They danced until the small hours at glamorous nightclubs and on hotel terraces. They gambled small sums at the casino in Monte-Carlo. And they often joined Mr. and Mrs. Hitchcock and Mr. and Mrs. Grant for dinner. "Hitch, of course, has found all the restaurants," Grace wrote to a friend that summer, "so we spend a great deal of time eating—and it is a great problem to remain decent-looking in a bathing suit!" Years later, she recalled, "You know how much Hitchcock enjoys eating. When we were working, he used to diet all week in anticipation of having a glorious meal on Saturday evening. He'd spend all week just thinking about it!"

"Hitchcock was at the height of his own vicarious romantic obsession with Grace," Oleg added, "but he didn't seem to resent my presence." Oleg's relationship with Grace, however, remained chaste, and so he decided to raise the matter in an exchange he recalled almost verbatim. It occurred when they were on a raft, floating lazily in the Mediterranean.

"Grace, this has been a long and strange relationship. I am tired of chasing about—enough is enough. There is no need for artifice any longer."

"Who are you, Mr. Cassini?" she asked. "I know that you are very wild, very pleasant, very extravagant and very dangerous— but who *are* you?"

Instead of a reply, he babbled about society, culture and sports. Late that night, when he drove Grace back to her hotel, he did not bid her good night at the door but spent the night in her suite. At this point his recollections sound like breathless phrases from an old romance novel: "She smelled of gardenias, exotic and pure. There was a translucent, pearl-like quality to her; everything about her was clear and fresh and fine—her skin, her scent, her hair. I was enraptured, aware only of the transcendence of the moment, the perfection that she was . . . in the intense emotional and physical chemistry we had found on the Riviera."

Now Grace became the comprehensive lover. She helped him plan their little escapes when she had a free afternoon or Saturday morning. They drove up tortuous, hilly roads; they shopped and visited country markets. They talked about food and wine, history and religion. They went to Mass every Sunday. "I've broken all my regulations with you," she told him, speaking neither boastfully nor contritely.

Just before they left France for California, Grace forced the issue as he had. They dined at a small but superb bistro on a pier, gazing at the boats in port and the twinkling lights in the harbor. As they sipped wine over a supper of grilled fish, Grace said softly to Oleg, "Oh, if only there was a man who could take me away from all this—take me to Tahiti, on a boat like one of these, away from the drudgery of this routine."

Cassini later admitted that he was content with the affair, and felt no inclination toward marriage. But "there was a Roman Catholic soul lurking inside Grace Kelly," he said, and the status quo was not sufficient for her. "I want to make my life with you," she said at last. "I want to be your wife." Fine, he said—so we'll get married. At once, she began to plan Oleg's introduction to her parents . . . and the wedding . . . and her gown . . . and having children.

But later Oleg confessed to her his disinclination to utter marriage vows. "Marriage to Grace Kelly was not something I'd truly anticipated. I had strong feeling for the girl, but I am not sure that marriage was what I really wanted." He added that he had several opportunities during the following year to "close the deal" and marry her, "but each time I acted indecisively." He had his first chance to hesitate when the production moved to California and he traveled separately, to New York. But a few weeks later he joined her in Hollywood.

"Oleg drives me to the [Paramount] studio every morning," Grace wrote during the final weeks of *To Catch a Thief,* "and he picks me up at night. Then we have dinner. . . . My father isn't very happy over the prospect of Oleg as a son-in-law. But the plan now is to be married the first part of October, so we can have some time together before he has his showings [of the fall fashion line]."

The inevitable meeting with the Kelly clan occurred in early September, immediately after the completion of *To Catch a Thief*. First, Oleg was introduced to Margaret in New York. Riding in a taxi, he and Grace encountered only a stony silence until Oleg seized on a literary reference and said cheerfully, "Well, here we are—the unholy trio!"

"You, Mr. Cassini, may be unholy," said Grace's mother, almost between clenched teeth. "I can assure you that Grace and I are not." This was worthy of a character in a play by George Kelly.

"We do not consider you good marriage material," Margaret continued coldly over lunch, counting the reasons on her gloved hand: he was divorced, he had a checkered past, he was a playboy. "I can see why Grace might have been swayed by you. You are charming and literate. But we believe Grace owes it to herself, her family and her religion to reconsider."

Grace did not challenge her mother in 1954. She remained optimistic even after this lunchtime fiasco, and insisted that Oleg come to meet her father and the rest of the family later that month at the Kelly summer home near Atlantic City. That weekend, as Oleg recalled, was "unforgettably unpleasant." Both Jack Kellys, senior and junior, completely ignored him, even to the point of refusing to answer his questions.

No sooner had Grace and Oleg fled back to Manhattan than the press descended on her family, who were all too willing to speak. "I don't approve of these oddballs she goes out with," grumbled Kell, as if Grace had brought home a sword-swallower instead of a wealthy, sophisticated and famous designer. "I wish she would go out with the more athletic type," interposed Papa. "But she doesn't listen to me anymore."

It was left to her mother to spell out the details, which she gladly did for the entire country: "The situation with Cassini had us all concerned," she told the syndicated press in early 1956. "Oleg was a charming man. His manners were continental, he had a wide acquaintance in international society, and he could tell a samba from a mambo. He was at Grace's side everywhere. He literally pursued her across the ocean to Europe. But we in the family were not too happy about it. We knew of his previous marriages—and the mere thought of Grace considering a divorced man was distasteful to us. We all felt she might well go against our wishes and marry him. I put it to him bluntly: 'Look here, Oleg—you're a charming escort, but in my opinion you are a very poor risk for a marriage.' "

And then Margaret Kelly said something that might have turned Grace's resentment into loud laughter: "Of course I never interfere, even when I do not approve."

According to Lizanne, Grace might have acted contrary to her parents' wishes: "If she had really wanted to marry him, I don't think you could have talked her out of it, but she didn't really want to." But Grace did not fully realize that she "didn't really want to [marry Oleg]" until almost a year later.

Meanwhile, notwithstanding the disapproval of her family, she and Oleg remained—in public as in private—very much a couple, despite occasional separations necessitated by work. They were photographed with Hitchcock, for example, at the New York and Los Angeles premieres of *Rear Window,* and they were often seen dining at this or that restaurant in both cities. More to the point, they were unofficially engaged: they had made a commitment to a wedding, and although the date was continually pushed back, their friends had no doubt about the nuptials, and the principals made no secret of their plans. Their perseverance prevailed until the autumn of 1955.

Regarding Grace's experiences with Alfred Hitchcock,

Oleg's judgment was sharp: "He was a complete autocrat. He believed anyone on a film (except him) could be replaced. I argued the opposite, the importance of individuals, especially the unique 'chemistry' generated by stars like Cary Grant and Grace Kelly. They could not be replaced. Hitchcock believed, though, that he could make anyone a star. He was wrong, and would spend the rest of his career [searching] for an actress who could replace Grace Kelly." John Michael Hayes agreed. "Had he been able, Hitch would have used Grace in his next ten pictures," he said in 1981. "I would say that all the actresses he subsequently cast were attempts to retrieve the image and feeling that Hitch carried around so reverentially about Grace."

Soon after, Hitchcock tried to fashion Vera Miles into another Grace Kelly, and most notably there was Tippi Hedren, who began working with Hitchcock in 1962. Hitchcock's colleague, the French director François Truffaut, wrote that "in casting Tippi Hedren in two of his films [*The Birds* and *Marnie*], he entertained the notion of transforming her into another Grace Kelly."* And there were others. He always told them a variant of something like "I will make you into the next Grace Kelly," and to the press he said the same about this or that ingénue: "I will make her into the next Grace Kelly." Conversely, he had no interest at all in women who could not be refashioned, or in whom he found no "chemistry," as he said—gifted actresses like Doris Day and Julie Andrews.

Hitchcock's attempt to re-create the image of a lost love is the premise of his most personal film—*Vertigo*. In the climactic moments of that spiritual testament to Hitch's own soul, Scottie (James Stewart) confronts Judy (Kim Novak) about her ex-

* Truffaut, who knew Hitchcock for twenty years, published a book-length series of interviews with the director in 1967; it was revised and expanded in 1983, three years after Hitchcock's death and a year before his own.

ploitative lover, who turned her into the replica of another woman: "He made you over, didn't he? He made you over just like I made you over—only better. Not only the clothes and the hair, but the looks and the manner and the words. Did he train you? Did he rehearse you? Did he tell you exactly what to do and what to say? You were a very apt pupil!"

Such was Alfred Hitchcock's conduct with several of his most talented leading ladies, his "pupils," after Grace. He tried to control their lives within and outside the studio, designing their personal as well as their professional wardrobes, and attempting to dictate where they went and with whom. But the more he acted this way, the more young women fled from his pathetic need to dominate. He was a brilliant artist, but a lonely and self-destructive man.

Vertigo was released in 1958, when Grace was a wife and mother and far removed from Hollywood. She agreed that it was among Hitch's masterworks, and then she paused and said, "I thought it was also very sad."

EIGHT

Crisis

I want to be at peace with myself.
— GRACE (AS PRINCESS ALEXANDRA) IN *THE SWAN*

ON OCTOBER 10, 1954, SENATOR JOHN F. KENNEDY entered the New York Hospital for Special Surgery. Ten days later, doctors performed a risky operation called a lumbar fusion, which was necessary to prevent permanent disability. The surgery itself was life-threatening, for the patient also suffered from the debilitating effects of Addison's disease; indeed, after the surgery, Kennedy contracted severe infections that were resistant to antibiotics. His parents and a priest were summoned, and his wife, Jacqueline, kept constant vigil at his bedside. No one expected the senator to survive.

The gravity of Kennedy's condition was not detailed in the daily press, but the news traveled in New York society. When Kennedy's condition improved slightly, Grace sent a note to Jackie, asking if she could visit the hospital. Mrs. Kennedy thought this was a marvelous idea, and she invited Grace to arrive wearing a nurse's uniform, for Jack had complained that all the nurses were homely old crones. Grace arrived to find a platoon of bustling attendants hovering over a bone-thin, frail and ashen patient; he was thirty-seven, but he looked much older—nothing like the picture of glowing energy normally presented by the media.

All in white and wearing the regulation nurse's cap, Grace entered the room, but Kennedy was heavily medicated and could neither recognize nor respond to her. "I must be losing it," Grace whispered to Jackie as she departed. Their little stunt had failed, but the actress and the senator's wife became fast friends, and later, Princess Grace and Prince Rainier frequently visited President and Mrs. John F. Kennedy at the White House.*

As her friend Judith Balaban Quine recalled, Grace usually thrived on excitement, chaos and overcrowded scheduling. "Grace was mature, and prematurely grown-up, yet we loved in her the dizzy, dopy, melting and swooning schoolgirl who was never out of sight for long." Sometimes Grace appeared withdrawn and indifferent in public, but with friends like Judy and Rita, she was warm, demonstrative and full of fun. Still, there remained throughout her adult life a constant, if mostly hidden, undercurrent of melancholy. She rarely seemed depressed and was fundamentally hopeful—but close friends sensed her subtle streak of wistfulness, or an occasional assault of "the blues." The precise source of this trait in her nature is difficult to locate.

---

* After a visit to Washington on May 24, 1961, the Prince and Princess of Monaco sent First Lady Jacqueline Kennedy a personal gift of a platinum and diamond necklace with matching earrings, which Mrs. Kennedy wore in private life and to various state dinners at the White House in 1962 and 1963.

Without her conscious awareness, it may have had to do with that element in the Catholic soul that is pessimistic about the world but optimistic about God.

No one who knew her believed that Grace felt religious guilt about her premarital sexual experiences, which were strictly proscribed by her religious education. She had, as she admitted, a tendency to fall in love repeatedly, and her failure to find the right man who would be her husband and the father of her children—and who would please her family, too—haunted her more than ever by the autumn of 1954. This was a different kind of guilt, of which she could not easily free herself, for it concerned not something she had done, but what she had failed to find in life. Grace marked her twenty-fifth birthday in November 1954, and while almost all her friends and relatives were married or engaged, she remained unattached. Hence, she was as reluctant to abandon hope for a life with Oleg as she was hesitant to finalize plans for the marriage. The unofficial engagement and their public courtship continued that season and into the new year. Just as Grace remained adamant in her refusal to accept Metro's offer of roles she considered unappealing, so she became more and more dependent on the thought of marriage to Oleg as a refuge from Hollywood and the Kellys.

On September 28, 1954, he sent his usual weekly bouquet of flowers to her Manhattan apartment. She kept the enclosed card, signed simply "O," on which he had written, *"Io ti amo e ti voglio sposare"*—"I love you and I want to marry you."

Meetings with Metro executives required Grace's presence in Hollywood in late autumn, but the discussions with Dore Schary and his colleagues were disappointing on both sides.

"Still don't know what the hell is going on or when I'll work," Grace wrote to Prudy.

From a suite at the Bel-Air hotel, she wrote to Oleg:

Darling—

I can't wait to see you, now that I know I want to marry you. We have so much to learn about each other—there are so many things I want you to know about me. We must be patient with each other and go slowly without wanting results too quickly. But we need each other and we must be completely honest, at all times.

I feel for the first time ready to approach love and marriage in an adult way. I never thought I could be capable of thinking and feeling this way. But in this last year, six pictures have taken so much from me physically and emotionally that it will take a while to recover. Please, darling, try to understand and to help me—I love you more every day and I hope you feel that way too. One time you said to me that you couldn't love me any more than you did then. That upset me terribly, because I so hope that we shall never stop growing and developing our minds and souls and love for God and each other, and that each day will bring us closer.

I love you and want to be your wife.

Grace

Grace was clearly in crisis—certainly more so than ever. A summary of her life, written to accompany a long photo essay and approved by her son Prince Albert for publication in 2006, notes that Grace was, at Christmas 1954,

physically exhausted and emotionally weary . . . sadder than ever. The pitiless California world that she never liked now seemed to her like hell. The "gentle Miss Kelly" became capricious, irritable and volatile. Fits of tears, a loss of appetite—this crisis was the worst anyone who knew her had seen. In California, she was isolated and everything around her seemed strange. Her life, her friends, her family and the film world disgusted her. She was even thinking of giving up her career, a crushing machine where only the box office mattered. Hollywood was the source of all she detested. She didn't want to live there any more or be subjected to the affronts of the headlines and the harassment of photographers. Nostalgic for New York, she left Los Angeles suddenly.

As Judith Quine said years later, "At that time, she wanted to build a happy married life—but she knew she couldn't do it hopping around the world, starring in films."

When Rita's work and imminent second marriage took her to New York, she and Grace gave up the West Hollywood apartment. With that, Grace signaled her desire to put California behind her by moving to a larger Manhattan residence. This she regarded as a major step in her life, for it involved the total redecoration of a grand New York apartment, which spanned the entire seventh floor of 988 Fifth Avenue. Grace may well have been anticipating her married life here, for it was a generously proportioned home.

With four exposures, ten-foot ceilings and crown moldings from the original 1925 décor, the apartment had a private elevator landing that opened onto a foyer. From there the apartment spread to four thousand square feet and eleven rooms, with four bedrooms, four and a half baths, a kitchen and laundry, living and dining rooms (both with wood-burning fireplaces), a library, two maids' rooms and no fewer than twelve spacious closets. There were extraordinary views of Central Park and the West Side, and vistas all the way north to the

George Washington Bridge. The rent for this apartment was among the highest charged in New York that year—$633.69 a month.* She moved in on February 1, 1955.

Grace invited decorator George Stacey to help locate new and old furniture, and together they found French antiques appropriate to the pale blue and off-white walls. She ordered fresh flowers to be delivered twice weekly, and she began to host small cocktail parties and dinners. To help with her busy life, she engaged a full-time secretary who moved into one of the suites. "I love this apartment," Grace told a friend one day. "But am I going to be living in it alone for the next twenty years, going back and forth from Los Angeles and movie locations?" Her single status was more bothersome that season: "I have been falling in love since I was fourteen—and my parents have never approved of anyone I was in love with."

SHE WAS awakened on the morning of February 12 with very good news: she had been nominated by the Academy of Motion Picture Arts and Sciences as the best actress of 1954, for her performance in *The Country Girl*. The other nominees were Dorothy Dandridge (for *Carmen Jones*), Judy Garland (for *A Star Is Born*), Audrey Hepburn (for *Sabrina*) and Jane Wyman (for *Magnificent Obsession*). Grace was, as the saying goes, cautiously optimistic: she very much admired the competition and she knew she could not depend on the backing of her home studio for encouraging publicity. In January she had again traveled to Culver City—at her own expense—for two days of meetings with Schary, but their discussions ended at an impasse.

---

* The apartment changed hands several times after Grace's departure. The building had been a cooperative for many years when the seventh-floor unit was sold, in 2006, for over $24 million.

Meanwhile, Henry Hathaway, her director on *Fourteen Hours,* wanted her back at Fox for a drama called *The Bottom of the Bottle.* Metro said no. George Stevens, at Warner Bros., was assembling his cast for an epic called *Giant,* based on the sprawling Edna Ferber novel. "I am reliably told," Ferber wrote from New York to the producer Henry Ginsberg at Warners, "that Grace K. is very anxious to play Leslie [in *Giant*], but Metro wants her for a Spencer Tracy picture, which she definitely does not want to do. As she now does pretty much as she pleases, I think she might do *Giant* if properly approached. This comes from someone here whom [*sic*] you know is very close to Tracy [i.e., Katharine Hepburn]." Metro said no again.

"Then they wanted to put me in a movie about Elizabeth Barrett Browning," Grace recalled years later. "I was twenty-five, and the story occurred when she was over forty and ill. I read the script and told them I was too young, and they said, 'No problem—we'll make her younger and prettier!' But I insisted that the whole beauty of the story was that this wonderful romance happened to an older woman who was fragile. 'No problem,' they said again. 'She'll be just as happy at twenty, and healthy!' You just couldn't reason with these men!" When Grace left Los Angeles for New York, she was told by an executive that she was persona non grata in Culver City. This pronouncement evoked no tears.

She was not at all surprised, therefore, when, on March 3, Metro sent Grace a notice that she had been put on suspension. Her refusal of multiple offers had pushed Schary and company to the breaking point, and she was told that her salary would be withheld until she came back to work on assignment; if she went to another studio, she would be "in danger of grave consequences"—a phrase governments ordinarily reserve for the threat of nuclear attack.

Then, without consulting her agents or attorneys, Grace took a very clever public relations step. Aware of her positive public image, and with her Oscar nomination still fresh in the news, she immediately informed the press about Metro's action against her—in advance of any public statement by the studio. When Schary was asked to comment, he could only rather sheepishly confirm her assertion.*

With that, Grace took her sister Peggy (whose marriage was foundering on the shoals of incompatibility and in a storm of alcoholic brawls), and together they left for a quiet Jamaican holiday. There they welcomed the photographer Howell Conant, who had already taken photos of Grace for the April issue of *Photoplay* magazine. In the pellucid waters of the Caribbean, on a private beach and in the sisters' bright, uncluttered rented villa, she and Conant together broke the mold of the standard-issue celebrity image. The results, published in *Collier's* magazine on June 24, were a landmark.

Up to this point in Hollywood history, the studios had employed their own photographers and had meticulously controlled the dissemination of actors' images, which were close to pure fantasy. The public could not get enough of the glamour photos taken, retouched and brilliantly corrected by such geniuses as Clarence Sinclair Bull, George Hurrell, Eugene Richee, Horst, George Hoyningen-Huene, John Engstead, Laszlo Willinger and a platoon of others who fed the dream machine. But Grace Kelly and Howell Conant had new ideas: they wanted to present her as a living human being—not a

---

* That season, Grace was finding her own voice in all departments of her life. Her agents had capitalized on her fame in a deal whereby Grace's picture was used in ads for Lux soap, the reason for her "movie star complexion." But to a Chicago *Sun-Times* journalist, Grace confided the real secret of her beauty: "Soap never touches my face!" She relied on plain cool water.

museum artifact—and the candid shots he took of her were just that: unposed, spontaneous, printed without cosmetic touch-ups or artificially flattering lights.

No star before Grace had ever posed with her hair wet as she rose from the water (an idea that Grace took from the pool scene in *The Bridges at Toko-Ri*). No star had ever been seen wearing her glasses. No star had been photographed without makeup, wearing an oversized shirt that did nothing to show off her figure. No star would have been shown munching an orange or lounging with a pillow. "You trusted Grace's beauty," Conant wrote in an extraordinary book of photos published in 1992. "You knew it wasn't built from clothes and makeup. In New York, Grace came over to my studio dressed in a sweater, a skirt and loafers. In Jamaica, she was no different: her hair [was] pulled back, [and she] dressed in a simple boy's shirt. This was Grace: natural, unpretentious." A close friendship developed, and Howell Conant became Grace's favorite photographer in the United States and Monaco up to the time of her death.

IN MARCH, Grace prepared for her appearance at the Academy Awards. As custom required, she went to Metro's wardrobe department for a consultation—after all, she was still under contract, even if she had been suspended from working. On the spot, Grace was told that she was unwelcome, an outlaw on the studio premises—a wholly unexpected, discourteous and short-sighted corporate gesture. Executives might have reasoned that *The Country Girl* was a Paramount picture, and that they need not concern themselves with promoting her in any way. With her usual unruffled poise, Grace smiled, adjusted her white gloves and asked if she could make a telephone call.

In her Paramount workroom, Edith Head answered her

private line and then put aside several obligations to work from Grace's own choice of fabric and design to come up with the clothes for Oscar night: a slim, floor-length aquamarine gown of French duchesse satin with a matching cloak and pastel blue slippers. White opera-length gloves completed the outfit.

At the Academy's rite of spring on March 30, William Holden stepped up to the podium to announce the award for best actress of 1954. Opening the envelope, he smiled broadly— "Grace Kelly, for *The Country Girl*!" This was the ultimate professional accolade, preceded by similar honors already tendered by the Hollywood Foreign Press Association (the Golden Globe), the National Board of Review and the New York Film Critics Circle; she was also nominated by BAFTA, the British Academy of Film and Television Arts. (Among seven nominations for the picture, George Seaton also won an Oscar, for best screenplay.)

When her name was read, Grace leaned over to Paramount executive Don Hartman: "Are you sure? Are you *sure*?" She went up to accept the statuette from Holden, stepped up to the microphone and quietly spoke her brief acknowledgment: "The thrill of this moment keeps me from saying what I really feel. I can only say thank you with all my heart to all who made this possible for me. Thank you." Backstage, clutching her Oscar and adjusting the yellow rosebuds she had inserted at the last minute into her blond chignon, Grace Kelly wept. At the victory dinner later, she was the winner everyone wanted to meet and congratulate. That night, *Life* magazine settled a deal to put her on the cover of the April 11 issue, wearing the same outfit. She returned to her suite at the Bel-Air hours later— "just the two of us, Oscar and I. It was the loneliest moment of my life." Three thousand miles away, Jack Kelly watched the Academy Awards on television and shook his head: "I can't believe it. I simply can't believe Grace won!"

In the years to come, she was often asked if that spring evening was the most gratifying, most exciting moment of her life. She never wavered: "No, not at all—it was the day when [her first child] Caroline, for the first time, began to walk. She took seven small steps by herself before reaching me and throwing herself into my arms." When another question was put to her, as it was hundreds of times, "How did it *feel* to win the Oscar?"—she smiled and said something polite. But to friends she confided the truth: "I was unhappy. I had fame, but you find that fame is awfully empty if you don't have someone to share it with." When Grace left America in 1956, the coveted statuette went with her, remaining on a small table in her room at the palace until her death; her son Albert then placed it in his living room.

WHERE WAS Oleg Cassini that March? As he later admitted, he was temporarily separated from Grace—"because of my terrible and often silly temper [and] some awful fights, most of which were my fault." The catalyst for the diminishment of their romance was in fact his unreasonable jealousy. There had been rumors he knew to be false—that Grace had had a brief romance with Bing Crosby—and he was furious that she still occasionally dined with Crosby in Los Angeles. "I behaved badly," Oleg said—and Grace agreed, as she wrote in a letter:

> *You have upset me so that I could die.*
> *It is incredible to me that having dinner with Lizanne and the Crosbys can make you behave like a schoolboy—If I went out with Bing alone you would be absolutely right—and I would never do that to begin with, because I have no interest in anyone but you—but this I shouldn't have to explain.*
> *Bing is a wonderful person and a very dear friend. I have*

*great respect for him and hope he will be our friend for
many years.*

*I told you he said that he was in love with me—but there
are many people he feels that way about, and after the emotional strain of playing Country Girl, this was only natural.
But Bing would never try to do anything about it. Unless he
thought I wanted it that way.*

*I have very few friends out here. Please don't ask me to
give up their friendships!*

But that was not the only incident that caused Grace to
reevaluate the affair with Oleg. On another occasion that
spring, she wanted to dine with Jay Kanter and Frank Sinatra,
to discuss a potential movie project. She told Oleg before the
evening was confirmed. But Oleg was furious, calling the dinner a pretext for Sinatra to initiate a romance. "I must explain
something to you right now, with no interruptions," Grace said
calmly while Cassini raged. "The extravagance of your jealousy did not displease me at first. But isn't it about time that
you stopped this silly behavior? It shows nothing but a lack of
confidence. I love you, but your anger isn't very endearing. Indeed, it is slowly destroying the warmth I've felt for you. If it is
so important to you, I won't go out with Sinatra. But please,
stop this behavior right now!"

Cassini was judging Grace by his own conduct, believing
that she was as frivolous (indeed, as promiscuous) as he—and
this mistaken presumption led him to jealous rages over matters he knew and later admitted had no foundation in reality.
That spring of 1955, he was, with his own hand, finishing off
an intense and important relationship that had been central to
their lives for a year—and that might otherwise have led to
marriage.

⁓

As if on cue, three distractions arose just as Grace was considering the emotional consequences of her cooling-off period from Oleg.

First, her agents had an uncharacteristically cheerful call from Dore Schary: *Congratulations to Grace on her well-deserved Oscar . . . we* said *that she was headed for the top . . . you* know *we have admired her all along . . . we just waited, in order to provide the right project for her. . . . We* love *her—why, she's just like* family. . . . And so it went—the usual Hollywood hypocritical double-talk in place of plain speaking. Now at last, Schary continued, the studio was convinced they had the right movie for Grace: *They just* know *she will love it, because she* said *she loved appearing in an abbreviated television version of the story in 1950—and of* course *all this business about the suspension—well, let's just forget about* that, *ha-ha-ha. . . .*

In fact, "the right movie" had not been Schary's idea at all, and Jay Kanter knew it, but he had the diplomatic good sense to listen and say nothing.

The day before her meeting at Metro the preceding January, Grace had invited George Kelly to lunch on the terrace of the Bel-Air Hotel. "As usual, we talked about books and the theatre," Grace told me, "and, also as usual, I mentioned the kinds of plays I dreamed of doing on the stage. George reminded me how much I had enjoyed acting in an abbreviated television version of Molnár's play *The Swan*. At that moment we both knew it could be a wonderful picture." During her meeting with Schary the next day, Grace proposed the idea. He promised to think about it, and now—during the phone conversation with Kanter—he presented it as if it were his own idea, and he asked that it be conveyed to Grace for her consideration.

The Swan, written in Hungarian in 1914, is the story of a beautiful princess in a small, unnamed European principality, torn between love and duty. In deference to her family and her station in life, she marries a prince who will inherit a kingdom, and at the finale, she (perhaps) glides happily ever after. Grace had read the 1923 English translation when she assumed the role of Alexandra in 1950; she appreciated the play's bittersweet understatement, its wit and irony, and she liked its poignant delicacy about the unrealistic expectations people often have of life. And so, on April 25, Grace signed the renewal of her option papers and agreed to return to Metro for *The Swan,* scheduled for production that autumn. To sweeten the deal, her studio announced that, for the first time in her career, Grace Kelly's name would appear first in the movie's opening credits; it does—but alongside the names of Alec Guinness and Louis Jourdan, and not alone on the screen.* With her Academy Award and the starring role of Princess Alexandra in the story, the studio could do no less—but they might have done more.

The timing of her first film since *To Catch a Thief* appealed to Grace. With four months to herself—from May through August 1955—she would be able at last to work full-time with George Stacey, finishing the redecoration of her new apartment. In addition, her sister Lizanne was to be married in June, and Grace wanted to help with all the preparations.

Then came a second distraction. Rupert Allan was acting as

---

* It has been repeatedly and wrongly claimed that Metro had the idea to produce *The Swan* after (and because of) the announcement of Grace's engagement to Prince Rainier. But this project was suggested by George Kelly, and his niece had brought it to Metro in January 1955—four months before her introduction to Rainier. Grace signed the contract to perform in the film three weeks before she first heard Rainier's name and was dragooned into meeting him for publicity purposes.

the liaison between the Cannes Film Festival and Hollywood studios. He rang Grace from Los Angeles with the news that the festival would like to include *The Country Girl* in early May, before its Paris opening on May 13, and they very much wanted Grace to make an appearance in Cannes. This idea held no interest for her at all. She was looking forward to her time at home and with her sister, and she told Rupert that the thought of crowds and interviews made her dizzy. Over several days, Rupert rang back with additional reasons for her to reconsider, but Grace was determined to preserve some distance from the world of movies. No, she told Rupert, thank you very much, but I will sit this one out. Perhaps another year?

And then came a third distraction, which changed everything. Jean-Pierre Aumont, with whom she had acted in the television drama about the Audubons, had returned briefly to New York after completing a French picture. With no fear of interference from Cassini, she readily accepted Jean-Pierre's dinner invitation and found him more than merely charming: he was also highly sophisticated, cultured, courtly and an attentive and caring listener—in other words, precisely the kind of companion Grace needed that spring.

Her Oscar had required her to change her telephone number, and for weeks she had been (as her character Lisa says in *Rear Window*) juggling wolves. A quiet dinner with Jean-Pierre occurred at just the right moment—and it was just a quiet dinner. But later, after he spent a night with Grace at her new apartment, he told her that he, too, had business in Cannes, and had planned to go to Paris to see his young nephews. Why shouldn't they meet in France a few weeks later? Grace acquiesced. From such casual, spontaneous decisions does one's destiny take shape, and what seems but a confluence of distractions alters the course of life.

By coincidence, Rupert rang the next day to importune Grace one more time: the festival would provide her with first-class airline tickets, he said, along with a suite at the Carlton Hotel, a limousine and driver at her disposal, and . . . But Grace interrupted him. She would be delighted to attend, and no more need be said about it. On April 30, she left New York and flew to Paris, intending to take the train from there to the south. "I had no idea," Rupert told me, "that Jean-Pierre would be waiting at the Cannes railway station to welcome her. These secrets were yet to be revealed."

But the subplots were only beginning.

At precisely the same time, the editors of France's *Paris-Match* magazine were huddled in their cramped offices near Champs-Elysées, trying to find an interesting way to cover the whirl of activities at Cannes. Pierre Galante, the magazine's movie editor, had the task of finding an angle for a photo story that would be newsworthy at home and abroad. Managing editor Gaston Bonheur, who had only just been informed that Miss Kelly was expected around May 3, said her presence was very welcome, but that on her own she would not provide the excitement they were after to attract a huge readership. Bonheur then asked Galante if he thought it would be possible to arrange a meeting between Miss Kelly and Prince Rainier III of Monaco—something along the lines of "Hollywood Movie Queen Meets Real-Life Prince."

Galante doubted such a meeting would be possible. While she was in Cannes, Miss Kelly's schedule had been planned to the minute, and the prince's business schedule alternated with capricious absences and impromptu holidays. Despite his misgivings, Galante and his wife—Olivia de Havilland, who had added two best-actress Oscars to her successful battle against the studio system—departed from the Gare de Lyon and headed for Cannes. As it happened, Grace held a reservation on the same train; she was traveling with her friend Gladys de Segonzac, who had helped with her wardrobe on *To Catch a Thief.*

A meeting between a prince and a foreigner not on an official visit was a delicate matter. The prince had to issue a formal invitation, which was rather like a command to be present—and it would be very nearly a catastrophe if the summons was turned down because of "other plans." Up to this point, Grace had no notion that there was a scheme to introduce her to Rainier of Monaco so that magazines could be sold.

Before the passengers disembarked the next morning, Grace asked Olivia what might be expected of her at the festival, where she ought to go and what she ought to do.

"How would you like to visit Monaco?" asked Pierre, as if the thought had just occurred to him. "You'll have to get away from the reporters for a little while or you'll collapse with exhaustion, and Monaco is delightful." With that, Pierre became a kind of travel agent for the small principality, speaking rhapsodically about the charm of the place. Grace replied that such a visit might be a pleasant interlude—if her schedule permitted.

In Cannes, Paramount's French representative welcomed Grace and escorted her to the Carlton Hotel. Lo! Among the celebrities gathering on the station platform to greet arriving guests was none other than Jean-Pierre Aumont, who followed Grace's car and arrived at the Carlton moments later. He found a few acquaintances in the lobby and corralled them for drinks while Grace dispatched the first of her interviews. Then Galante arrived with the news that Grace's schedule would indeed allow her some free time the next afternoon, and they could all drive to meet Prince Rainier and pose for some photographs. In the best traffic conditions (which rarely prevailed), the drive from Cannes to Monaco would take no less than an hour and a half.

"I don't see why it's so important for me to meet the

prince," Grace said, "but if you think it's such a good idea, I'll do it." Calls were put through to the palace, and the report came back that Prince Rainier would be pleased to welcome Miss Kelly at four o'clock on May 6. The next morning Grace told Galante, "Oh, this is quite impossible—I simply can't go to Monaco today. I've had a call that I must return to Cannes at five-thirty to host a reception for the American contingent. You'll have to cancel the prince." Galante made another call to the palace, and after a brief delay, the prince's secretary said that His Serene Highness was entertaining guests at his villa in Beaulieu, but he would make every effort to return to the palace at three instead of four to accommodate Miss Kelly's schedule. More rearrangements were made, and at last things looked favorable.

Minutes before three o'clock on Friday, May 6, Grace, Pierre, Olivia and Paramount's French representative arrived at the palace in Monaco. The prince had been delayed in Beaulieu, but his guests, waiting at the palace, were assured his return was imminent. An aide gave Grace and her companions a tour of the palace. Tea was offered. No Rainier. At fifteen minutes before four o'clock, Grace and her small party waited anxiously in the palace courtyard. "I think it's very rude of him to keep us waiting like this," she said quietly. "I cannot be late for the reception—let's get out of here."

And then, as the tower clock struck four, the apologetic Prince Rainier hurried through a portico to greet his guests. "Would you like to visit the palace?" he asked.

"We just have," Grace replied.

He suggested a stroll through the gardens, and cameras clicked from a discreet distance. Thirty minutes later, polite thank-yous and good-byes were said, and Grace and company raced back to Cannes. "Well, he's very charming," Grace said to Pierre and Olivia, and that was that. *Paris-Match* had their photos, the issue would be a sellout, and Grace was a half hour late to the reception. Late that evening she joined Jean-Pierre Aumont for supper, and when all Grace's duties at the Cannes Film Festival had been fulfilled a few days later, she prolonged her visit to France to spend more time with him.

The 2006 summary of Grace's life, approved by her son, Prince Albert, contains this account of her relationship with Aumont that May of 1955: "They spent their days together, and their apparent friendship hid a complicit love affair. Looking to escape from the paparazzi, they took refuge at the Montana reserve in La Napoule, outside Cannes. Even so, they were pursued by photographers and journalists, and this lunch *à deux* resulted in a memorable photo of the couple."

Within days, "everyone was talking about her 'future marriage' to Jean-Pierre Aumont." The couple retreated to Paris, where "she spent many happy days with Jean-Pierre Aumont. Hidden from the press in his La Malmaison home, she tasted the joys of a peaceful life, happy and surrounded by children, the actor's nephews." The love affair quickly deepened into something quite serious, and very soon the American press reported that Grace and Jean-Pierre "held and kissed each other's hands in cozy rendezvous." Asked if marriage was in the forecast, he was diplomatic but not coy: "She is an adorable and sensational woman any man would be proud and pleased to marry. But whether the feelings are reciprocal is up to her to say."

Another contingent of the press followed up on the Monaco visit. What did the bachelor prince think of Miss Kelly? "I had not yet visited the United States," Rainier said, "and this was one of the first occasions I had to meet an American girl. She spoke clear English and was very calm, very agreeable, but my feelings went no further than that. It was merely 'hello' and 'good-bye.' . . . Certainly no thoughts of marriage crossed my mind!"

◠

IN A DIFFERENT context, marriage (but not to Rainier) was very much on Grace's mind when she returned to America and helped her sister prepare for her wedding. On Saturday, June 25, 1955, Lizanne's twenty-second birthday, she was married to Donald LeVine at the Kellys' parish church, St. Bridget's. Grace was the bridesmaid and Peggy matron of honor. Margaret and John Kelly had disapproved of Peggy's marriage to a Protestant, and they had expressed their doubts about Lizanne's marriage to a Jew. It was no surprise that the continued vetting of Grace's beaux continued more insistently than ever.

Lizanne's wedding was a turning point in Grace's life. According to Lizanne, "She thought she was missing something, and she wanted to get married and be a mother, too." Grace spent much of the summer at the family's seaside home, where the place was filled with children and young married couples. At twenty-five, she was more than eager to be married—and, as she had said, she felt that she was "aging much too quickly." To Judy Kanter, Grace confided that "the wedding was so sweet . . . and all those sweet children . . . I want all of that . . . before I'm just everyone's spinster Aunt Grace." When Judy asked about Jean-Pierre, Grace smiled: it had been a lovely springtime dalliance, but there was no serious prospect of marriage and the affair had ended, with mutual respect and affection. Years later, Aumont was asked if Grace was one of the great loves of his life. "No," he replied, "but it was a very tender friendship."

The tabloid press, ever eager for lubricious tales of Hollywood, began an assault on previously untouchable leading ladies in 1955. *Rave* magazine was one of the boldest, and in March it published an article about Grace called "She-Wolf Deluxe," which listed a legion of lovers whose marriages Grace had supposedly destroyed. The content was so libelous that her father initiated legal proceedings—an action he withdrew when he learned that the editor, one Victor Huntington Rowland, had legally declared bankruptcy. "My son and I will settle it in our own way without a lawsuit," Jack Kelly said. "We'll take him on." The matter went no further, except that (with appropriate changes) it found its way into the screenplay for Grace's last Hollywood film, *High Society*.

Metro, meanwhile, was casting a film version of Tennessee Williams's controversial, prize-winning play *Cat on a Hot Tin Roof*, still running in New York. On July 9, the studio announced that it had bought the rights specifically for Grace to play the leading role of the sex-starved Maggie, but the movie could not be made until the Broadway run had ended. That did not occur until November 1956, after Grace had quit Hollywood, had married and was expecting her first child. The role of Maggie, perhaps more suitably, went to Elizabeth Taylor.

NINE

Playing the Princess

I want to be a queen.
　　—GRACE (AS PRINCESS ALEXANDRA) IN *THE SWAN*

THEIR FIRST EXCHANGE OF LETTERS CROSSED IN THE
international mails.

After returning to America, Grace wrote a formal
note of appreciation to Prince Rainier III, thanking him for the
welcome he had extended to her. At precisely the same time,
Rainier wrote Miss Grace Kelly a formal note of thanks for in-
terrupting her busy professional schedule to visit him. So began
a lively and frequent correspondence—an epistolary courtship
instead of one conducted in person. According to Rainier, he
and Grace "revealed more and more with each letter." They
wrote about the world and they wrote about life, about themselves, their feelings and their histories. It had been easy for
him to find lovers, Rainier admitted (as it had been for her)—
"but my greatest difficulty was knowing a girl long enough and
intimately enough to find out if we [were] really soul mates as
well as lovers." In their letters over seven months, they had

time to become pen pals and then friends, "long before they ever held hands," as he added.

In the letters, as Rainier recalled, they gradually came to see the similarities in their different backgrounds. They were both public figures uncomfortable with their status as celebrities. They were both serious Catholics with more than a mere Sunday sense of religion: they made no public displays, but faith was more than an inherited tradition—it was at the core of their lives. Their friends knew that religious practices were not burdensome obligations for these two; they were free and purposeful expressions of a deep if mysterious commitment. And they both had enough experience to distinguish mere infatuation from love. Rainier found Grace gentle, poised and unaffected, and he shared her sense of irony, her fey (and occasionally risqué) humor. She found him warm and unpretentious, and he had the kind of European charm and sophistication she found irresistible in men—and of course, even during their brief introduction, there had been an immediate and intense mutual attraction. They came to believe that they were destined to be a couple.

"I didn't save them," Rainier said about the letters Grace sent before their marriage. "Maybe I should have, but that's not the way I am. I don't keep things like that." As for the letters he sent to her, he remained uncertain if she kept them—and if she did, he had no idea of their location, even when he and the children sorted through her personal effects after her death. "Even if I could find the letters," he said in 1987, "I simply couldn't let anyone trespass." In any case, what happened at the second encounter of Grace and Rainier indicates that by the end of the year—lacking any meeting beyond the afternoon of May 6—they had become sufficiently acquainted in writing to give more than whimsical consideration to the prospect of marriage.

Grace never discussed this early correspondence, but she did say, "I was especially impressed with Rainier's long view of things—he saw the large picture, the context. He didn't look only to the moment, but to the meaning and the effects of relationships. We found we had a lot in common, and we had the same needs and hopes for our future, too. I was dissatisfied with my life, and he with his."

The prince, who marked his thirty-second birthday on May 31, 1955, had governed Monaco's half square mile and four hundred acres—half the size of New York's Central Park—since 1949. To readers of international glossy magazines, he was unfairly portrayed as a bland, sporting bachelor prince, the claimant to one of Europe's oldest thrones, occupied uninterruptedly for seven centuries by the Grimaldi family. Contrary to the superficial and misleading description of him merely as a leisure-time sailor and racing-car enthusiast, he was in fact an educated, intelligent man with a highly enlightened business sense and solid modern ideas about the financial and social development of Monaco. But he was also surrounded by counselors dedicated to the conservative status quo and to their own comfortable employment. Hence (like Grace) he had to exercise a certain caution in the choice of friends and confidants.

Since the end of his six-year romantic affair with the French actress Giselle Pascal in 1953, Rainier had been living (in his words) "a lonely, empty bachelor's life.... I cannot go out without being followed, watched and gossiped about. Every time I am seen with a girl, someone starts a rumor about a love affair." That May of 1955, as he told a visiting American journalist, "I met your lovely American actress, Miss Grace Kelly. Next day, I read in the press that I was going to marry her. That sort of thing embarrasses both of us. It is very difficult to be natural and at ease when you are secretly wondering whether something will come of the friendship, and when the whole world is openly speculating about marriage!"

Misperceptions, rumors and frank inaccuracies were the bases of Rainier's unfortunate image outside Monaco, which is usually considered to be synonymous with Monte-Carlo. But they are not identical places, nor is Monte-Carlo ("Mount Charles," named for Rainier's ancestor Charles III) the location of the royal palace.* Monte-Carlo (the new town) is rather one of Monaco's several administrative areas; the others are Le Larvotto (the beach), La Condamine (the harbor), Fontvieille (the industrial sector) and Monaco-Ville (the old town), where the palace had been built as a fortification, jutting nine hundred yards out over the Mediterranean. Known for its gambling casino, luxurious hotels and expensive shops, Monte-Carlo, on the other hand, for centuries attracted Europe's royals and aristocrats, as well as the merely wealthy and a disturbing complement of disreputable characters; it was for a very long time, as Somerset Maugham famously said, "a sunny place for shady people."

Rainier was dutifully trying to change that reputation in the 1950s. He contrived, for example, to break the vast financial power held in Monte-Carlo by Aristotle Onassis. The Greek shipbuilding magnate controlled the major shares of the Société des Bains de Mer, the corporation owning the legendary casino of Monte-Carlo as well as Monaco's most lucrative hotels and real estate parcels. "We can't go on catering only to the super-super rich," Rainier said. Unlike the seasonal visitors, the population (about 20,000 citizens) was middle class, and most citizens were employed within Monaco or nearby, in France or Italy, on whose borders the tiny principality had nestled since the thirteenth century.

The citizens were a diverse lot, but they were united by one concern: according to a treaty with France signed in 1861,

---

* Contrary to popular usage, the proper spelling of Monte-Carlo must include the hyphen.

Monaco would fall under French rule as a protectorate if the princely monarch died without a male heir. That would make the Monégasques liable to French taxes (Monaco has no sales tax, inheritance tax or income tax) and to French military conscription (Monaco has no standing army). In 1955, only the good health of thirty-two-year-old Rainier stood between the people of Monaco and French control—and he had neither an heir nor a prospective bride on the horizon.*

"I must get married and raise a family," the prince said that year, evidently without a candidate in mind. "I told my people that I was keenly sensitive to the political implications of my bachelorhood—but I told them not to overlook the human factor, the duty of a man to fulfill himself as a human being by taking a wife he loves. I will not marry except for love. I will not agree to a loveless marriage of convenience." He wanted, Rainier said with admirable frankness, a wife who would be a soul mate as well as a lover, and he detailed the obstacles in reaching that goal. "My life is public and regulated. I must attend many formal receptions, and the palace protocol is quite severe"—as, he said, his wife would immediately discover. There was also the issue of his extraordinary wealth, which made it difficult to know whether anyone loved or even liked him for his own sake or for the material benefits attending their association with him.†

Despite an unhappy background, Rainier had matured without emotional or psychological disabilities. He had spent an

---

* Monaco is a principality, not a kingdom—hence its sovereign is a prince, not a king, and his spouse is a princess, not a queen.

† In 2008, a report by *Forbes* magazine listed Prince Albert II of Monaco (son of Rainier and Grace) as the ninth-richest monarch in the world, with a personal fortune estimated at $1.4 billion; most of it was derived from real estate, art, antique cars, stamps and a large share of the Société des Bains de Mer. Queen Elizabeth II of England was placed lower—twelfth on the list, with a personal fortune of merely $650 million.

unstable, deeply troubled childhood as the son of the French count Pierre de Polignac and Princess Charlotte of Monaco, the illegitimate daughter of Prince Louis II. When Rainier was seven years old, Charlotte ran off with an Italian doctor, abandoning both Rainier and his older sister, Princess Antoinette. Charlotte was divorced from Pierre in 1933 and yielded her right of succession—which had, despite her illegitimacy, been granted to her by the government in 1919. Thus the throne would pass to her ten-year-old son, Rainier—not to the older Antoinette, for the Monégasque constitution favored a male over a female heir.

In his mother's absence, Rainier became a withdrawn, sullen boy with an eating disorder that led to severe obesity. At the age of eight, he was shipped off to a British boarding school, where he mastered perfect, unaccented English and learned to cope with crushing loneliness. A passion for sports resolved the eating disorder and its unfortunate consequences, and Rainier went on to secondary school in Switzerland, then to the University of Montpellier (France), and finally to the Institut d'Etudes Politiques in Paris. During World War II, Rainier served as an artillery officer in the French army, displaying such courage during the battle for Alsace that he was awarded the Croix de Guerre and was made a chevalier in the Legion of Honor.

Deprived of familial affection or even transient attention, young Rainier engaged in a series of wild love affairs and dangerous sports—until the spring of 1955, when a thirty-minute rendezvous with an American actress touched something in him. For the first time in his life (so he told the palace chaplain, an American Catholic priest named Francis Tucker), he felt he had really met the right woman. Whatever inchoate feelings Grace harbored were not confided to anyone—not to her sisters or her mother, not even to close friends. In the absence of any expressed sentiments about the prince of Monaco between

May and December, it is impossible to know or to presume what Grace's feelings may have been.

Rainier's sister Antoinette did not take her disenfranchisement graciously. After divorcing her first husband and taking up with a jewel thief, she concocted a scheme to depose her brother and declare herself regent, on the basis that she had a son to inherit the throne, whereas her brother Rainier was unmarried. Apparently mad for power, she simultaneously circulated the rumor that Giselle Pascal was sterile, and this perfidy effectively forced Rainier to end his relationship with the French actress, to whom he was about to propose marriage. Pascal then married in 1955 and bore a healthy daughter. Antoinette, for whom eccentricity is too mild a description, was later banished from Monaco.

IN SEPTEMBER, Grace returned from New York to Hollywood, where she began work on *The Swan*. On the fifteenth and sixteenth of that month, she had hair and makeup tests, and then there was a week of long hours at the studio, for her wardrobe fittings with Helen Rose, head of the costume department. "I've always been interested in fashion and textile design," Grace said, "and Helen was a diplomat. She knew how to steer actresses away from a favorite color or line if it did not suit them or the role. I also observed her tactfully get a producer or director, who was fixed on a certain idea, to change his mind if that particular thing was unflattering for the star. I knew very little of the period [of *The Swan*], so I did some research in New York before going out to California for my fittings. The Empire look had come back into fashion for just a few years leading up to the 1914 war, and it was an enchanting look. I was thrilled when I saw Helen's sketches and some of the exquisite fabrics she had selected."

"There were costumes in every conceivable situation," Helen Rose recalled about the film, set in 1910 in a mythical European kingdom. "There was a riding habit, and a fencing costume, negligees, afternoon frocks and ball gowns. I used beautiful fabrics on all the costumes, the finest I could find. I never saw a star as thrilled as Grace the day we fitted the white chiffon ball gown. She stood before the mirror, gently touching the embroidered camellias and saying, 'How simply marvelous, Helen—what talented people you have here at MGM!' For weeks, several skilled women had sat at embroidery frames, carefully working by hand each petal of every flower. The ball gown was indeed fit for a princess."

After preparations in Culver City, the production, under the Hungarian-born director Charles Vidor, moved to the Biltmore House, near Asheville, North Carolina, for three weeks of exterior filming at the largest private home ever built in the United States. Begun in 1889 and completed seven years later, George Vanderbilt's residential extravaganza had been designed by architect Richard Morris Hunt in imitation of three Loire Valley châteaux. When finished, Biltmore House featured four acres of floor space and 250 rooms, including thirty-four bedrooms, forty-three bathrooms and sixty-five fireplaces. The swimming pool, gymnasium, bowling alley, servants' quarters and kitchens were located below ground level, while Frederick Law Olmsted, creator of New York's Central Park, designed 125,000 acres of gardens and parklands. No one could have chosen a lovelier setting for the European palace of *The Swan*.

John Dighton's screenplay follows very closely the text of Molnár's play. Princess Alexandra (Grace), her mother, Princess Beatrice (Jessie Royce Landis), her great-aunt Symphorosa (Estelle Winwood) and her younger brothers (Van Dyke Parks and Christopher Cook) live in the castle of a country that lost its status as a kingdom at the time of Napoleon. Beatrice is eager to make a match between Alexandra and a distant cousin, Prince Albert (Alec Guinness), who will one day inherit a throne as king of a neighboring country. The marriage of Albert and Alexandra will effect the fulfillment of Beatrice's long-cherished dream—the family will at last have "a throne of their own" again, and her beloved daughter will be a queen. Nor is Alexandra apathetic to this idea: she, too, likes the idea of becoming the wife of a future king, although she has not yet met Albert and fears that her shyness will be unappealing to him.

When the prince arrives for a four-day visit with Beatrice and her family, he prefers sports and shooting activities to time with Alexandra. Albert is a wise, kind and unpretentious royal bachelor, refined and aware of his royal destiny but without any desire to manipulate or exploit others. His apparent indifference to Alexandra seems to augur poorly for an engagement, and so Beatrice takes a desperate measure, hatching a scheme to make Albert jealous. She forces Alexandra to ask the family's tutor, handsome young Nicholas Agi (Louis Jourdan), to come to the ball in Albert's honor. Alexandra will feign romantic interest in the teacher, thus arousing Albert's interest. Albert will then see Alexandra's beauty and charm, Nicholas will be duly returned to his servant status and Beatrice's hope will be fulfilled as Alexandra becomes engaged to a future king.

But there are complications. From the time of his arrival at the castle some time earlier, Nicholas has been secretly in love with Alexandra, and after expressing his devotion to her, he is deeply hurt and offended to learn that he has been used as a device to propel her into another's arms. Alexandra, who regrets her complicity, is moved to discover that intelligent, attractive Nicholas has harbored an ardent passion. This is her first experience of love, and she is ecstatic—and far too naïve in her belief that she can abandon her quest for a throne by yielding to this romance with an employee. At the bittersweet, completely realistic conclusion, Nicholas leaves the castle and Alexandra accepts that it is only with Albert that her own aspirations and her family's future destiny can be realized.

The film of *The Swan,* like the Molnár play, is far more emotionally complex and more mature in its stance toward love than can be conveyed in a summary. Ostensibly a romantic fable, it is actually high comedy, puncturing social pretenses and exaggerated expectations of life gently and without bombast or cruelty. *The Swan* is also a remarkably earnest depiction of the shallow, fading monarchical pretensions of minor European royalty. Written in 1914, as the fires of the Great War were being stoked in Molnár's native Hungary and were soon to engulf all of Europe, the play presents Beatrice as hopelessly self-absorbed, but not wicked. Her treatment of Nicholas is inexcusable, as Albert and his comical but endearing mother the queen (Agnes Moorehead) make clear. But in his departure, Nicholas is clearly moving on to brighter fields.

There are three constellations of characters in *The Swan*—a celestial metaphor reinforced by frequent references to telescopes, stars, astronomy lessons and the vastness of the universe. Beatrice and her household represent an old and now inadequate way of life. Albert and his mother stand for a kind of royalty that can still be relevant in a modern world—a working family mindful of the need for a new social order. And Nicholas and Alexandra (a noteworthy choice of names in light of the couple then still reigning in Russia) represent the unlikely lovers.

Like the play, the film sparkles with delicate humor that leavens the gravity with which it explores the nature of romantic love in a rapidly changing world dominated by class struggles. In this regard, Alexandra is not simply a foolish, inexperienced young woman. She is a sympathetic soul who, in the course of the story, moves through the stages of a moral education, comporting herself at first with charming awkwardness, then relying on her idea of what it is to be a love-struck maiden, and finally accepting that her ambitions and her vocation require sacrifices she has not yet considered.

In 1923 the great Eva Le Gallienne created the role for the American premiere, and then the play was indifferently adapted to the screen in 1925 and 1930. It lay all but forgotten until—at the instigation of a judicious uncle and his shrewd niece—Metro transformed it into a lush Technicolor film that remains an acutely touching and alluring adult romance. The Hungarian director Charles Vidor, admirably familiar with the literary sensibility of his compatriot Molnár, also understood the tangle of characters, and he never lost sight of the complexities in his deceptively simple, uncluttered management of the actors in their vast and lavish settings.

The performances are uniformly first-rate. In his American movie debut, Alec Guinness portrays the prince with the proper combination of wry bemusement, astuteness and comic gentility. Jessie Royce Landis (also Grace's mother in *To Catch a Thief*) had no equal in her ability to convey hollow pomposity as only an amusingly venial fault. Louis Jourdan, as the lovesick, mistreated academic, knew how to play a young man at the mercy of his emotions. His love scenes with Grace in the carriage by moonlight and on the terrace are lessons in the fine art of making such moments both credible and affecting. Estelle Winwood, in a role that could easily have been relegated to mere comic relief, gave Symphorosa a daffy wisdom as she insists, "I don't like the twentieth century." And Brian Aherne, improbably cast as Beatrice's brother, a worldly-wise Franciscan monk who has abandoned the world but not his wisdom, turns the character of Father Hyacinth into a new Friar Laurence from *Romeo and Juliet.* He reminds everyone that compassion is the best axis for any romantic constellation.

For much of her time onscreen, Grace remains silent, or speaks but a few words. But we see her listening, we watch her subtle reactions and confusions, and her muted passion is the cyclorama against which everyone must play. The performance is like a pantomime in a silent movie: she communicates every emotion with only the slightest changes in facial expression. Some of this subtlety she learned from her trio of Hitchcock films, but much of it came from a deep understanding of Alexandra—"a woman I thought I really had under my skin," as she told me. Certainly she was never more lovingly photographed than in *The Swan*.

It was perhaps no wonder that the industry's trade journal *The Hollywood Reporter* proclaimed that with this achievement she was "on the threshold of becoming the next Garbo," for this was a performance of deep repose and admirable tranquillity. Grace's features were neither immobile nor masklike, and perhaps it is no exaggeration to assert that she acted with markedly more warmth than Garbo. It was precisely this tenderness that raised her portrait of Alexandra above the level of a thesis-character. She made it impossible, for example, to discount her declaration of love to Nicholas: "I've never seen a man in love—and he happens to be in love with me. Oh, Nicholas, if I am afraid of you, I want always to be afraid. I want to be so good to you. I want to tell you everything that's in my heart. I want to look after you and spoil you and—oh, *here*—eat something!" Rarely has a standard love scene been so gently and movingly lifted above stereotypes. In *The Swan,* Grace is at last, as Hitchcock had hoped she would one day become, "the character around whom the whole film is built."

BEFORE THE FIRST scenes were filmed, Dore Schary summoned assistant director Ridgeway Callow and told him, "I want Grace Kelly treated like a star." Callow hadn't the remotest idea what that meant, and so he decided to treat Miss Kelly the way he would treat a good friend who had a difficult assignment—using practical jokes to relax her, and refusing to behave as if she were . . . well, a princess. "We gave her a dog's life on the picture," Callow recalled, "and she loved every minute of it. We short-sheeted her repeatedly in her hotel room when we were on location in North Carolina. We played many tricks on her, she played many tricks on us, and after the picture was over, she wrote a note to Dore Schary, saying that she enjoyed the picture tremendously. We played more tricks on her than anybody we ever worked with. She certainly was not temperamental. She wasn't regal at all—she kidded around all the time."

Howell Conant, who documented the making of the film in a brilliant set of color photographs for Metro and for Grace, also recalled her sense of fun. Aware that Guinness had received a rather bold letter from a fan named Alice, Grace had "Alice" page him repeatedly in the hotel lobby.

Guinness decided on suitable retribution. Jessie Royce Landis had given him a tomahawk from a local souvenir shop, and when he departed for a brief holiday, he tipped the concierge to slip the weapon into Grace's bed. "It became a sort of running gag between Grace and myself," according to Guinness, "although neither of us ever mentioned it. A few years after she had married Prince Rainier, I returned home from an evening performance in London and, getting into bed, found the identical tomahawk between the sheets. My wife knew nothing about it. I waited two or three years and then, hearing by chance that Grace was going to do a tour of poetry readings in the U.S. with the English actor John Westbrook, whom I had never met, I telephoned him to ask if he would be prepared to help me with a little scheme. Sportingly he agreed, so I got the tomahawk to him through a third party [and] the thing was placed in Grace's bed. I had almost forgotten about it until I went to Hollywood in 1979. Grace was in Monaco, but after the ceremony, I found the tomahawk in my bed at the Beverly Wilshire Hotel."

And so it went until Grace's death. "She had this extraordinary sense of humor," according to Louis Jourdan, "first of all, about herself, never taking herself seriously." But Conant also recalled another side of Grace that autumn: she was often "remote, quiet, pensive." Her colleagues, and visiting friends like Judy Kanter and Gant Gaither, believed that her moments of reserve, and even her sudden brief periods of withdrawal into an atypical solitude, had to do with concern over her next picture. On November 27, Metro announced that Grace was joining Bing Crosby and Frank Sinatra in the cast of *High Society,* a musical remake of *The Philadelphia Story.* The production of *High Society* was scheduled for early 1956, and that seemed to be the source of Grace's apprehension. Metro's executives were finally coming to their senses in the matter of Grace Kelly, but time had run out for them: unknown to everyone, her epistolary romance with Rainier was moving her in another direction— away from Metro and out of Hollywood forever.

The reason for her "remote, quiet and pensive" manner was clarified after *The Swan* was completed. During the film's production, no one in America knew that, in late October, Rainier had privately decided to ask Grace Kelly to be his wife. "I knew what I wanted to do," the prince said years later. "But I couldn't just assume she'd marry me. I had to ask her. So I went to the States to see her."

He arrived in New York on December 15, accompanied by his chaplain and his personal physician—traveling companions whose presence briefly seemed to support Rainier's stated insistence that he was going to Johns Hopkins University Medical Center for an annual checkup, and was then going to visit friends in Baltimore. The press, picking up the scent of imminent news about the eligible bachelor prince, bombarded him with questions about a secret romance with some American girl, but Rainier laughed and said no, they were off the track.

For once, of course, they were very much on the track, and their suspicions were leading them in the right direction. But so far they had no clues as to who might be Rainier's inamorata. In November he had spoken with the proper authorities in Monaco, for his possible marriage was an affair of state and not merely a personal matter. But Grace's name was not mentioned.

Rainier proceeded to Johns Hopkins for a three-day medical examination. In Baltimore he stayed with friends of the Kellys whom he already knew, and together with them, he was invited to Henry Avenue for Christmas dinner. Grace, having just finished *The Swan,* had raced home to join her family and was seated next to the prince at the holiday table. Still, there was silence about any romance.

On December 27, Rainier and Grace popped up among holiday crowds in Manhattan. He was seen entering and leaving her Fifth Avenue apartment at all hours, and on December 28 he put to her the question that had prompted his long journey. According to Rainier, it was very simple: "Will you marry me?" And she replied, "Yes."

Rainier had everything Grace had ever loved in a man—and he was so much more, as she confided to a close friend. "He's enormously sweet and kind. He's very shy but he's also very strong. He wants a close and loving family, just as I do. It's even more important to him than to most men, because he had a terribly lonely childhood. He's very bright, has a wonderful sense of humor, makes me giggle and is very, very handsome. I love his eyes. I could look into them for hours. He has a beautiful voice. He's a good person. And I love him."

As Rainier began to share stories about his royal ancestors, Grace might have been amused to learn that she would not be the first American to marry a reigning prince of Monaco. The second wife of Rainier's great-grandfather, Prince Albert I, was Mary Alice Heine, daughter of a prosperous New Orleans building contractor and the wealthy widow of the Duc de Richelieu. She was sharp at business and helped her husband put the principality on a sound financial footing; and she turned Monaco into a world-class European cultural center, founding and supporting its opera, theatre and ballet companies. Princess Alice was also, it seems, a feisty and independent little number, and was widely suspected to be the mistress of the composer Isidore de Lara. Whether factual or not, this intrigue caused her acrimonious separation from Albert, but they never divorced. She subsequently lived in splendid banishment at Claridge's Hotel in London, where Isidore de Lara also took a suite.

GRACE'S FATHER addressed Rainier bluntly: "Royalty doesn't mean anything to us. I hope you won't run around the way some princes do, because if you do, you'll lose a mighty fine girl." As usual, brother Kell had only sports on his mind when asked his opinion of Rainier: "I don't think we can make a sculler out of him. He's not tall enough."

As for Margaret Kelly, she insisted that the marriage be performed in Philadelphia: "That's how it is in America," she said. "The girl's parents arrange the wedding, and Grace always promised me she wanted that." But Rainier—and, for the first time, Grace—explained that theirs would not be an ordinary wedding: Grace would become Princess of Monaco, wife of a head of state, and she would assume responsibilities to the government and to the citizens of Monaco.

"I made up my own mind and didn't ask my parents for

permission to marry Rainier," Grace said later. "I had asked them once or twice before, and it hadn't worked out. This time, I knew I had to make my own decision—and I did." The announcement to the press and the world had to be delayed until Rainier petitioned Grace's parents and obtained the proper permission, demanded by protocol, from his Monégasque council and the Minister of State. The official proclamation of forthcoming nuptials was made on Thursday, January 5, 1956—first in Monaco and then, a few hours later, by Jack Kelly at a Philadelphia luncheon. Next day, the matter was front-page news all over the United States.

Grace did not want her closest friends to learn of her engagement from news reports. "She rang me in New York and invited me over to her apartment for drinks," recalled Rita. "And she said, 'I want you to meet my prince'—so of course I thought she simply meant the man of her dreams. Well, I was soon in for a surprise."

"Neither of us was a child," Rainier said years later. "We both understood what marriage meant. Both of us had gone through difficult times, but both of us had learned from those difficult times that what we were looking for was marriage. We discussed it and we thought about it, and after we saw each other again in Philadelphia, I think we both realized that what we wanted was to make our lives together."

At Cartier in New York, Rainier bought Grace a 10.47-carat, emerald-cut diamond engagement ring, mounted in platinum. She wore it as her character's engagement ring in *High Society,* and director Charles Walters favored it with a sparkling close-up. Metro at once announced that Grace's entire wardrobe from *High Society* would be hers to keep—and that they would also pay for her wedding dress, commissioning Helen Rose to confer with Grace and to create whatever she desired, at whatever cost. "Of course I was very grateful for the studio's generosity," Grace said years later, "but I must admit that Rainier and I would have been happy to be married in our own ordinary, casual clothes in a secluded chapel somewhere. After all, I would have married him even if he was some small-town mayor."

As the news continued to fill the front pages throughout January, February and March, Margaret Kelly twittered away to the press. She signed off on a series of syndicated newspaper articles, written with her permission but (as she admitted) without her first reading the text. Margaret and her *amanuensis,* Richard Gehman, trumpeted some facts about Grace's early years, her love life and her temperament. Grace was furious. She did, however, have to laugh aloud when her mother circulated the news, "My daughter is going to marry the Prince of Morocco!" Peggy and Lizanne corrected her—*"Mon*aco, Mother dear—*Mon*aco!" But Margaret was adamant: "I just can't imagine Gracie riding camels in the deserts of Morocco!" The girls opened an atlas, there was a brief geography lesson, and the matter was clarified. But until the main event—"the wedding of the century," as news editors were insisting—Margaret Kelly was not entirely confident that her daughter was not relocating to the sands of North Africa.

The press began to gather round during Christmas week, and the Kellys decided to give only one group interview, at their home, with Rainier present.

What would be Grace's married name?

Grimaldi, Grace replied: "The Grimaldi family occupies the royal house of Monaco and has ever since the thirteenth century."

"But that sounds *Italian!*" Margaret Kelly whispered to Peggy. "I thought he was *French!*"

"Well, you see, Mother, he's neither Italian nor French. I'll explain the background to you later."

"Never mind that!" Margaret shot back. "Tell them what your name will be, Grace, dear."

"Grace Grimaldi," her daughter replied.

Actually, it was more complicated than that, interjected Father Tucker. She would be Her Serene Highness Princess Grace of Monaco—legally, Grace Kelly Grimaldi.

What about her movie career?

"Well, I still have a contract with MGM, and I have to do two more pictures. Of course I'm going to continue with my work—I'm never going to stop acting!"

"I think it would be better if she did not attempt to continue in films," Rainier said quietly but firmly. "I have to live there in Monaco, and she will live there. That wouldn't work out." As for films in Europe: "I don't think so. She will have enough to do as Princess. But she will not be involved in the administration of Monaco."

Would the couple have a big family?

Grace smiled and hesitated, so her mother obligingly chirped, "I should say a lot! I'm a grandmother and I love a family."

And with that, Rainier decided to end the media intrusion for the day. "After all," he said to Father Tucker as they repaired to Jack Kelly's den for a drink, "*I* don't belong to MGM."

PART III

fade-Out

1956—1982

TEN

High Society Rearranged

I don't want to be worshiped—I want to be loved!
—GRACE (AS TRACY LORD) IN *HIGH SOCIETY*

LOVED ACTING — WORKING IN THE THEATRE AND IN PIC-
tures. But I really didn't like being a movie star. I loved working at my craft, but I didn't like everything that went with the
public's idea of what a movie star ought to be." Grace endured
but never enjoyed the publicity that attended her movie stardom. Just so, she tolerated but took no pleasure in the exposure
that attended her engagement, her marriage—and, indeed,
that dogged the rest of her life.

On January 6, the day after the announcement of her engagement, the long leading story on page one of the *New York
Times* began the media frenzy: "Prince of Monaco to Wed
Grace Kelly" ran the headline—with the subtitle "Movie Star
Will Live in Principality—No Date Is Set." The story ran to
several columns. Following that account, four months of stories began to flood the American press. Tidbits ran daily in
newspapers from coast to coast. There were feature stories in

weekly and monthly magazines. Interviews were conducted with anyone who, it seemed, had even a remote connection or had sold her a newspaper on a street corner. Everyone had something to say.

On January 16, *Time* magazine, usually far cooler about such things, published a long story ("The Philadelphia Princess") and then somehow managed to justify another feature or at least an item about Grace every week during the first seven months of the year. On April 9, *Life* put her on its cover, in costume for *The Swan* ("Grace Kelly—Education of a Princess, for a Movie and for Real") and ran a seven-page photo essay about the preparations for her departure.

Perhaps it was inevitable, therefore, that, before the year ended, a Broadway musical—*Happy Hunting,* starring Ethel Merman—satirized the royal wedding: "We're up to here with the wedding of the year," belted the chorus in gleeful disdain. The show was set in Monaco, described in one song as a "pint-sized, pinpoint, pre-shrunk, postage-stamp principality," to which an earthy Philadelphia matron (Merman) comes in search of a princely groom for her daughter. With a group of classmates from the American Academy of Dramatic Arts, I went to a performance during Christmas week 1956. Like most reviewers, we were not amused, but perhaps we had to go on believing that the wedding was too sacred for ridicule—even if, by then, Grace had left the country.

The public was insatiable for any and every detail, and decades later, those particulars seem more amusing than significant:

JANUARY 8: "Miss Kelly left New York at 5.30 p.m. yesterday aboard the *Commodore Vanderbilt* [train] for Hollywood. The Prince of Monaco will drive to Wilmington. He will attend Mass there tomorrow."

JANUARY 9: "Whether Miss Kelly will be permitted to bring her dog aboard an airplane or a steamship has not been confirmed. . . ."

JANUARY 10: "The Prince of Monaco hopes to marry Grace Kelly in the United States, in deference to his bride, her family and the American people. Meanwhile, the prince left Wilmington by automobile for Palm Beach, Florida."

JANUARY 11: "Grace Kelly on Coast—She Says Plans for Marriage to Prince Are Still not Set . . . but her father indicated he would like to have the wedding in the bride's home parish, which is the custom. Mrs. Kelly was neutral."

JANUARY 15: "Rainier Going West—Prince Plans a Trip Across U.S. Before Wedding. . . . The Prince told a reporter that he planned a leisurely motor trip across the United States to Hollywood when he leaves Palm Beach in about a week. Miss Kelly is in Hollywood. 'I want to see this country, and I especially want to see Arizona,' he said. He did not elaborate on his interest in Arizona."

JANUARY 16: "The Cabinet chief of Prince Rainier III today settled a dispute: the civil and religious ceremonies of the marriage will be in Monte-Carlo, not in the United States." [The reporter made a common error: the rituals were not scheduled to be held in Monte-Carlo, but in the palace and in the cathedral, both in Monaco-Ville.]

JANUARY 17 [The story in its entirety]: "Rainier Wedding Date Not Set." Mrs. John B. Kelly, mother of Grace Kelly, said today that the time and place of her daughter's marriage to Prince Rainier III of Monaco had not been decided."

Things were becoming ridiculous.

FEBRUARY 2: [The story in its entirety]: Headline—
"Prince Rainier in Auto Mishap. . . . While driving to see
Grace Kelly in Hollywood last night, Prince Rainier's car
lightly tapped the car in front."

Should anyone have doubted it, the daily reports demonstrated that deeply buried in the American psyche was an ata-
vistic reverence for kings and queens, princes and princesses,
who seemed more fascinating to those living in a republic than
to those in a constitutional monarchy. After all, women movie
stars were called "movie queens"; Clark Gable was known as
"the king"; and John Wayne was hailed as "the duke." It was
common in America to hear a doting father call his little
daughter "princess," although for some reason, even the dear-
est little boys were not called "princes."

What of the pageants past counting, with girls "crowned" as
"queens" of a football season as they pinned plastic tiaras in
their hair? And how else to explain *Queen for a Day,* the radio
and TV quiz show that had a run of twenty-five years and featured women from deprived or downright destitute circumstances who were hauled up onto a stage, draped in a red velvet
robe, presented with a shimmering crown and long-stemmed
roses and given vacations and nights on the town with their
husbands or escorts? "Make *every* woman a queen, for every
single day!" cried the host, and the crowd went wild.

ON THE EVENING of January 6, hours after news of the engagement had broken, Grace and Rainier attended an "Imperial
Ball" at New York's Waldorf-Astoria Hotel, where the ball-
room had been quickly redecorated to suggest the prince's

palace in Monaco. The event, already planned as a fundraiser for the Veterans Administration hospitals, became the first great social occasion of the year. A fashion show that evening was followed by a ballet performance, and then the prince and his fiancée descended from an elaborately furnished box to the stage, where they cranked a revolving container filled with hundreds of ticket stubs. Grace drew out the name of the lucky winner—none other than Senator John F. Kennedy, who gave the prize (a diamond and sapphire ring) to his wife.

GRACE WAS back in Culver City before the end of January, coping with a tornado of activities: makeup and wardrobe tests for *High Society;* voice lessons before she and Bing Crosby recorded Cole Porter's "True Love" for the movie; requests for interviews; intensive French lessons; meetings about palace protocol with consular representatives from Monaco; and appointments with a platoon of designers, artists, musicians, chefs and hair stylists. Rainier was with her in Los Angeles for almost the entire shooting time of *High Society,* which wrapped on March 3.

The Philadelphia Story, on which *High Society* was based, had been a Broadway hit with Katharine Hepburn, who also appeared in the 1940 movie version. Screenwriter John Patrick made very few changes to Philip Barry's original text and Donald Ogden Stewart's first screenplay, and the result—with songs by Cole Porter—was a literate, sharp and clever musical that eventually became Metro's biggest hit of 1956.

The story is well known. Tracy Lord (Grace) has divorced popular singer and composer C. K. Dexter-Haven (Crosby) and is about to marry a handsome, social-climbing, monumentally self-righteous bore named George Kittredge (John Lund). At the same time, Tracy's relationship with her father (Sidney Blackmer) is threatened by his philandering—conduct so blatant that a scandal magazine called *Spy* has threatened to publish a story about his antics. This can be prevented only if Tracy allows a photographer and a reporter from *Spy* (Celeste Holm and Frank Sinatra, as Liz Imbrie and Mike Connor) to document her wedding. She agrees reluctantly in order to save her mother (Margalo Gillmore) from embarrassment.

The heart of the story concerns the maturing of Tracy Lord. She finally realizes that her unpretentious ex-husband, who is still in love with her, is far preferable to her fatuous and moralistic fiancé. Contrary to a customary pattern in comedy, Dexter—a man from the upper classes who is patient, gallant and compassionate—is more desirable than George, a hard-working man risen from the ranks, who is a prig. At a formal party the night before her wedding, Tracy drinks too much champagne and thinks that she might really be in love with Mike (Sinatra). In the woozy light of dawn, however, when George wrongly accuses her of a sexual escapade, she sees that George is not right for her, and Dexter replaces George at the altar.

Unlike most movie musicals, *High Society* relies on character, situation and dialogue—not on absurdly splashy numbers with singers and dancers cavorting on a great sound stage or in the water. On the contrary, it has a literate sense of high comedy, without any facile sermons about the idle rich. The major point of both *The Philadelphia Story* and *High Society* is that Tracy learns to harmonize her social poise with a maturing humanity, and to soften her uncompromising attitudes to her father and her ex-husband by confronting her own frailties. These points are made clear in two strong—indeed, almost cruel—speeches by Dexter and her father, in which they accuse her of moral inflexibility and a frightful lack of feeling.

In the tradition of high comedy, *High Society* exploits the glamorous but fading wealth of Newport, Rhode Island, and

...us finery precisely in order to
... . In this regard, her mother is
...d makes no moral judgments
...mes to his senses and returns
...r, Caroline (Lydia Reed)—a
...ents the bright, unstuffy new

...ysical stunts but on verbal wit
...plays of Oscar Wilde *(The Im-*
...Coward *(Private Lives),* S. N.
..., Samuel Taylor *(Sabrina Fair)*
...are often the pretensions of the
...ten exploit the comic tradition
...revelations of double lives—
elements as old as ancient Greek comedy and adaptable to later
circumstances.

As the actress Maria Aitken has written, high comedy "uses society's most sophisticated accomplishment—intellect and wit—to mock society itself; the glitter reveals the grubbiness." In this regard, *High Society* is not a languorous, effete, verbose exercise in social theses. Its themes are sex, money and social status, and, in the best tradition of high comedy, it reveals something truthful yet suspect in human nature. All this is presented as an entertainment, for high comedy requires special talents and makes heavy demands on actors, who must perform without pretense or mannerisms and find the right alchemy of elegance and vocal nuance.

Director Charles Walters enlisted a number of veterans to ensure the success of *High Society*'s tone. Margalo Gillmore, as Grace's mother, had decades of theatrical experience behind her (notably, in 1929, as Helen Pettigrew, the role Grace later assumed in the TV version of *Berkeley Square*). Louis Calhern, as lecherous Uncle Willie, added subtle touches of humor to a role that could have been frankly distasteful. Bing Crosby had demonstrated surprising depths as the self-destructive alcoholic in *The Country Girl;* here, he pitched comic dialogue the way he sang—naturally and without apparent calculation. Early in the picture, Frank Sinatra seems uncomfortable, and his drunk scene is embarrassingly unbelievable. He was saved from sheer buffoonery only by Grace's depiction of a woman unaccustomed to champagne. From the dance-floor sequence to her damp return from a moonlight swim, her acting was infused with hilariously understated inflections. "She was," said costar Celeste Holm, "the least self-conscious actress I ever met."

For its success, *High Society* depends entirely on an audience's acceptance of Tracy Lord as a reserved, demanding socialite whose coolness (like that of Princess Alexandra in *The Swan,* also high comedy) is warmed by another's patient love.

"It was one of my most enjoyable experiences," Grace recalled. "I was in love, I was engaged, I was singing a song called 'True Love'—it was all wonderful, and I remember the cast as a group of amiable professionals. We had such fun making that picture. At last, I thought maybe I could put it all together acting Tracy Lord. I was never happy with my singing—it seemed awfully tentative to me when I heard our playback of 'True Love'—but our director left us alone in all the long scenes of dialogue. Maybe because I was about to leave Hollywood, I felt relaxed and could just let the character have her way—I didn't impose myself on her. You know, the original story was set in Philadelphia. Well, I knew all about those Main Line snobs, but you couldn't look down on them or condemn them, or else the character [of Tracy] would have become insufferably arrogant. I tried to find the point where her haughtiness was a cover for insecurity, and for the pain she felt over her father's thoughtless behavior."

Grace was, as usual, hypercritical about her singing: a trained vocalist would have turned the song into an implausible movie cliché. But her singing with Crosby had the kind of charming apprehension that later characterized Audrey Hepburn's rendition of "Moon River," in *Breakfast at Tiffany's*. Grace sang with touching wistfulness—not in a full-throated, over-confident mezzo. The record of "True Love" sold a million copies.

But in one respect, she was on the mark: she did "let the character have her way." When Tracy emerges, hung over and shielding her eyes from the sunlight, Grace finds the right variations in tone to make a few simple words supremely amusing: "Isn't it a fine day?" she asks bravely, even though the day is not fine for her at all. "Is everybody fine?" she continues at once, although she can scarcely think of anything but her headache. "That's fine!" And then: "Do you like my dress? It's so heavy." The dress is multi-layered chiffon, as light as air, but (as the later cliché runs) we feel her pain. Put together with only the millisecond of a pause between each remark, the lines emerge as genuinely droll:

"Isn't it a fine day? Is everybody fine? That's fine . . . My dress—it's so heavy."

This sort of comedy is unlikely to appeal to moviegoers who prefer slapstick, burlesque, diversions laced with crude double entendres, sexual slang, stinging sarcasm, cruel invective, noisy commotion and pratfalls. All these are absent from high comedy. Audiences in 1956 loved the movie, although American critics then and later wrote off Grace's performance, missing the delicacy of her portrayal as Tracy and the nuance with which she conveyed a character by raising an eyebrow or a hand, ever so slightly bending her head and listening, with comic restraint, to the commands she will soon counter. When George Kittredge says that he worships and adores her, that he wants to put her on a pedestal and keep her there, the director kept his camera on Grace's confused, then sad, features. Without breaking her eye contact with him, she gently pleads, "I don't want to be worshiped—I want to be loved!" And we believe her.

FOR A FEW years, Grace was a kind of American ideal: she had the manners, dress and diction of the social élite, but there was a democratic person underneath—she had a quick sense of fun and a healthy, passionate nature. Despite her aristocratic bearing, she was "one of the girls." In each of her films, she played characters with a touching and credible longing for socially inferior men—women whose principles were humanized by being united with feelings. Because it was her last American picture, one can only wonder how Grace might have continued as the major exponent of modern high comedy—just as she could have matured as a dramatic actress, as *The Country Girl* presaged. She was at the peak of her youthful beauty, and that is sometimes an impediment for viewers who think good looks mean less talent.

ALTHOUGH THE film was completed on March 3, Grace remained in Hollywood to record some radio ads for the picture, to bid farewell to a few friends and to dispatch a professional duty. The previous year, she had won the Academy Award as best actress, and now custom required her to present the Oscar for best actor. This she did on the twenty-first, handing the statuette to Ernest Borgnine for his performance in *Marty*. Grace then rushed back to New York on the morning of the twenty-second in order to attend the wedding of her good friend Rita Gam to publisher Thomas Guinzberg on the twenty-third.

That left her with no more than eleven days to shop, pack, spend the Easter weekend in Philadelphia with the family and manage countless details before she sailed from America, onboard the S.S. *Constitution,* on April 4.

Rainier had departed for Monaco on March 16, as there were countless details to supervise at the palace in preparation for the civil ceremony on April 18 and the nuptial mass the following day. During the time of their brief separation, he sent Grace notes and *billets doux* almost daily. "My darling," he wrote one day, "This is to tell in a very mild way how terribly much I love you, miss you, need you and want you near me always. Safe trip, my love. Rest, relax and think of me, burning myself out with this terrible longing of you, *for* you! I love you so.—Rainier."

Grace was not marrying a man who was remote and unemotional, as the pundits wrongly presumed in light of his refined public manner and infrequent, calm statements to the press; indeed, they made precisely the kind of faulty judgment so often leveled against her. Like the prince, she had, as she said, "been accused of being cold, snobbish, distant. Those who know me well know that I'm nothing of the sort—if anything, the opposite is true!"

"My real life began with my marriage," Grace said. "Sometimes, looking back after so many years, I think I really hated Hollywood without knowing it. I had lots of acquaintances there, and people I enjoyed working with and learned a lot from. But I found a great deal of fear among people in Hollywood— fear of not succeeding, and fear of succeeding but then losing the success. I've often said that it was a pitiless place, full of insecure people who had crippling problems. The unhappiness out there was like the smog—it covered everything.

"And I didn't want to have to go along with all those illusions about youth when I was older. I had to be in my makeup chair at seven in the morning when I was twenty-six. Rita Hay-worth [who was thirty-seven] told me she had to be ready at six. I heard that Joan Crawford and Bette Davis [fifty and forty-seven, respectively] had to show up at five. What did that predict for me, if I stayed in the business any longer?"

"THE DAY we left New York," Grace recalled, "our ship was surrounded in fog. And that's the way I felt—as if I were sail-ing off into the unknown. The trip was just bedlam, [with] mounting hysteria everywhere from the members of the press who were on board. I had been through several unhappy ro-mances, and although I had become a star, I was feeling lost and confused. I didn't want to drift into my thirties without knowing where I was going in my personal life. I looked out into the fog, wondering, 'What is going to happen to me? What will this new life be like?' I had never met [Rainier's] family, except for his father [who had visited her in California], and I had no idea how the rest of the family and the Court would ac-cept me. What sort of world was waiting for me on the other side of that fog?"

For one thing, she was entering a world whose ways were completely different from everything familiar. Grace was mov-ing to a place where a foreign language was spoken, to a royal life where strange, ancient customs not only prevailed but were held in reverence, where formalities ruled all but the most pri-vate moments and where demands were made that often out-weighed the privileges. After years of effort, she later came to consider herself a working woman—someone like a public re-lations manager whose "boss" just happened to be her husband, the monarch of a small but self-sustaining parcel of Europe.

Those first days in April 1956 fueled the fame she had so

much distrusted in Hollywood—in fact, her marriage made her an *international* celebrity. But she took her responsibilities with the utmost gravity, finding—as Alfred Hitchcock told me with a sly grin—"the best role of her life." Hitchcock was right, except that now there was nothing separating the role from the player. Grace had *pretended* to be Amy Kane, Lisa Fremont, Georgie Elgin, Tracy Lord and the others—but Grace *was* a princess, and princesses do not live happily ever after, except in fairy tales. "I certainly don't think of my life as a fairy tale," she said not long before her sudden death. "I think of myself as a modern, contemporary woman who has had to deal with all kinds of problems that many women today have to deal with. I am still trying to cope."

The marriage of Miss Grace Patricia Kelly to His Serene Highness Prince Rainier III of Monaco was universally described as "the wedding of the century" (a phrase repeated twenty-five years later, when Prince Charles married Lady Diana Spencer). It could not be described as an intimate event, with 1,600 reporters and photographers (more than the number who covered all of World War II) flooding into Monaco, six hundred guests jammed into a small cathedral that holds only four hundred, and 1,500 guests invited to the palace reception. "Most of them," according to Grace, "wanted extra tickets for the balls and the dinners and the two weddings. To make everything worse, the weather was just foul, and the palace wasn't ready to be lived in yet." In addition, there were thousands of gate-crashers everywhere, and jewel thieves invaded every Monte-Carlo hotel.

Her wedding was, Grace said, "so hectic and so quick and frantic—there was no time to think about it. Things just happened, and you reacted on the moment. It's hard to describe the frenzy of it all—it was really kind of nightmarish. I remember looking at those first weeks as if I was just a visitor, a guest at my own wedding—but unlike guests, I couldn't go home when all the fuss and furor became too much."

"They told me that they just hated their wedding day," said their daughter, Princess Caroline, "and they never looked at any photographs of it. They had wanted a small wedding with just the families present. But they couldn't do that, and it turned out to be a mob scene." That was true, Grace said: "I didn't even read a press clipping for over a year, because the whole thing was just a nightmare, really. A few private moments, of course, were marvelous. But it was a difficult time to go through, for the prince and myself." Rainier agreed: "If it had been up to me, the wedding would have been held in the palace chapel, which seats twenty-one people."

When the turmoil of the wedding was over, a long and difficult period of adjustment began. First, she was enormously homesick for her friends and family, and for the familiarities of the American way of life. Then there was resentment from the traditionalists, from the Court and from the palace employees, who were committed to a rigid protocol. The people of Monaco were polite but wary of an American from Hollywood, and Grace found that, for a long time, her liberty was greatly curtailed—she could not, for example, simply go out for a stroll in the village. Tourists crowded her, and in the 1960s, the world-wide epidemic of kidnappings made it impossible for her to enjoy outings with her children unless they were accompanied by a phalanx of bodyguards.

Grace's friends remained precious to her throughout her life. Judith Quine might have spoken for many when she wrote of Grace's friendship: "No admonitions for not writing, though letters from her pals were very important to her. No questions asked. No explanations required. No judgments passed. Forthcoming expressions of sympathy and unity when most appropriate. Instant invitations to visit when most feasible. Offers of fun and friendship when both were most needed. Though Grace's position had become more elevated since we first met, the gifts of her friendship were no less exalted than they had always been. We did not use the expression 'unconditional love' in those days, but that's what Grace was good at giving."

"She came back from our honeymoon to what must have looked rather a grim situation," Rainier recalled, "but she faced up to it marvelously. There was not only the challenge of turning a palace into a home, but the very big problem of becoming accepted, liked and respected by the Monégasques and other local residents. Then there was the language difficulty. And it was hard for her to be cut off from her family and friends. She was very homesick for a long time, and even now [in 1974], she still finds it difficult to make friends. Looking back, I was probably too impatient that she should fit in and feel at ease. Often I didn't understand her outlook on things."

"I had always lived in big cities," Grace said. "I had also spent nearly ten years acting—so it was quite a change from an actor's life to civilian life, so to speak. My real difficulty was to become a normal person after being an actress for so long. For me, at that time, a normal person was someone who made films!"

"We do not do it that way" was a response Grace heard repeatedly from one or another staff member when she made a decision or a suggestion about something as minor as a table setting or the arrangement of flowers. She needed several years to find her own voice, and to be able to reply gently, "Well, we will do it this way now, thank you." Especially during the first year, when she was virtually cold-shouldered by the entire palace staff, Grace might have felt like the second Mrs. de Winter in

Rebecca, and only after a long and awkward period was her word or request taken seriously by her staff. For a very long time she felt like a displaced person, not just an expatriate.

By palace custom—to her astonishment—no man was permitted to visit her in the private apartments. Hence, when, for example, a dress designer or perfumer arrived, the representatives had to be women. This was outrageous to her, for she felt that she was under suspicion of impropriety. No, Rainier replied, this has been a palace regulation since . . . forever. It took her eleven years to change that custom.

Grace's common sense told her that many centuries-old traditions were absurd—like the requirement that every woman coming to see her had to wear a hat. "I thought it was ridiculous, that a woman would have to go out and buy a hat just to come to lunch. So I abolished that custom—and what a stir *that* caused. People were just appalled!"

But the biggest adjustment, she said, "was being married to a foreigner. There were so many changes to be made all at once, and at first I missed the easier American attitude toward things."

Years later, Grace was forthright about the early years in Monaco. "I had to separate myself from what had been Grace Kelly, and that was very difficult for me. But I could not be two people—an American actress and the wife of the Prince of Monaco. So, during those first years, I lost my identity. My husband and his life absorbed me until the children came, and it helped when I began service work in Monaco. Then, gradually, I joined up with myself again."

Contrary to the swirl of wild rumors during the rest of her life, the marriage was a success. "Of course there were stormy periods, as there are in any marriage," Grace said. "But we discuss things, and neither of us broods or sulks." Close friends like Judy Kanter recalled that "Rainier was moody and quick-tempered, and he took some of that out on Grace, because he knew that she would still love him. He once said that a good marriage was not an eternal romantic liaison, but a long conversation." Grace loved her prince: "I married the man, and not what he represented. I fell in love with him without giving a thought to anything else."

"She came here with fresh ideas," said her husband, "and these were not necessarily the views I always had. Sometimes this caused difficulties. One example: My staff had never done a buffet or a dinner with small tables as she suggested, instead of the big, formal table. I hadn't imagined anything ever changing, but there it was. Eventually, I thought this was a good idea—but the staff, oh . . . !" After twenty years, Rainier thought Grace enjoyed "some parts" of being a princess, "but she also gets sick of it at times, and she admitted to me that sometimes when she's at a meeting, listening to people talking stupidities, she feels like exploding. That is probably the hardest thing about her job—never being able to let go."

This was not helped by the fact that their leisure time together was limited, and they were often too busy with official duties to enjoy the quiet, private hours every couple requires. Eventually they insisted on spending more time at their three-bedroom villa, Rocagel, near La Turbie, a half-hour drive just over the French border. There they shut the door on the world and rarely took servants. Grace cooked, knitted and perfected her skills at artistic arrangements of pressed dried flowers—indeed, she turned a casual hobby into a refined craft. As for Rainier, he happily tended a small farm there and indulged his hobby of fixing antique cars and doing metalwork. "I don't know what would have happened without our country retreat," Grace said. "Or I *do* know, but I don't want to think about it!"

Grace tried to make frequent visits to America to visit

family and friends, but that became difficult after the birth of her three children—Caroline in 1957, Albert the following year and Stéphanie in 1965. She and Rainier returned to Philadelphia when her father died in June 1960. According to the press, his fortune was estimated at $18 million. The truth is that his will distributed the sum of $1.1 million among his wife and four children.

EVERYONE WHO knew the Grimaldis, as well as casual visitors and those who had a glimpse of the family at home or away, realized that Rainier and Grace were devoted and attentive parents. "I didn't ever want them to be strangers relegated to the other end of the house," Grace said, refusing to copy the ways of parents she had seen in Hollywood and in many European homes. She got down on the floor or the grass to play games with them; they always took their meals with their parents; Grace helped them with homework; and a certain discipline prevented them (at least until their teenage years) from imitating the worst habits of spoiled, wealthy children. Skillfully and unselfconsciously combining her American ways with a palace lifestyle, she was loved and respected by both her children and her "subjects," whom she greeted warmly, as if they were old acquaintances.

A DECADE AFTER the marriage, Monaco's economic situation and its public image had much improved. Before Grace arrived, there had been a decline in tourism; the lucrative casino had deteriorated; doubtful characters were buying up real estate and funneling ill-gotten gains into their accounts in Monaco's banks; and the attitude toward Rainier of most Monégasques was as suspicious as that of most Europeans.

But Grace's presence, and her close collaboration with her husband on every project (which he came to welcome), changed everything. By the late 1960s the government had a large surplus; tourism increased from 77,000 visitors a year to ten times that number; and she revived the principality as a major center for opera, ballet, concerts and plays. "She brought in poets and dramatists," recalled the British writer Anthony Burgess, a resident of Monaco. "She also made it a center of cultural conferences, with an annual television convention, amateur drama festivals and poetry readings." And there were her beloved flower festivals, to which she invited people regardless of their talent or financial status—the only requirement was a love of flowers and a desire to create something pretty.

In 1954, 95 percent of Monaco's budget came from gambling; by 1965 that contribution was less than 4 percent, for the Grimaldis together had shifted the income from the casino to tourism, banking, real estate and culture. Grace had the idea of opening the palace for guided tours during the summer, when she and the family were away; and for the first time in many years, middle-class tourists joined European high society as they returned to Monaco in great numbers. More important, in 1962 Rainier announced that he and his council had drawn up a new constitution that greatly reduced his power and ended autocratic rule; the old constitution, he said, had hindered the administrative and political life of the country.

In the 1970s, Grace dismissed the bodyguards who tracked her every step—and within days, locals felt comfortable in going right up to their princess, greeting her and asking about the family. To the horror of some die-hard conservatives, it was not unusual to see Grace and one of her children, or Grace and a visiting friend or relative, sipping tea or a glass of wine at a local café. More shocking still was the sight of her and the children at the public beach. But eventually the idea of a family in the palace took hold, and the residents of Monaco approved. Even when Grace's daughters entertained a youthful, free-wheeling lifestyle, their mother was held in such affectionate respect that people said, "Well, she's got the problems all mothers have these days." It's no exaggeration to say that in comparison with some other ruling families in Europe, Grace was far more important to her adopted country, and much more loved. Always hating to drive a car, she preferred local taxis to official limousines. "She spoke with five popes and I don't know how many world rulers," a Monégasque taxi driver said, "and yet she knew immediately how to put me at ease. She spoke with people on their own level."

By 1963, to the surprise of journalists from Paris, Grace was fluent in French. But she was always aware of people's feelings. During our first visits, Grace always addressed her staff in English out of deference to me as a fellow American. But when she realized that I spoke French, too, she reverted to that language out of deference to her staff. After that, we frequently laughed over the complexities of this or that French idiom or syntax. During one hot August afternoon, she asked a palace attendant to bring us cold drinks. For a moment we both forgot how to say "sparkling water" in French—and so Grace simply turned to her helper and said in English, "Oh, Pierre, please bring us some fizzy water."

When she offered me a tour of the private quarters, I was surprised at its simplicity. There were 250 rooms at the *palais princier,* but the family occupied only one small portion of it: a living and dining room, a small library doubling as Grace's office, three bedrooms and baths, two dressing rooms and a small kitchen, where Grace cooked breakfast for her children and (more often than the staff expected) prepared dinner, too. The nursery adjoined the bedroom, and after Stéphanie's childhood, it was converted into a family room. The entire residence was not much larger than a suburban apartment.

In addition to full-time motherhood, Grace revived and personally directed the principality's Red Cross and supervised the renovation of a crumbling local medical facility. When it was completed, it was a first-rate hospital. She passionately defended breastfeeding and became a representative for the international organization La Leche. Very close to her heart were the Garden Club of Monaco, the International Arts Foundation and her Princess Grace Foundation, which encouraged young people's involvement in the arts.

Grace also set an example of volunteerism by regular visits to patients, and to the homes of the elderly, where she sat and chatted; she never merely walked through a ward or clinic with a wave and a smile. Anthony Burgess became a friend of Grace, who took every opportunity for a serious talk about books and the arts. "I observed her concern for the older and poorer Monégasques," Burgess recalled, "all of whom she knew by name. She spoke not only French, but also the local dialect. The kisses she bestowed on the old ladies seemed tokens of genuine affection. There was nothing glacial about her."

Grace's fundamental compassion is well illustrated by her friendship with Josephine Baker. Years after the infamous racist incident at the Stork Club, Baker's career foundered in bankruptcy. Hounded by creditors, the singer was ill and in desperate circumstances by the end of 1974. When she heard of this, Grace brought her from Paris to Monaco, where she offered Josephine a villa and financial support for her and her dozen adopted children. Grace was a constant visitor to her old friend, encouraging her to return to the stage in a revue of her great songs. Grace then enlisted the participation of Jacqueline Onassis, and together they financed Baker's triumphant Paris comeback in early April 1975. The Rainiers were at the sold-out performance, along with many admiring celebrities.

Soon after, Josephine Baker was found lying peacefully in bed, surrounded by clippings of her rave reviews. She had gone into a coma after a massive stroke, and two days later she died in a Paris hospital, on April 12. She was sixty-eight. After the funeral at the Church of the Madeleine, Grace paid all expenses and arranged for the remains to be brought down to Monaco for burial.

Just as any talk of prejudice had angered her as a child, so her rage against racism was always evident in adulthood. In addition to her strong friendships with Josephine Baker, Coretta Scott King and Louis Armstrong (who appeared with her in *High Society*), lesser-known men and women were helped by the long arm of Grace's friendship.

LIKE THAT of Audrey Hepburn and Jacqueline Onassis, Grace's stardom depended on a mysterious amalgam of presence and reserve—of accessibility and distance. These women gave themselves to the camera, but they knew that they had to hold something of themselves back. This was not hypocrisy—it was merely self-preservation.

Stardom or no, these women did not enjoy unalloyed bliss in their marriages. For a period in the 1970s, friends of the Grimaldis knew that the couple had grown apart. "There's absolutely no doubt about that," said Gwen Robyns, who knew Grace well. "They put up a façade that they were together, but they were not." Grace loved ballet, opera, theatre and the arts, and she had a serious interest in horticulture that extended farther than the occasional pastime of a wealthy matron. Rainier, meanwhile, was preoccupied with matters of state and finance—he had to keep Monaco running.

Whatever her private difficulties, her beauty remained undiminished. When the writer Roderick Mann asked Grace the secret of her beauty at the time of her fortieth birthday, she replied that she never thought of herself as "a great beauty. I think I'm quite nice-looking, but that's about it. Frankly, I've always hated being known for my looks. I'd much rather be known for my ability. One of my few regrets is that I wasn't able to develop more fully as an actress. I stopped acting before I could do that. But that was my choice. I just hope I've developed as a person, instead. That's what's important to me—to fulfill my role as a wife and mother and princess—not [to be] beautiful, but whether I have more character than I used to [have]." She was not, she added, "terribly pleased at being forty . . . because I feel I should be so much more grown-up and wiser about the world than I am."

By 1980 the Grimaldis were, according to Robyns, "enjoying one another on a completely different level from before." However tested the marriage had been, "it was certainly going to work out for the future." Grace was "the pivot and center of that family, and no one realized how much she had given all of them until she was gone." Those were sentiments with which Grace's longtime friends wholly agreed; they were never out of the orbit of her life for very long.

The entire program of her private and public life was not easy. She had left everything—her family, her country, her friends and her profession—and she had left them for something of which she knew absolutely nothing. For years she had to fit in, submit, make do, conform, deny herself, learn a language and antique customs, and do everything with a smile. The births of her children gave her the most joy and sense of purpose, just as her several miscarriages pitched her into black depressions from which she emerged only after many months of withdrawal from public appearances.

EPISODES OF profound depression were infrequent. But there were many periods of melancholy and of loneliness, despite her efforts and her good works, and these feelings came upon her more often as the years passed. As early as the autumn of 1965, at the time of her thirty-sixth birthday, she told an interviewer, "I don't expect to be happy, and I don't look for happiness. So perhaps I am content in life, in a way. I understand myself, but I also argue with myself, all the time. So I guess I'm not really at peace. But I have many unfulfilled ambitions in life, and if I can keep my health and strength and manage to pull myself out of bed in the morning, some of them may be realized." After 1970, letters to friends were often pointed requests for news "of where I am not," and mild complaints that she felt "out of things."

At such times, she turned to her friends and her faith. "She was basically a deeply religious person," Rita Gam said, "and she understood the true role of religion in modern life. She did everything by example, to make it important for others, without referring to any particular denomination. And she had no neurotic religious guilt. She was very tolerant of people, and very liberal—not politically, but humanly. That was a part of her authentic piety."

Grace's melancholy and her loneliness derived from the fact that she desperately missed her career—especially after her children were grown and were away at school. She might indeed have "hated" Hollywood, as she said. But she also "loved acting," and she retained, as she always said, happy memories of the work, which outweighed her unpleasant recollections of the place.

Despite Rainier's early insistence that she give up her career, Grace never believed that her "Mediterranean husband, the head man, the one who says yes or no" would impose a permanent ban. "She never thought she would have to give up acting forever," Rita continued, "and she often spoke about finding the right moment to return to the movies. With each year, she missed it more and more, something awful. She needed some of her old life back, and she was hungry for good conversation."

In June 1962, Rita won the best actress award at the Berlin Film Festival for her performance in *No Exit,* and after the honors she visited Grace in Monaco. "Her excitement about my success typified all that was so special about her. But I sensed behind her loving and generous celebration a tinge of actor's envy." That same year, the photographer Eve Arnold came to Monaco to work on a CBS documentary. "I got the distinct feeling that Grace felt trapped," Arnold recalled. "It wasn't the fairy tale one had expected." As Oleg Cassini later said, "They were living in a gilded cage, but she wanted to be respected as an actress."

Alfred Hitchcock had the impression that "there would be a temporary interval [in her movie acting] after her marriage and the birth of a few required children—but then we would welcome the return of the native."

Hitch's plan to bring her back took the form of offering Grace the title role in *Marnie,* in 1962. She accepted—and then reneged. The fact itself is well known, but the reasons for Grace's sudden withdrawal, and the timing of it, have been misrepresented for decades.

Many explanations have been put forward, some of them partly supported by Rainier's account and others fabricated wholesale by inventive writers. The actual situation can be properly understood only by considering the timeline of events.

On the afternoon of March 19, 1962, a palace spokesman announced that Her Serene Highness would travel with her husband and children to the United States from August to November that year for the filming of Alfred Hitchcock's motion picture *Marnie*. No other details were mentioned. This news broke in America the next day, when the *New York Times* reported it, along with a photograph of the Princess of Monaco and a comment from Hitchcock that he very much looked forward "to making a movie again with Miss Kelly, who is a wonderful actress." This was, according to the later conventional wisdom, the news story that at once evoked the wrath of the Monégasque people and that forced Rainier to tell his wife to abandon her plans, for it was considered unseemly for their princess to play the role of a frigid compulsive thief, and to appear in love scenes with the actor Sean Connery.

But such objections were never raised, nor could they have been: no one knew at the time what *Marnie* was to be about, and Connery had not even been mentioned for the role of Marnie's husband. "Grace told me," recalled her friend Jacqueline Monsigny, "that at the time of the *Marnie* debacle, Rainier never told her to withdraw, he never forbade her participation—nor was there any public outcry. As Grace told us, 'It was I who decided not to do it.' "

The fact is that Grace did not withdraw from the picture until June 6; an interview with her to that effect appeared in the newspaper *Nice-Matin* the next day, in which she simply confirmed that she had informed Hitchcock of her withdrawal around June 1. As for the public's opinion of her original plan to appear in the movie, Grace mentioned only "an unfavorable reaction," without adding specifics.

Rainier had from the start supported his wife's decision to accept Hitchcock's offer. "She and I talked about it," he said in 1997. "We also talked to Hitchcock about it. She was very anxious to get back into the swing of things, and by that point, I didn't see anything wrong with it." In fact, Rainier suggested that since Grace would be working during the summer and autumn, he and the children could accompany her for a family holiday—which would serve the double function of stifling any hypothetical rumors (1) of his disapproval and (2) of any marital problems prompting Grace's return, alone, to Hollywood. Grace then announced that her fee for the film would go to a charity for destitute children. As for her credit in the film and in advertising, Rainier saw no problem in her billing as Grace Kelly, "because that's the name she worked under."

But after March 19, there were exchanges of both phone calls and letters between Hitch and Grace, detailing the problems of timing—of producing *Marnie* that autumn.

On March 19, when the original announcement was made, Hitch was about to direct *The Birds,* which began principal photography the following Monday, March 22. On Tuesday, Hitchcock's office announced that *Marnie* would have to be postponed for at least a year.

There were several reasons for this delay.

First of all, *The Birds* was the most technically challenging picture of Hitchcock's career, and soon it was very clear that the picture would not be completed until July at the earliest. But in a sense, that was only the beginning—the picture would require eight months of postproduction, editing, laboratory work, special effects and sound scoring. *The Birds* was not released until late March 1963.

Another problem that delayed *Marnie* was the screenplay, based on Winston Graham's recently published novel in England. First, Joseph Stefano, who had written the screenplay for Hitch's *Psycho,* had written a treatment. His version was considered and rejected, and Evan Hunter, who wrote the script for *The Birds,* then accepted the job and began working with Hitchcock. But writer and director seriously disagreed about both character and plot, and to Hunter's astonishment, he was informed that he was fired, and that airline tickets for him and his family to return to their home on the East Coast could be collected the following day.

From that point, *Marnie* was the most troubled of Hitchcock's movies. Jay Presson Allen, a novice screenwriter, was hired at a bargain rate, the writing of the screenplay plodded along by fits and starts—and *Marnie,* it was clear, would not begin filming for over a year. In fact, the first scenes were not filmed until November 1963, and the picture was released during the summer of 1964.

Of themselves, these postponements would not have made Grace's participation impossible. Why, then, did she so abruptly withdraw in early June 1962? The main reason was never given, but it can be pieced together by a careful study of certain vital correspondence.

In early April, after she had accepted Hitch's offer, Grace had learned that she was pregnant, and in mid-June she miscarried. On July 9 she wrote to Prudy Wise that she "had the great sadness of losing the baby two weeks ago [i.e., in mid-June]. It was just at the three-month mark. It was a terrible experience and has left me shaken both mentally and physically." (She suffered a total of three miscarriages.) "The three-month mark" would place the conception in mid- to late March. This explains Grace's acceptance of Hitchcock's offer on March 19, before she knew of her pregnancy; it also justified her decision to withdraw on June 1, after the pregnancy had been confirmed but was not going well. An August commencement of *Marnie* (which of course never occurred) would have then been impossible.

For all her talent, it must also be said that Grace would have been wrong for this picture. But the outcome of this debacle was fortunate for both the movie and its eventual star. The role went to Tippi Hedren, who had no prior public image to overcome.

Grace's performance would have brought legions to the box office—but it would have been impossible to believe her in the role of a frigid compulsive thief, and audiences would have been merely watching the Princess of Monaco—twice a mother by 1963—playing the part. How did she look, how did she speak? How much did she resemble the Grace of 1956? Tippi Hedren, on the other hand, had acted previously only in *The Birds,* and audiences easily accepted her convincing portrait of a strange and finally sympathetic woman named Marnie—a role, not incidentally, that she performed to perfection.

The matter of Grace's pregnancy was not considered appropriate to be made public, so the official reason for her withdrawal was later given as an outcry from the Monégasque press, and from certain citizens who thought that Grace's participation in *Marnie* heralded her permanent return to Hollywood. That would have been unacceptable, and Rainier's advisers would have counseled strongly against such a step, which would, some said, have delighted the French president, Charles de Gaulle, by its implication of trouble in paradise.

The political situation involving de Gaulle and Rainier was later given as another reason for her withdrawal. De Gaulle's government was locked in a proverbial battle royal with Rainier. The French president was insisting upon the cancellation of a 1951 convention governing French-Monégasque relations so that taxes could be levied against French residents in Monaco, and the revenue be forwarded to Paris. Rainier refused to leave the principality while the matter remained unsettled, and he preferred that his wife remain at home, too, for de Gaulle had threatened to cut off Monaco's water, electricity and telephone services, all of which were supplied and controlled across the French border. Grace joined her husband in the standoff with de Gaulle, and they remained in the palace until the dispute was settled—in Rainier's favor, as it turned

out. But this political situation did not occur until later in the
year, after she had already turned down the role because of
pregnancy.

On June 18, 1962, more than two weeks after she informed
Hitch of her withdrawal from *Marnie,* Grace wrote a letter of
apology: "It was heartbreaking for me to have to leave the picture. I was so excited about doing it and particularly about working with you again. When we meet I would like to explain to you
all of the reasons, which is difficult to do by letter or through a
third party. It is unfortunate that it had to happen this way and I
am deeply sorry—Thank you, dear Hitch, for being so understanding and helpful. I hate disappointing you. I also hate the
fact that there are probably many other 'cattle' who could play
the part equally as well—despite that, I hope to remain one of
your 'sacred cows.' —With deep affection, Grace."

Hitch's handwritten reply arrived a week later: "Yes, it was
sad, wasn't it. I was looking forward so much to the fun and
pleasure of our doing a picture again. Without a doubt, I think
you made not only the best decision, but the only one. After all,
it was 'only a movie.' Alma joins me in sending our most fond-
est and affectionate thoughts for you. —Hitch.

"P.S. Enclosed is a recording I have made for R. to be played
privately. —H."*

THERE WAS some saber rattling from Hollywood. Joseph R.
Vogel, then president of Metro, had read that Hitch wanted
Grace for a movie, and wrote, from his headquarters in New
York City, on March 28:

"When Miss Kelly left the country to become Princess

---

* Hitch occasionally sent cassettes of bawdy songs and risqué tales to
Rainier, as to others—hence, "to be played privately."

Grace there were four and one-half years unfulfilled on her contract [with Metro]. The unexpired portion of her contract represented and represents an important but unused asset of this company. . . . As an illustration of how our interests were adversely affected by our inability to avail ourselves of Miss Kelly's services, James Stewart, Joshua Logan [as director] and Miss Kelly were cast and set for *Designing Woman*. Miss Kelly then withdrew and this package . . . was upset. Instead, substitutes had to be made hastily with unsatisfactory results. Since that time, we have respected Princess Grace's retirement. Furthermore, when she requested, we consented to her appearance in the documentary film *Invitation to Monte Carlo*.

"So long as Princess Grace remained in retirement, we felt that we had little alternative but to sit by with an unfilled commitment, although I did call on her in 1960 to endeavor to accomplish the very thing you appear to have been successful in doing, if the press reports are true. While the return of Princess Grace to the motion picture scene is most welcome, we do believe that in all sense of fairness and equity, her return should be made with the participation of Metro-Goldwyn-Mayer.

"I must say in all sincerity that there are very few, if any, independent producers whose standards and integrity are such that I feel I could write in this vein. I shall appreciate your consideration of the foregoing and would be very pleased to hear from you."

Hitchcock replied on April 5: "Thank you for your letter of March 28. As the matter of the picture with Princess Grace has only just arisen so far as I'm concerned, I'm afraid that it would be premature for me to discuss it at this time. May I communicate with you further when the various matters connected with the preparations for this picture are resolved?"

"FOLLOWING THIS episode," according to an account authorized by the palace many years later, "she was very sad and stayed locked in her room for several days." For years afterward, her family sensed Grace's regret at giving up her film career. "At different times, she felt she would have liked to do something more, and that she didn't finish what she had set out to do," said her son. Among Grace's unfinished projects included two plays. She told her friend Gant Gaither she would love to play the title role in *Hedda Gabler* as the young girl she felt Hedda should be; another was the lead in Uncle George's *Behold the Bridegroom,* which had once been successful for Judith Anderson on Broadway.

Her screen appearances after 1962 were limited to narrating travelogue documentaries about Monaco or the palace, and a voice-over narration for *The Children of Theatre Street,* in 1976. This was a noble but tedious exploration of the difficulties imposed on children as they struggle to pursue a successful career in Leningrad at the Vaganova Choreographic Institute, one of the finest ballet schools in the world. (The documentary was nominated for an Academy Award.) Then, in early 1980, she narrated a religious film of Bible readings, and in 1982 she again hosted two brief religious programs of readings and hymns ("The Nativity" and "The Seven Last Words"). In all these, Grace recited her lines with unaffected sentiment and looked more like an ordinary, devout pilgrim than like a princess. "She looked incredibly beautiful and she was, as always, totally professional and marvelous to everyone," according to producer Frank O'Connor.

These were respectable projects, but appearing in them did not mean acting a role. "Privately, she harbored a sense of loss," said Judy Quine in 1989, adding that Grace felt that one day the pressure would ease, and she would be able to return to movie acting—"but it never did."

From the 1960s to the time of her death in 1982, journalists, interviewers and friends put to Grace the same question, time after time: When would she return to the screen? A selection of her replies reveals her wisdom and experience.

In October 1969: "I certainly do miss acting, whether it's in Hollywood or in the theater. I loved acting. I loved my job as an actress. But if you want to do it well, acting is something that takes a great deal of time and concentration and there's a great deal of competition. When you're acting, you have to think of yourself first, and when you're a mother, you just can't do that. My situation is even more complicated, being Princess of Monaco and married to a head of state. But it is very nice, when one approaches my advanced age [forty!], to think they would still like to have me."

In June 1982: "My former agent, Jay Kanter, sent me the script [for the movie *The Turning Point*] and told me I could have either of the two parts, which were eventually played by Anne Bancroft and Shirley MacLaine. He hoped I would return to the screen, but my answer was 'no.' The acting profession isn't looked on in Monaco as it is in the United States. In America, performers can have public and private lives and keep them apart. But as the wife of Prince Rainier, I can have but one public life—that of being his princess."

In July 1982: "I'm flattered that people could think I could go back to the theatre or making pictures. But that would be a very difficult decision to make after twenty-six years of being away from it all. . . . It's all changed very much. I'm not sure I could work there anymore."

Would she *never* return to perform again? She smiled. "I still have my original makeup kit from the American Academy of Dramatic Arts. It's buried in one of my closets, probably covered with dust. Perhaps one day I will take it out again—and then, maybe I won't."

The closest she ever came to a reinvolvement with old Hollywood came in the spring of 1976, when she was offered and accepted a position to join the board of directors of Twentieth Century-Fox. This kept her coming and going from Monaco or Paris (where she resided during the girls' schooldays) to New York or Los Angeles for about two years. To their surprise, the Fox executives found that her questions at the meetings raised significant issues, for Grace had developed a finely sharpened business sense; likewise, her creative ideas were never to be summarily dismissed.*

She could not, however, accept movie offers—roles that included the empress in *Nicholas and Alexandra*. In her continuing frustration over her feeling that she had not been fully responsive to her talent, Grace had further periods of dark melancholy as the children grew and went off to their own lives. When her old friend Peggy Lee sang "Is That All There Is?" Grace knew the heartache behind every phrase. "It should not be forgotten," runs the text of the official family celebration of her career, "that behind that perfect ease in the exercise of her role [as princess] were hidden a delightful sense of humour and, at times, discreet bouts of melancholy. Protocol and duties weighed heavily on her existence."

Rainier was aware of his wife's unhappiness, as he said as early as 1966. "There have been times when the Princess has been a little melancholy—which I understand—after having performed an art very successfully, only to be separated from it completely. She has been prevented not only from acting herself, but also from watching other actors, whom we do not have

---

* Hitchcock claimed to speak for many when he told me Grace accepted the position with Fox "because it gives her free first-class airfare to come and go." I corrected him gently: there was never anything like a cash shortage in the Grimaldi accounts. "Oh, you'd be surprised," he replied. He was wrong.

much occasion to see here. If we lived in New York or London or Paris, she would still be able to keep up with acting activities. But she found herself cut off from this."

In September 1976, Grace made (as the *New York Times* raved) a triumphant return to the entertainment world, at the Edinburgh International Festival. With the actors Richard Kiley and Richard Pasco, she participated in "The American Heritage," prepared in honor of the U.S. bicentennial. Grace recited poems by Anne Bradstreet, Carl Sandburg, Ogden Nash, T. S. Eliot and Robert Frost. This engagement was so successful ("it was just sheer fun, that's all," she told me) that Grace continued her stage appearances in a program devised by John Carroll that played on stages in Pittsburgh, Minneapolis, Philadelphia, Princeton, Harvard and Washington, D.C.

That program was called "Birds, Beasts and Flowers," and Grace alternated with Pasco in reading texts that drew attention to the World Wildlife Fund. As the *New York Times* critic wrote wistfully, "Perhaps it will encourage Princess Grace to attempt a real performance." The critic suggested she play Lady Anne to Pasco's Richard III, or Titania to his Oberon.

The staged poetry readings continued sporadically from 1976 through 1981 and were a source of great pleasure for Grace and her audiences. She canceled them early in 1982 when she suffered the first of a series of severe headaches that seemed to be migraines but were not. No cause or remedy could be found, except that her blood pressure was abnormally high, and she could not tolerate the side effects of most antihypertensive medications then available to her. The headaches came and went, but her blood pressure was not well controlled. These ailments were the first signs that she was suffering from a vascular disease, just like several members of her family.

The headaches were almost paralyzing during the summer of 1982, when she had a demanding schedule of travel and activities both professional and familial. As she was driving down with Stéphanie from Rocagel to Monaco on September 13, 1982, she apparently felt a piercing pain in her skull, and for a second or two she blacked out. Her car swerved violently, and when she fully regained her awareness, she was momentarily disoriented. Instead of the brake, Grace pressed her foot on the accelerator (or had perhaps lost the use of her legs). Just at that moment, there was a hairpin turn on the roadway, and the car careened straight ahead and over a precipice. Stéphanie survived the crash, but Grace did not. While driving, she had suffered a slight brain hemorrhage, the incident (called a transient ischemic attack) that often precedes a larger, morbid event; the second stroke, a massive one, was caused by the violent tumble and crash of the car.

Grace was placed on mechanical life support at the hospital in Monaco. Next day, a team of doctors concluded that she had suffered catastrophic, irreversible brain damage. Her family made the agonizing but necessary decision to remove the artificial devices maintaining her heart and lungs. On September 14, 1982, Grace Kelly Grimaldi, Her Serene Highness the Princess of Monaco, wife of Rainier and mother of three children, was pronounced dead. She was fifty-two years old.

SHE HAD been feeling well two years earlier, in 1980, just when an idea for a magnificent professional project came along.

Jacqueline Monsigny is a successful French novelist, the author of more than two dozen books and once the presenter of a popular TV talk show in Paris. Invited to a television conference in Monaco, she and her husband, the actor Edward Meeks, had been introduced to Grace, who was delighted to meet a talented French television hostess and another American living in France. She had also seen Edward on television, most recently in the dramatic series *Les Globe-Trotters*. A friendship was established, and many times in the coming years, Grace invited Jacqueline and Edward to Monaco if there was a benefit or a movie event, or to dine at her Paris apartment on the Avenue Foch. Often Rainier and the children were present.

In Grace's Paris apartment, early in 1980, Grace told them she would like to appear in an original movie, probably produced for international television, in which she would act opposite Edward as her leading man. It was to be directed by Robert Dornhelm (who had directed *The Children of Theatre Street*)—and Grace would like the screenplay to be written by Jacqueline. "This was like a dream come true for us," Edward and Jacqueline said in 2007, "but it wasn't an easy task. What sort of thing did she have in mind?"

They discussed the theme and plot for some time. Jacqueline knew at once that it wouldn't be appropriate for the project to be a love story or a thriller—that might be going too far with Rainier. "But then Grace came up with the perfect idea for a story about the annual Monaco Flower Show, at which she always presided. The princess would play herself in a comedy of mistaken identity." In short order, Jacqueline came up with a fast-paced screenplay that celebrated the flower show while telling a hilarious story.

The plot concerns an internationally famous astrophysicist from America named Professor Nelson (played by Meeks), who has come to Monte-Carlo for a scientific conference. He is met at the Nice airport by a limousine driver, who tells him, "The princess will be so delighted to meet you at last." The professor is surprised but gratified at this unexpected reception.

Nelson is taken at once to the palace gardens, where Princess Grace mistakes him for a journalist named Wilson, who writes travel articles. She welcomes him most warmly and does not pause for breath as she enthusiastically describes the annual flower show and the contestants in various competitions of floral arrangements—"Why, even my husband is trying his hand!" (as we see later, when Rainier makes a wordless cameo finishing a decoration). Each time Nelson tries to tell her who he is, she chatters on about the competition and the joy that everyone can take from beautiful flowers and simple plants. Finally he manages to say that he really doesn't have an atom of talent for floral arrangement, and he'd better move along to his other business.

"Nonsense," says Grace with an irresistible smile. "You will do very well, Professor Wilson. We know all about your great talent as a journalist." Once again, we hear Nelson's thoughts off-camera: "Talent? She thinks I'm some journalist named Wilson, representing the press! How do I get out of this?"

The film's irresistible humor is derived from the situation of authentic high comedy: no one understands anyone else—languages are confused, words within the same language have equivocal meanings, and identities shift and change. Jacqueline Monsigny wrote in the finest tradition of light French farce: one thinks of the jumbled characters in Molière, for example, and the hilarious episodes in the comedies of Feydeau. Edward Meeks, trained as an American actor, played Nelson/Wilson with absolute gravity, the straight man to Grace's comic role—as herself. The result is a masterpiece of underplaying. It is, in other words, the stuff of great comedy, right up to its very warm and human conclusion.

Nelson learns that the scientific conference has been postponed for a few days, and so, because he is at the benevolent mercy of Princess Grace, there is nothing for him to do but to enter into the spirit of the flower show. As he had predicted, he does not come up with anything very attractive or even presentable, and he tries to escape. But Grace and her driver catch up with him, and their final dialogue in her car is a fitting coda to her career:

PROFESSOR NELSON (EDWARD MEEKS). I should have told you from the beginning, but let me put it straight now. I am not the journalist Wilson. I am not interested in flowers, vegetables or, for that matter, anything else that grows on this earth. At least I wasn't until I met you, ma'am. I tried to tell you so many times—my field is astrophysics: stars, comets, satellites, space research. And my name is—

GRACE. Yes—it's Professor Nelson.

PROFESSOR NELSON. You knew my name?

GRACE. Everybody knew your name. Why, you're as famous as Sarah Bernhardt. But when I heard that your lecture was postponed until Monday, I decided to rearrange things. I know it was naughty of me, but I don't regret it. Tell me, Professor, why can't a scientist—especially one who studies the stars and the heavens—find a little bit of glory in a simple flower, or a lovely bunch or grapes, or even a carrot?

PROFESSOR NELSON. But you saw my flower arrangement!

GRACE. It was an effort from the heart, wasn't it? And don't tell me you didn't enjoy feeling your heart beat just a little bit faster for a change. I saw you! You enjoyed what you were doing. You became involved. Why, you noticed things you never even saw before. And that, Professor, was what I was hoping would happen. Even disappointment is better than no emotion at all. So don't regret it—even if you did make a mistake.

AND WITH THAT, the movie called *Rearranged* ends. It was less than a half hour long, but additions were planned.

The film was made entirely in Monaco. There were, as Jacqueline and Edward recalled, no problems with unions, and just a small crew attended. "Grace was involved in everything and made us all into a family around her. Then she organized a premiere with about five hundred people. She wanted to see how her husband and some of the notables of Monaco would react to it. Everyone loved it, and later, with Rainier's encouragement, Grace took it to a TV network in New York. They adored it, too, and they wanted us to add about fifteen minutes more, so it could be an hour-long TV special. This was the first movie in which Grace had acted in twenty-five years, and there was wild excitement among the executives. When she returned from New York, she told us that she had also shown the rough cut to Frank Sinatra and Cary Grant—'They loved it!' she said."

After Grace returned from New York, Edward, Jacqueline and Dornhelm sat with her, watched the footage they had, took notes and began to extend their little comedy into an hour's length. The director suggested that there ought to be at least one scene in which Grace wears a tiara or diadem, to emphasize her status. But Grace was adamant: "No," she insisted, "that would only be pretentious, and I don't want that."

Jacqueline and Edward felt that Grace "was proceeding in such an intelligent way with this project. The children were grown, and she wanted to have a more creative life at last. But she didn't want the people of Monaco to think they were going to lose out, or that she was reverting to her movie-star status."

While Grace was in New York, a reporter from *Paris-Match* heard about the picture and rang Edward to ask what it was about. He said he would speak with the princess, and he rang Grace to ask how to proceed. She replied, "Tell them it's something that we've already done, that the people of Monaco have already seen it, that it's virtually completed, and everyone knows about it." Edward relayed her words, and of course the reporter was completely baffled. Grace's priorities were, as Edward and Jacqueline said, "in this order—her family, always first; then Monaco, America and France."

In July and August 1982, Grace was very busy. She and her family took a cruise to the North Pole. She was also planning the annual Red Cross gala, to which she invited Edward as master of ceremonies. After the plans for that benefit were finalized, he and Jacqueline went on a holiday to Los Angeles. "Call me when you return," Grace told them, "and we'll film the added scenes for our movie."

ON SEPTEMBER 5, Grace wrote to Rita Gam, then living and working in Beverly Hills. The letter was, as always to friends, in her own hand: "I am just reading the revised script for ABC [for the network's dramatic movie about her life, in which Cheryl Ladd played Grace]. I think it will be all right. Of course I dislike the whole idea and feel slightly like someone coming home to find that burglars have entered and gone through all of one's personal belongings. But they are trying to do it well, and it will be fairly accurate. You come out in it very well [i.e., an actress who represented Rita].

"We went on a wonderful cruise into the Arctic Circle. It was very exciting and quite mysterious. But I have spent a month battling with a persistent bronchitis—which I hope will leave soon, as I am doing a poetry programme Sept. 28 at Windsor in St. George's Chapel and then early Oct. will join [actor-director] Sam Wanamaker for a little tour of four cities to find some well-heeled donors for the Globe Theatre Project in London. Then in Paris until December. I expect to be in California in March. Hope we meet somewhere along the line. Meanwhile, much love, dear girl, and hang in there!—Grace."

❧

Rearranged was never completed as planned, but in its twenty-seven-minute version, it is a perfect gem. Grace still lit up the screen, and her sense of comedic timing served her and the movie perfectly. She had lost nothing of her talent; if anything, the years had sharpened it and given her a depth and poignancy that would have left audiences worldwide like the private guests in Monaco—cheering wildly and wanting more.

When Jacqueline and Edward later approached Rainier with a request to have the film distributed, "he was completely submerged in grief," according to Jacqueline, "and he probably didn't want to stir up painful memories." The prince politely but firmly denied them and any businessmen permission to circulate the film. "We had no intention of seeking any profit from it," Jacqueline added, "but we very sincerely thought that, to honor the princess's memory, the public could discover underappreciated aspects of her real personality and talent, which was simple, charming, always subtle and full of good humor." The master negative of *Rearranged* remains locked in the vaults of the palace, very likely forever.

In June 1982, before leaving for her family cruise, Grace sent her own 35-millimeter copy of *Rearranged* to Edward: "I entrust our little film to you for the summer, Ed. Please have some videocassettes made—that will make it easier for it to be seen [by potential distributors] in the Secam, Pal and NTSC formats when we return, rather than the 35-millimeter version, which requires a projection room."

On July 22, Grace gave, as it happened, her last interview. Toward the end, she was asked, "How would you like to be remembered?" She hesitated and glanced aside for a moment before replying.

"I would like to be remembered as a person who accomplished something, who was kind and loving. I would like to leave behind me the memory of a human being who behaved properly and tried to help others."

NOTES

Unless otherwise noted, all quotations from Grace Kelly Grimaldi are drawn from my recorded conversations with her. Details of interviews with others are supplied at the first citation only; subsequent quotations from the same source derive from the identical interview with that source unless stated to the contrary.

ONE

12. *We could have been members*   Stephen Birmingham, "Princess Grace: The Fairy Tale 25 Years Later," *McCall's,* March 1981.

13. *My other children*   Mrs. John B. Kelly, as told to Richard Gehman, in a series of syndicated newspaper articles published in dozens of American newspapers for ten days beginning January 15, 1956. These sentences appeared in the installments dated January 15 and 16. Hereafter designated Kelly/Gehman.

14. *Grace could change her voice*   Robyns, p. 27.

14. *I hate to see*   Grace's poem has been widely published—see, e.g., "The Girl in White Gloves," *Time,* January 31, 1955.

15. *They've latched on to*   Gaither, p. 7.

16. *I had a good stiff*   Robyns, p. 23.

16. *the Prussian general*   Lewis, pp. 172, 180; see also Englund, p. 29n.

16. *My mother was the disciplinarian*   Curtis Bill Pepper, "Princess Grace's Problems as a Mother," *McCall's,* December 1974.

17. *She was so myopic*   Conant, p. 17.

17. *My older sister*   Pepper, "Princess Grace's Problems."

17. *Of the four*   Lewis, p. 161.

17. *I thought it would be*   Isabella Taves, "The Seven Graces," *McCall's,* January 1955, 70.

17. *According to him*   Rupert Allan to the author, October 1, 1990.

18. *a very nice man*   Lizanne Le Vine, in *Grace Kelly: The American Princess,* A Wombat Production, written and produced by Gene Feldman and Suzette Winter (1987); hereafter designated Feldman/Winter.

18. *I used to help*   Princess Grace of Monaco, *My Book of Flowers,* pp. 7–8.

18. *Grace admired her father*   Rita Gam to the author, May 7, 2007.

18. *As a child*   Feldman/Winter.

19. *Jack Kelly didn't*   Marian Christy, "I Remember Grace Kelly When . . . ," *Boston Globe,* July 2, 1989.

19. *He kept their cars*   Lewis, p. 182.

19. *Gracie asked my opinions*   Robyns, pp. 28–29.

20. *Little flower*   Grace's lyric was reprinted, e.g., by Quine, p. 401.

21. *Aside from going to Mass*   Lizanne Kelly LeVine, in *Hello!* (UK), no. 222 (Oct. 3, 1992): 60; hereafter, LeVine/*Hello!*

21. *My dad*   Lewis, p. 158.

25. *I won't put my plays*   "Where Are They Now?" *Newsweek,* February 2, 1970.

26. *I am so proud*   Robyns, p. 21.

26. *My dear, before you*   Lewis, p. 25.

28. *Grace's first date*   Kelly/Gehman, January 16, 1956.

29. *My sister Lizanne*   Gaither, p. 34.

30. *There was never any doubt*   John Underwood, "No Bird, No Plane, Just Superjack," *Sports Illustrated,* May 10, 1971.

30. *It was a failure*   Ibid.

30. *I could never understand*   Ibid.

30. *messed up his only son's life*   Lewis, p. 14.

31. *Daddy was uncomfortable*   LeVine/*Hello!,* p. 63.

31. *Jack Kelly saw acting*   Christy, "I Remember . . ."

31. *She wouldn't let her Uncle George*   Pete Martin, "The Luckiest Girl in Hollywood," *The Saturday Evening Post,* October 30, 1954.

32. *I rebelled*   Pepper, "Princess Grace's Problems."

32. *Oh, Jack*   Feldman/Winter.

32. *I hear some of*   Martin, "The Luckiest Girl."

TWO

36. *If a girl put*   Dee Wedemeyer, "Barbizon, at 49: A Tradition Survives," *New York Times,* March 13, 1977.

36. *She kept a great deal*   Robyns, p. 51.

37. *Grace's usual outfit*   "Grace Kelly," *A&E Biography,* ABC News Productions: Lisa Zeff, executive producer; Adam K. Sternberg, producer (1998); hereafter, *A&E Biography.*

37. Grace kept the comments on her audition for entrance to the American Academy of Dramatic Arts; see Dherbier and Verlhac, p. 32.

39. *She absolutely did not*   Feldman/Winter.

40. *It came as no surprise*   LeVine/*Hello!*

41. *Honey, . . . you can*   Kelly/Gehman, installment of January 18, 1956.

41. *The whole situation*   Excerpts from Grace's correspondence with Prudy Wise are quoted in Kinsella and Kinsella, p. 30; the entire letter is printed (in French), in "Grace: Lettres secrètes," *Paris-Match,* March 24, 1994.

42. *That Grace Kelly*   Gaither, p. 13.

42. *daughter of John B. Kelly*   Program for the week of July 25, 1949, at the Bucks County Playhouse, New Hope, PA.

42. *a very gorgeous-looking thing*   Kelly, pp. 62–63.

43. *For a young lady*   The unsourced quotation is cited in McCallum, p. 200.

43. *I've always thought*   Martin, "The Luckiest Girl."

43. *I thought all the success*   Taves, "The Seven Graces."

44. *thunderbolt of wrath and hatred*   Brooks Atkinson, "At the Theatre: *The Father,*" *New York Times,* November 17, 1949.

45. *a naturalness*   Quoted in Mitterrand, p. 285.

45. *She got the part*   Budd Schulberg, "The Other Princess Grace," *Ladies Home Journal,* May 1977.

46. *Grace's father wanted her*   Christy, "I Remember . . ."

49. *She quickly*   Gaither, p. 24.

50. *Despite the quickness*   Feldman/Winter.

50. *had talent and attractiveness*   Taves, "The Seven Graces."

50. *Everyone in the production company*   Herbert Coleman to the author, August 1, 1981.

52. On the factual basis of *Fourteen Hours,* see Joel Sayre, "The Man on the Ledge," *The New Yorker,* April 16, 1949.

54. *Those movie people*   Martin, "The Luckiest Girl"; see also Taves, "The Seven Graces."

55. *In two senses*   Cary Grant to the author, March 4, 1979.

56. *We've got a new girl*   *Time,* January 31, 1955.

56. *The living room*   Quine, p. 36.

THREE

59. *that it would*   Gaither, p. 17.

60. *If she had been raven-haired*   Ibid.

63. The friendship between Grace and Josephine Baker is well documented and was known to her family and friends. Her cousin, John Lehman, spoke of it on *Larry King Live,* CNN (TV), September 3, 2003.

63. *The film is to be shown*   Robyns, p. 28.

66. *In the 1950s*   Quine, p. 81.

67. The quotations from Stanley Kramer are excerpted from interviews I conducted with him in 1977, when I was preparing a book about him and his career—*Stanley Kramer Film Maker* (1977).

68. *We still needed*   Fred Zinnemann and I discussed his films several times in person during 1977, 1978 and 1979, and I was fortunate to maintain a lively correspondence with him. On January 24, 1978, Zinnemann sent me a long and courteous letter, responding in detail to my questions about *High Noon.* We spoke further in person in New York in November 1982, at a reception following a private, prerelease screening of his last film, *Five Days One Summer.*

72. *He and Grace*   Feldman/Winter.

77. *This movie was*   Ibid.

77. *When I watched*   HSH Prince Albert of Monaco, interviewed for the 2008 Lionsgate DVD of *High Noon.*

78. *Grace was not self-confident*   Duncan, p. 30.

79. *seems to mean*   Zinnemann, pp. 96–97.

80. *Less is more*   The quotations from Meisner and about his technique are cited on the website of the Neighborhood Play-

house School of the Theatre: www.neighborhoodplayhouse
.org/meisner/html.

80. *living truthfully*   Silverberg, p. 9.

81. *Are you still in love*   Kinsella and Kinsella, p. 62.

88. *I thought Grace's voice*   A&E Biography.

89. For background on *Mogambo,* see, e.g., Schary, pp. 260ff., and
     Sinden, pp. 204–28.

90. *This dame has*   Schary, p. 260.

FOUR

95. *It was a lush*   Dore Schary, "Who Made Miss Kelly?" *Satur-
     day Review,* October 20, 1956.

95. *We had trouble*   Ibid.

96. *Grace proceeded*   Sinden, pp. 204–5.

97. *Clark's eyes*   Gardner, p. 183.

97. *When I was younger*   Curtis Bill Pepper, "Princess Grace of
     Monaco," *Vogue,* December 1971.

99. On the difficulties of filming *Mogambo,* see Morgan Hudgins,
     "Bivouac on the Trail of 'Mogambo' in Africa," *New York
     Times,* January 4, 1953.

100. *He had by instinct*   For Henry Fonda's remarks, see, e.g., his
     entry on the website IMDB, the Internet Movie Database.

100. *the meanest man*   Server, p. 254.

100. *Clark, whose chest*   Sinden, p. 210.

103. *Grace Kelly's blond beauty*   Time, October 12, 1953.

104. *tyrant*   Harris, p. 329.

104. *Grace Kelly is all right*   Bosley Crowther, in the *New York
     Times,* October 2, 1953.

104. *Ava and I*   Ibid.

106. *You shouldn't criticize*   Kinsella and Kinsella, p. 73.

106. *You know, the girl*   Taves, "The Seven Graces."

106. *She was pretty much*   Schary, "Who Made Miss Kelly?"

FIVE

109. *The best way to do it*   This was Hitchcock's sole comment at
     the conclusion of the Lincoln Center Film Society's tribute to

him in New York on April 29, 1974. Grace was at his side that evening, and I was in the audience.

118. *All I had to do*   Martin, "The Luckiest Girl."

120. *she disappeared*   Aljean Harmetz, "Hollywood's Lovely But Lonely Lady," *New York Times,* September 16, 1982.

122. *On November 12*   Oleg Cassini's 1953 telegram to Grace was publicly exhibited by her family at the exhibition in her memory held at the Grimaldi Forum, Monte-Carlo, in August 2007. Cassini's autobiography is important for an account of his relationship with Grace, but the dates noted therein are very often inaccurate (and some of the events clearly fabricated). He claims, for example, that they first met in 1954—an error that the telegram, for one thing, contradicts.

123. *I saw her only in profile*   Cassini, pp. 238–39.

124. *make her look*   Head and Calistro, pp. 107–9.

125. *but in fact*   Quine, p. 295.

129. *symmetry*   Truffaut, p. 216.

133. *Everybody wants a new*   Martin, "The Luckiest Girl."

136. *fascinating*   Bosley Crowther, in *New York Times,* August 5, 1954.

137. *I don't understand*   Ibid.

137. *There hasn't been*   Ibid.

138. *had to be accepted*   Thomas Harris, "The Building of Popular Images—Grace Kelly and Marilyn Monroe," *Studies in Public Communication* 1 (1957), reprinted in Gledhill, pp. 40–44. I am indebted to Harris's brief but provocative essay.

138. *There's Grace Kelly*   *Vogue,* October 1954.

139. *I think it's nobody's business*   "The Girl in White Gloves," *Time.* January 31, 1955.

139. *She was anything but cold*   Dewey, p. 373.

SIX

142. *Twenty-four—and aging*   Grace Kelly to Hedda Hopper, May 1954; see the Hopper Papers at the Academy of Motion Picture Arts and Sciences Library, Beverly Hills.

142. *I don't know*   Mitterrand, p. 78.

142. *Who is the real Grace Kelly*   See also Taves, "The Seven Graces."
143. *Grace had taken*   Rita Gam to the author, May 5, 2007. See also Gam, pp. 17–26, and her essay "That Special Grace," *McCall's,* January 1983. Rita was also interviewed for Feldman/Winter; and she spoke about Grace on *Larry King Live,* September 3, 2003.
144. *She was a weak*   Quine, p. 39.
147. *She had an ability*   Feldman/Winter.
147. *She succumbed*   Dherbier and Verlhac, p. 11.
148. *Grace doesn't throw*   *Time,* January 31, 1955.
151. *rocked to the core*   Quine, p. 48.
154. *I'll never open*   Martin, "The Luckiest Girl"; see also Schulberg, "The Other Princess Grace."
154. *Grace called me up*   *Larry King Live,* September 3, 2003.
155. *I was happy*   Head and Calistro, p. 108.
155. *A lot of actresses would say*   *Time,* January 31, 1955.
156. On the background for *The Country Girl,* see, e.g., the Turner Classic Movies Database.
159. *Miss Kelly will get her share*   *New York Times,* December 16, 1954.
160. The amusing seven-point summary of *Green Fire* may be found in *Time,* January 10, 1955.
160. *It was a dog*   Lewis, p. 262.
161. *Hitchcock wanted*   Granger, p. 305.
162. *They're doing the same*   Grace Kelly to Hedda Hopper, in the Hopper Collection at the Academy of Motion Picture Arts and Sciences, Beverly Hills.
162. *Grace had always been*   John Ericson to the author, May 18, 2008.
163. *I had the misfortune*   *New York Times,* September 16, 1982.
167. *I finished* Green Fire   Oscar Godbout, "Star on the Ascendant," *New York Times,* November 7, 1954.

SEVEN

176. *Alfred Hitchcock fell in love*   Mitterrand, p. 275.
176. My observations on Hitchcock's complex attitude to Grace are

found, in a slightly different form, in Spoto, *Spellbound by Beauty: Alfred Hitchcock and His Leading Ladies,* pp. 203–13.

177. *She is cool*   Bosley Crowther, in the *New York Times,* August 5, 1955.

178. *Grace can play*   Martin, "The Luckiest Girl."

179. *Those were the most*   Oleg Cassini, *A&E Biography.*

179. *My work*   Cassini treated the affair with Grace in his book, pp. 237–68.

179. *We have lunch and dinner*   Grace to Prudy Wise, quoted in Kinsella and Kinsella, p. 131.

179. *Hitch, of course*   Ibid.

180. *You know how much*   Roderick Mann, "Princess Grace: How a Royal Beauty Stays Beautiful," *Ladies Home Journal,* May 1970.

181. *Oleg drives me*   Kinsella and Kinsella, pp. 135–36.

182. *I don't approve*   *Time,* January 31, 1955.

183. *The situation with Cassini*   Kelly/Gehman, January 21 and January 15, 1956, installments.

183. *If she had really*   Lizanne Kelly LeVine, on *Larry King Live,* September 3, 2003.

184. *in casting*   Truffaut, p. 327.

EIGHT

187. For details of Grace's visit to John F. Kennedy's sickroom, see Spoto, *Jacqueline Bouvier Kennedy Onassis: A Life,* pp. 109–110.

188. *Grace was mature*   Quine, p. 50.

190. *Still don't know*   Kinsella and Kinsella, p. 142.

190. The letter from Grace to Oleg is reproduced in Cassini, p. 263.

190. *physically exhausted*   Laurence Aiach, in Dherbier and Verlhac, p. 12.

191. *At that time*   Christy, "I Remember . . .".

192. *I love this apartment*   Quine, p. 98.

193. *I am reliably told*   Undated handwritten letter from Edna Ferber to Henry Ginsberg, in Folder 596 (the casting folder for *Giant*) in Collection 1343, the Hedda Hopper Papers at the Academy of Motion Picture Arts and Sciences, Beverly Hills.

194. *Soap never touches*   *Time,* March 7, 1955.

195. *You trusted Grace's beauty*   Conant, p. 25.

196. *I can't believe it*   McCallum, p. 211.

197. *No, not at all*   Quoted many times—e.g., in Conant, p. 84.

197. *I was unhappy*   Schulberg, "The Other Princess Grace."

197. *because of my terrible*   Cassini, p. 265. Grace's letter is reproduced on the same page of his book.

198. *I must explain*   Ibid., p. 266.

202. Pierre Galante's account of May 1955 was documented in his article "The Day Grace Kelly Met Prince Rainier," *Good Housekeeping,* May 1983.

205. *They spent their days*   Dherbier and Verlhac, p. 12.

205. *She is an adorable*   *Time,* May 23, 1955.

205. *I had not yet visited*   Prince Rainier, with Peter Hawkins, "Prince Rainier Tells of 'Our Life Together,' " *Good Housekeeping,* March 1967—an extract from the Hawkins book.

206. *She thought she was missing*   Feldman/Winter.

206. *the wedding was so sweet*   Quine, pp. 107, 109.

206. *No, . . . but it was a very*   Englund, p. 180n.

207. *My son and I*   *Time,* August 1, 1955.

NINE

209. *revealed more and more*   Quoted in Robinson, pp. 73ff. Robinson's book, published in 1989, is both important and trustworthy, for it was based on extended interviews with Rainier, Caroline, Albert and Stéphanie. All subsequent quotations attributed to Rainier and the children derived from the Robinson interviews unless otherwise noted. For summaries of Rainier's life before Grace, there are many sources. Among the books, those by Hawkins and Robinson were written with the prince's cooperation and authorization. The periodical literature is vast—e.g., David Schoenbrun, "Where Will the Prince Find His Princess?" *Collier's,* December 9, 1955; "Peppery Ruler: Prince Rainier," *New York Times,* March 18, 1967; Maurice Zolotow, "Grace of Monaco," *Cosmopolitan,* December 1961; Peter Carlson, "Living with the Memories," *People* (USA), November 15, 1982.

211. *I met your lovely*   Schoenbrun, "Where Will the Prince . . ."

212. *We can't go on*   "Peppery Ruler," *New York Times.*

213. *I must get married*   Ibid.

215. *I've always been interested*   Grace, quoted in Rose, p. 105.

216. *There were costumes*   Ibid., p. 103.

220. *I want Grace Kelly*   From the American Film Institute's oral history with Ridgeway Callow, interviewed by Rudy Behlmer in Beverly Hills, California, in 1976; transcript on deposit at the Academy of Motion Picture Arts and Sciences, Beverly Hills.

221. On Grace having Guinness paged by "Alice," see Conant, p. 35.

221. *It became a sort*   Guinness, pp. 214–15.

222. *She had this*   Quoted in Duncan and Hopp, p. 153.

222. *remote, quiet, pensive*   Conant, p. 29.

222. *I knew what I wanted*   Robinson, p. 74.

223. *He's enormously sweet*   Quine, p. 116.

224. *Royalty doesn't mean*   "The Philadelphia Princess," *Time,* January 16, 1956.

224. *I don't think*   Ibid.

224. *I made up my own mind*   Schulberg, "The Other Princess Grace."

225. *Neither of us was*   Robinson, pp. 79–80.

227. *Well, I still have a contract*   Zolotow, "Grace of Monaco."

227. *I think it would be better*   *New York Times,* January 27, 1956.

227. *I should say*   Milton Bracker, "Prince of Monaco to Wed Grace Kelly," *New York Times,* January 6, 1956.

TEN

231. *I loved acting*   Grace, in an interview with Pierre Salinger for ABC television, July 22, 1982. See also Pepper, "Princess Grace of Monaco."

235. On the Barry play, see Christian H. Moe, "The Philadelphia Story," in Hawkins-Dady, pp. 603–6.

237. *uses society's*   From the back cover of Aitken.

238. *She was . . . the least*   Jack Kroll, with Scott Sullivan, "Portrait of a Lady," *Newsweek,* September 27, 1982.

241. *My darling*   Rainier's note to Grace in March 1956 was made public at the exhibition in the Grimaldi Forum and printed in the celebratory book—see Mitterrand, p. 141.

241. *been accused*   Ibid., p. 137.

242. *The day we left New York*   Schulberg, "The Other Princess Grace"; see also R. T. Kahn, "Amazing Grace," *Ladies Home Journal,* September 1982.

243. *I certainly don't think*   "A Life of Grace," *People* (USA), September 27, 1982.

244. *They told me*   Princess Caroline, *A&E Biography.*

244. *No admonitions*   Quine, p. 230.

245. *She came back*   Rainier, with Hawkins, " 'Our Life Together' "; see also Douglas Keay, "Life with Grace: An Exclusive Interview with Prince Rainier," *Ladies Home Journal,* May 1974.

245. *I had always lived*   "Interview with Princess Grace," *Playboy,* January 1966; see also Dherbier and Verlhac, p. 124.

246. *I had to separate*   Pepper, "Princess Grace of Monaco."

246. *Of course there were stormy*   Ibid.

246. *Rainier was moody*   Christy, "I Remember . . ."

247. *I married the man*   Mitterrand, p. 268.

248. *I didn't ever want*   Conant, p. 79.

249. *She brought in*   Anthony Burgess, "Grace Adieu," *Observer Magazine,* September 29, 1982.

252. *There's absolutely no doubt*   *A&E Biography.*

253. *a great beauty*   Mann, "Princess Grace: How a Royal Beauty . . ."

254. *I don't expect*   "Interview with Princess Grace," *Playboy.*

254. *of where I am not*   Kinsella and Kinsella, p. 180.

254. *Mediterranean husband*   Judy Klemesrud, "Princess Grace Makes a Movie—But It's No Comeback," *New York Times,* December 18, 1977.

255. *Her excitement*   Gam, p. 26.

255. *I got the distinct feeling*   *People* (USA), February 12, 1996.

255. *They were living*   Ibid.

256. *She and I talked*   For Rainier's comments on the *Marnie* issue, see Robinson, pp. 197–98.

258. *had the great sadness*   Kinsella and Kinsella, p. 206.

260. The letters from Joseph Vogel and Alfred Hitchcock are contained in the *Marnie* files at the Academy of Motion Picture Arts and Sciences, Beverly Hills.

262. *Following this episode*   Dherbier and Verlhac, p. 16.

262. *At different times*   Matthew Campbell, "Remembering My Fairytale Mother," *Sunday Times* (UK), May 27, 2007.

262. *She looked incredibly*   Producer Frank O'Connor to Rainier, October 20, 1982.

262. *Privately, she harbored*   Christy, "I Remember . . ."

263. *I certainly do miss acting*   "Princess Grace Turns 40," *Look,* December 16, 1969.

264. *It should not be forgotten*   Mitterrand, p. 282.

264. *There have been times*   Rainier with Hawkins, " 'Our Life Together.' "

266. Stéphanie spoke once on the record about the accident; see Robinson, pp. 214, 268–73.

267. *This was like*   Edward Meeks to the author, November 24, 2007.

272. *he was completely submerged*   Monsigny, pp. 222–23 (translated by the author).

272. *How would you like*   Pierre Salinger for ABC-TV (USA); available on DVD: ABC News Classics Productions, 2007.

BIBLIOGRAPHY

Aitken, Maria. *Style: Acting in High Comedy*. New York: Applause Theatre Books, 1996.

Barry, Philip. *The Philadelphia Story*. New York: Samuel French, 1969.

Cassini, Oleg. *In My Own Fashion*. New York: Simon and Schuster, 1987.

Conant, Howell. *Grace*. New York: Random House, 1992.

Dewey, Donald. *James Stewart: A Biography*. Atlanta: Turner Publications, 1996.

Dherbier, Yann-Brice, and Pierre-Henri Verlhac. *Grace Kelly—A Life in Pictures*. London: Pavilion, 2006.

Drummond, Phillip. *High Noon*. London: BFI Publishing/British Film Institute, 1997.

Duncan, Paul, ed., and Glenn Hopp (text). *Movie Icons: Grace Kelly*. Cologne: Taschen, 2007.

Englund, Steven. *Grace of Monaco: An Interpretive Biography*. New York: Zebra/Kensington, 1985.

Finler, Joel W. *The Hollywood Story*. London: Wallflower, 2003.

Gaither, Gant. *Princess of Monaco: The Story of Grace Kelly*. New York: Hillman/Bartholomew House, 1961.

Gam, Rita. *Actress to Actress*. New York: Nick Lyons, 1986.

Gardner, Ava. *Ava: My Story*. New York: Bantam, 1990.

Gledhill, Christine. *Stardom—Industry of Desire*. London: Routledge, 1991.

Grace Kelly—Princesse du Cinéma (no author or editor credited). Paris: Stanislas Choko, 2007.

Grace of Monaco, Princess, with Gwen Robyns. *My Book of Flowers*. New York: Doubleday, 1980.

Granger, Stewart. *Sparks Fly Upward.* New York: G. P. Putnam's Sons, 1981.

Graves, Mark A. *George Kelly: A Research and Production Sourcebook.* Westport, CT: Greenwood Press, 1999.

Guinness, Alec. *Blessings in Disguise.* New York: Knopf, 1986.

Harris, Warren G. *Clark Gable: A Biography.* New York: Harmony, 2002.

Hart-Davis, Phyllida. *Grace: The Story of a Princess.* London: Willow/Collins, 1982.

Hartnoll, Phyllis, ed. *The Oxford Companion to the Theatre,* 4th edition. Oxford: Oxford University Press, 1983.

Hawkins, Peter. *Prince Rainier of Monaco—His Authorised and Exclusive Story.* London: William Kimber, 1966.

Hawkins-Dady, Mark, ed. *The International Dictionary of Theatre,* vol. 1: *Plays.* Farmington Hills, Michigan: St. James Press/Gale, 1992.

Head, Edith, and Paddy Calistro. *Edith Head's Hollywood.* New York: E. P. Dutton, 1983.

Jakes, John, ed. *A Century of Great Western Stories.* New York: Forge/Tom Doherty, 2000.

Kelly, George. *Three Plays: The Torch-Bearers, The Show-Off, Craig's Wife.* New York: Limelight/Proscenium, 1999.

Kinsella, Terry, and Angelika Kinsella, eds. *With Love—Gracie.* Westlake Village, CA: A Piece of History, 1994.

Knott, Frederick. *Dial "M" for Murder.* New York: Dramatists Play Service, 1982.

Lacey, Robert. *Grace.* New York: Berkley, 1996.

Lewis, Arthur H. *Those Philadelphia Kellys—With a Touch of Grace.* New York: William Morrow, 1977.

Marchant, William. *To Be Continued.* New York: Dramatists Play Service, 1980.

McCallum, John. *That Kelly Family.* New York: A. S. Barnes, 1957.

McGilligan, Patrick. *Alfred Hitchcock: A Life in Darkness and Light.* New York: ReganBooks, 2003.

Michener, James A. *The Bridges at Toko-Ri.* New York: Ballantine, 1982.

Mitterrand, Frédéric. *The Grace Kelly Years—Princess of Monaco.* Monaco: Grimaldi Forum/Skira Editore, 2007.

Molnár, Ferenc. *The Swan*. New York: Longmans, Green, 1929.

Monsigny, Jacqueline. *Chère Princesse Grace—Souvenirs*. Neuilly-sur-Seine: Michel Lafon, 2002.

Odets, Clifford. *The Country Girl*. New York: Dramatists Play Service, 1979.

Quine, Judith Balaban. *The Bridesmaids: Grace Kelly, Princess of Monaco, and Six Intimate Friends*. New York: Weidenfeld & Nicolson, 1989.

Robinson, Jeffrey. *Rainier and Grace: An Intimate Portrait*. New York: Atlantic Monthly, 1989.

Robyns, Gwen. *Princess Grace*. London: W. H. Allen, 1982.

Rose, Helen. *Just Make Them Beautiful*. Santa Monica, CA: Dennis-Landman, 1976.

Schary, Dore. *Heyday*. Boston: Little, Brown, 1979.

Server, Lee. *Ava Gardner: "Love Is Nothing."* New York: St. Martin's Press, 2006.

Silverberg, Larry. *The Sanford Meisner Approach: An Actor's Workbook*. Manchester and Lyme, New Hampshire: Smith and Kraus, 1994.

Sinden, Donald. *A Touch of the Memoirs*. London: Hodder & Stoughton, 1982.

Spoto, Donald. *The Art of Alfred Hitchcock;* preface by Princess Grace of Monaco. New York: Doubleday Anchor, 1999 (centennial edition); first edition, New York: Hopkinson & Blake, 1976, and London: W. H. Allen, 1976.

———. *Camerado: Hollywood and the American Man*. New York: New American Library, 1978.

———. *The Dark Side of Genius: The Life of Alfred Hitchcock*. New York: DaCapo/HarperCollins, 1999 (centennial edition); first edition, Boston: Little, Brown, 1983, and London: Collins, 1983.

———. *Enchantment: The Life of Audrey Hepburn*. London: Hutchinson, 2006, and New York: Harmony Books, 2006.

———. *Jacqueline Bouvier Kennedy Onassis: A Life*. New York: St. Martin's Press, 2000.

———. *Marilyn Monroe: The Biography*. New York: HarperCollins, 1993, and London: Chatto & Windus, 1993.

———. *Notorious: The Life of Ingrid Bergman*. New York and London: HarperCollins, 1997.

————. *Spellbound by Beauty: Alfred Hitchcock and His Leading Ladies.* London: Hutchinson, 2008, and New York: Harmony Books, 2008.

————. *Stanley Kramer, Film Maker.* New York: G. P. Putnam's Sons, 1978.

Strindberg, August, translated by Edith and Warner Oland. *The Father.* Mineola, NY: Dover Publications, 2003.

Truffaut, François. *Hitchcock* (revised edition). New York: Simon & Schuster, 1983.

Vineberg, Steve. *High Comedy in American Movies.* New York: Rowman & Littlefield, 2005.

Zinnemann, Fred. *Fred Zinnemann, An Autobiography—A Life in the Movies.* New York: Robert Stewart/Scribner's, 1992.

INDEX